To Exist is to Resist

Black Feminism in Europe

Edited by
Akwugo Emejulu and Francesca Sobande

PLUTO PRESS

First published 2019 by Pluto Press
345 Archway Road, London N6 5AA

www.plutobooks.com

British Library Cataloguing in Publication Data
A catalogue record for this book is available from the British Library

ISBN   978 0 7453 3948 1   Hardback
ISBN   978 0 7453 3947 4   Paperback
ISBN   978 1 7868 0457 0   PDF eBook
ISBN   978 1 7868 0459 4   Kindle eBook
ISBN   978 1 7868 0458 7   EPUB eBook

This book is printed on paper suitable for recycling and made from fully
managed and sustained forest sources. Logging, pulping and manufacturing
processes are expected to conform to the environmental standards of the
country of origin.

Typeset by Stanford DTP Services, Northampton, England

Simultaneously printed in the United Kingdom and United States of America

Contents

Figures

PART I

Introduction

1

Introduction: On the Problems and Possibilities of European Black Feminism and Afrofeminism

Akwugo Emejulu and Francesca Sobande

How might we theorise and practise Black feminism and Afrofeminism in Europe today? This is a provocative question for Black women, as our politics are too often erased from or misrecognised in the European imagination.[1] We define Black feminism as a praxis that identifies women racialised as Black as knowing agents for social change. Black feminism is both a theory and a politics of affirmation and liberation. Black feminism names and valorises the knowledge production and lived experiences of different Black women derived from our class, gender identity, legal status and sexuality, for example. This insistence on Black women as human, as agents and as knowers is critical to any kind of Black feminist thought. It radically dissents from and subverts the hegemonic constructions of Black women as either irrelevant and invisible objects or alien Others who disrupt the taken for granted racialised and gendered social and economic order. Crucially, Black feminism is also a politics of liberation. Our struggle for our humanity is revolutionary political action that imagines another world is possible beyond the plunder, exploitation and expropriation that are the bedrock of liberal democracies. It is important to stress that Black feminism does not merely operate against violence and exclusion but creates and fosters a different way of seeing and being in this world. Black feminism is always a creative and dynamic production of thinking and living otherwise.

We can trace Black feminism back to the earliest days of slavery and colonialism. Where the historical record survives, we find the narratives of displaced and enslaved Black women analysing the violence of their everyday lives and resisting those forces of dehumanisation to assert their belonging in humanity. From abolition to anti-colonial movements,

Black women have been at the forefront of liberation struggles and have made clear that no emancipatory movement is to be taken seriously unless the specific oppression faced by Black women – based on race, class, gender and sexuality – are addressed. This enduring lesson from Sojourner Truth to Jeanne and Paulette Nardal to Claudia Jones to May Ayim has yet to be learned.

Feminism has always been an uncomfortable coalition between Black and white women. Because white women benefit from white supremacy, they can be, at best, unreliable actors for liberation and at worst, active and willing agents for Black women's oppression. Black feminism is oftentimes positioned as a reaction to white-dominated feminism but this is a gross misreading of Black feminist history and theory. In fact, Black women have always been leaders of women's liberation and have had to struggle against and defeat white women so that everyone – and not just white men and women – can be free. Any honest history of white women's roles in abolition, for example, and how their experiences in this movement radicalised them to demand the vote – ahead of Black men and Black women – demonstrates the point. Black feminism is in no way an afterthought or a derivative of white feminism but rather a radical praxis for the liberation of everyone – starting with Black women.

However, Black feminism is too often limited in how it conceives of itself and Black women. Black women in Europe must struggle for our humanity while simultaneously negotiating the dominant discourses of racial, gender and intersectional politics of North American Black feminists that make it difficult to name and take action on our particular racialised, gendered and classed experiences in a European context. Because the United States is the global hegemonic power, it imposes and transmits its values and culture across the world. Much of what we understand as American culture is actually Black American culture popularised through social movements and social media. Black American culture is a key way the United States exercises its soft power. In the Black diaspora, Black American culture looms large and has a tendency to crowd out and misunderstand other histories and understandings of Blackness and resistance. For example, pretty much everyone knows the basic story of the American Civil Rights Movement and some of its key players from Rosa Parks to Martin Luther King Jr. However, the same popular knowledge does not exist about liberation struggles outside (and against) the United States and from which American activists drew inspiration. So, there is a constant tension within the Black diaspora of having

Black American politics and culture dominate, with little reciprocal knowledge about the long history of anti-imperialist and anti-colonial struggles in Europe and against various European empires. Thus we read Angela Davis and Kwame Turé but less so Aimé Césaire and Gail Lewis. This lacuna matters greatly to how we think about Blackness, solidarity and resistance. These dynamics are re-enforced by the domination of the English language, which further preferences American, and to a lesser extent, British texts.

Black feminism is also entangled in these power relations. Too often, when we think about Black feminist theory and activism, we look to the particular Black American experience and seek to universalise and apply it to Europe. This is a mistake on two levels. First, by trying to import American race politics to Europe, this signals that race and racialisation is somehow fundamentally foreign and outside the European experience. This is all too convenient and robs European Black feminists of a key analytical tool to name and act on our oppression. If racial injustice is understood on American terms and as an American export, there is no incentive to dismantle the distinct European racialised social order. Second, this importation of the American experience silences the actually existing experiences and histories of European Black feminists resisting racist and sexist domination. These dynamics also erase the long histories of anti-imperialist struggles of Black feminists located across various European empires.

Further, the linguistic divides between English-speaking Black feminists of Britain and North America drown out the perspectives and experiences of Black women in Continental Europe. In parallel to Black feminism, Afrofeminism – particularly in francophone Europe – has been the space for many Continental European Black women to collectively learn, organise and mobilise for their interests. There are many similarities between Black feminism and Afrofeminism but Afrofeminism insists on grounding analysis and action in the particular and specific histories of colonialism, racial formation and gender hierarchy of the various European nation-states in which Black women live. Thus, when we speak of European Black feminism, we must ensure that the lived experiences and theorising of Black women on the continent and across different countries and languages is at the forefront of our work. We are, of course, in no way devaluing or disrespecting Black American feminist theorists who have shaped our praxis such as bell hooks, Patricia Hill Collins and the Combahee River Collective. Rather, this book attempts to talk back against both American domination and European silence about Black feminism and create a space for a different kind of dialogue – one that this is led by and for Black women in Europe.

Locating Black feminist and Afrofeminist politics in Europe is provocative because it is radical counter-storytelling about whose knowledge counts, whose politics matter and who gets to be part of the 'European story'. European Black feminist and Afrofeminist politics are nothing new. Indeed, they refract the story of the Enlightenment, colonialism and modernity. The 'Europe' of secular liberalism is not possible without the subjugation of colonised people. European Black feminist and Afrofeminist politics has been at the heart of anti-slavery, anti-colonial and socialist politics on the continent. This book helps to correct the record and place Black feminism and Afrofeminism firmly within contemporary European politics.

Black feminism and Afrofeminism have been so influential that they have helped to inspire the thinking and politics of non-Black women of colour in Europe. For this edited volume, we wanted to bring together the best writing about Black feminism and Afrofeminism as a way to showcase the creativity of resistance and demonstrate the possibilities of intersectional solidarity across race, class, gender, legal status and language. To be clear, we do not use 'women of colour' as a synonym for Black women nor are we engaging in the politics of 'political Blackness' in this text. Rather, we are attempting to demonstrate that solidarity is possible despite anti-Blackness. We do not reify or fetishise the category of 'women of colour'. Solidarity between different racialised women can never be taken for granted – it must be fought for and in this creative tension exists the possibilities for new insights. In this text we wanted to demonstrate that there are patterns of experiences and analyses that create the conditions for fruitful coalitions. These coalitions might falter but we think the struggle for solidarity across difference is central to any Black feminist politics. As such, this edited volume brings together activists, artists and scholars to explore how Black women and other women of colour from across Europe:

- theorise Black feminism and Afrofeminism from European perspectives
- build and sustain activist spaces for survival and resistance
- challenge, subvert and transform hegemonic socialist, feminist, populist and/or anarchist politics

- develop transnational alliances and intersectional and intergenerational coalitions for equality and social justice
- engage with creative practice as a means of activism and self-preservation.

Black women and women of colour in Europe have always maintained critical spaces of analysis and activism based on our race, class, gender, sexuality, disability, legal status and other categories of difference. This edited collection fills an important gap in knowledge about how Black women and women of colour, as active agents and authors of our lives, conceive our differing social positionings in various European countries, how we organise and mobilise for our shared interests and how we might collectively imagine a Black feminist Europe.

Part II, *Resistance, Solidarity and Coalition-Building*, explores how women of colour in five different countries undertake their Black feminist and Afrofeminist activism for social change. Viki Zaphiriou-Zarifi explores the creative strategies African migrant women activists undertake to assert their inclusion in Greek society. Staying in southern Europe, Nadia Nadesan examines the struggles for recognition and solidarity of newly formed queer and Afrofeminist activist networks in Spain. Cyn Awori Othieno and Annette Davis on behalf of Mwasi Collectif, the premier Afrofeminst activist network in France and perhaps in Europe, engage in the classic Black feminist practice of counter-storytelling to recount the history of French Afrofeminist activism since the early twentieth century. Connected to Mwasi's struggles, we move to Belgium where Nicole Grégoire and Modi Ntambwe explore the changing strategies of younger Afrofeminist activists as they shift away from older activists' integrationist approaches. Part II concludes with a view from Scotland from Claire Heuchan in which she discusses her writing, her well-trafficked blog and how Black feminist activism transforms in digital spaces.

In Part III, *Emotions, Affect and Intimate Relations*, we shift our Black feminist and Afrofeminst gaze from public to private space. Gabriella Beckles-Raymond discusses the multiple meanings of home for the Black British women of the Caribbean diaspora. In a dispatch from Switzerland, Pamela Ohene-Nyako explores how her founding of Afrolitt', a platform for literature lovers, helps build community, solidarity and critical cultural knowledge among women of colour. Johanna Lukate examines the fraught politics of Black women's hair in Germany and how Black women's hair is oftentimes used as a proxy for belonging and inclusion. Writing from a British perspective, Ego Ahaiwe Sowinski and Nazmia Jamal discuss what love, friendship and allyship might mean for women of colour. Another contributor from Belgium, but this time from a Flemish standpoint, Lubumbe Van de Velde explores the violent cultural practices of *Zwarte Piet* and how Black motherhood must be mobilised against it. Part III concludes with an interview that France-based Alecia McKenzie conducted with the late Eartha Kitt and explores what Kitt and her art represented in McKenzie's childhood home.

Part IV, *Surviving the Academy*, reflects challenges and expressions of Black feminist resistance in relation to life in academia. Writing from a British perspective, Yesim Deveci, inspired by Audre Lorde, discusses the risks and resistance involved in daring to speak and act otherwise as a woman of colour in academia. This radical practice of 'talking back' is continued by the Cruel Ironies Collective where they explore the implications of exclusion and misrecognition in the Dutch academy. Melody Howse offers incisive analysis of the formation of new and resistant spaces that emerge from an initial sense of feeling out of place and time in German academia. Part IV's spirit of survival is also evident in the words of Sadiah Qureshi, inspired by trailblazing Black feminist theorists, who provides a manifesto for navigating academia as a woman of colour. Extending this part's examination of institutional whiteness, Oda-Kange Diallo discusses such issues and their particularities in Danish academia. Part IV concludes with Chijioke Obasi's critique of the potential limitations of Black feminism when outlining the ingredients of an Africanist Sista-hood in Britain.

In Part V, *Digital and Creative Labour*, Kesiena Boom writes about tensions between the self-empowering nature of personal online essays and their capacity to perpetuate the commodification of Black women's pain. Continuing the commentary concerning creative labour and resistance, Tia-Monique Uzor explores the role of dance in the collective movements of African diasporic women in Britain. In addition, Dorett Jones documents past and present ways that Black women are filming their resistance and taking control of the lens, through which their lives are viewed. Part V concludes with Stacie CC Graham's account of the varied healing and activist creative practices of Black women across Europe.

In reading this edited volume, we hope that you reflect on the similarities of experiences across linguistic, cultural and national borders, as well as the nuanced differences that are documented. We urge you to consider how the various local contexts produce specific kinds of violence – and resistances. It is in that space between the particularity of difference and the similarity of experience that a new world can be born, and that Black feminism and Afrofeminism can continue to evolve and tell another story about Europe.

NOTE

1. L. Bassel and A. Emejulu, 2017. *Minority Women and Austerity: Survival and Resistance in France and Britain*. Policy Press, Bristol. B. Bryan, S. Dadzie and S. Scafe (eds), 1985. *The Heart of the Race: Black Women's Lives in Britain*. Virago, London. C. Boyce Davies, 2007. *Left of Karl Marx: The Political Life of Black Communist Claudia Jones*. Duke University Press, Durham. K. Oguntoye, M. Opitz and D. Schultz (eds), 1992. *Showing Our Colours: Afro-German Women Speak Out*. University of Massachusetts Press, Amherst. T.D. Sharpley-Whiting, 2000. 'Femme Négritude: Jane Nardal, *La Dépêche Africaine*, and the francophone New Negro'. *Souls: Critical Journal of Black Politics & Culture* 2(4), pp. 8–17. F. Sobande, forthcoming 2020. *The Digital Lives of Black Women in Britain*. Palgrave Macmillan, London. G. Wekker, 2016. *White Innocence: Paradoxes of Colonialism and Race*. Duke University Press, Durham.

PART II

Resistance, Solidarity and Coalition-Building

2

The Collective Mobilisation of African Women in Athens 'United We Stand'

Viki Zaphiriou-Zarifi

We have been suffering for long time. We have our own austerity measure for long time. (Lauretta Macauley, President of the United African Women's Organization, Greece)

As the above quote reminds us, long before the current economic crisis, African women in Greece have faced the ordinary, institutionalised social and economic inequalities based on race, class, gender, religion and legal status that individual women deal with every day.[1] In recent years, however, austerity, high unemployment and increasing anti-migrant sentiment have intensified the vulnerability of this and other already marginalised groups in multiple ways. In a context in which national identity and belonging are racialised as white, and in which migrant women are invisible as active independent agents, processes of gendered racialisation operate to make African women hyper-visible in particular stereotypical ways: as oppressed wives and mothers, uneducated domestic workers, and sexualised and/or dangerous Others.

With a focus on the activism of the United African Women's Organization (UAWO) this chapter explores how African women in Athens are collectively mobilising to counter the exclusionary processes they face in their everyday lives. Applying an 'acts of citizenship' framework of analysis, the chapter illustrates some of the ways in which women are attempting to challenge, and potentially transform, the categories of recognition available to them. Claiming citizenship rights for non-citizens creatively, performatively and in multiple spaces, UAWO's activism resonates greatly with the notion of 'acts of citizenship' as formulated by Isin and Nielsen.[2] According to Isin, such acts are 'those deeds by which actors constitute themselves (and others) as subjects of rights'.[3] Thus, subjects who are not citizens may *act* as citizens, thereby constituting themselves as those with 'the right to claim rights'.[4] Crucially, this expands the idea of citizenship to include those acts through which claims are articulated in new sites of contestation, belonging, identification and struggle. No longer limited to traditional sites of citizenship, these acts are performed in and through bodies, in the media and on the internet, at the borders and on the streets.[5]

THE UNITED AFRICAN WOMEN'S ORGANIZATION:
RECIPROCITY, ADVOCACY AND VOICE

UAWO emerged from a recognition that, despite inevitable differences, 'African women in Greece' occupy a particular position of intersectional disadvantage vis-à-vis Greek society and state. Run by African women for African women, UAWO can perhaps best be described as a bridge between the informal social networks women have developed and depend upon in their everyday lives and the more formal non-governmental organisation (NGO) landscape. Through a combination of self-advocacy work, political campaigning and cultural activities, UAWO provides an important collective space from which women can make rights-based claims for themselves, address practical needs, and perform a kind of affective politics that not only counters isolation but also collectivises problems and their possible resolution.[6]

By calling upon a cultural identity, UAWO deliberately creates a sense of 'groupness' with others. The double common bond of shared experiences 'back home' and as African women in Athens contributes to a clarity and certainty of identity that life in Greece cannot provide.[7] Hana, who is from Sierra Leone and has lived in Greece for 29 years, described UAWO thus:

> it's like our refuge home. You know, we feel comfortable … We safe. We see ourselves all the same, whether we are from Cameroon, Sierra Leone, Nigeria, we are all just the same. We all have something common. So we able to relate and say our problems you know in one word that we understand and we feel safe.

As both a 'home' where women 'feel comfortable' and a hub of activism from which many political actions are born, to many women UAWO is that 'homeplace' hooks describes as 'a site of resistance and liberation struggle …' 'that space where we return for renewal and self-recovery, where we can heal our wounds and become whole'.[8] Lauretta emphasised this in a speech she made on International Women's Day in 2009:

> We say 'united we stand' and we mean it. We stand and we endure because we have something that makes us strong and helps us stand upright. And this is our organization, which is our home and family …

In a context in which the mere presence of African migrants has been constructed as a threat to the nation, this statement of togetherness alone can be seen as an expression of resistance to the non-integrative, othering policies of the state. By helping women to claim a sense of 'in placeness', UAWO seeks to counter the processes and practices that keep these women in a state of permanent insecurity.[9]

UAWO's approach is in stark contrast to and, indeed, challenges those that seek to conduct politics in generalised terms and neutralised language – in ways that avoid the individualised or personal account. At conferences, political meetings, parliamentary debates and so on, many of these women, as marginal Others, lack the authority of political, academic or institutional discourses.

What they do have, however, is the passion of experience and remembrance. Not 'the authority of experience' which, hooks warns, is all too often used to silence and exclude, but the 'spirit that orders those words, that testifies that, behind them – underneath, every where – there is a lived reality'.[10] When women get up to speak about their own experiences, they are claiming to know their truth. Theirs is the particular knowledge that comes from suffering that is, according to hooks, 'a way of knowing that is often expressed through the body, what it knows, what has been deeply inscribed on it through experience'.[11] It is this passion of experience and remembrance that Hana refers to when she explains why African women must represent themselves:

> We really feel it and we know it more than any other group that will represent us – just reading it and saying it … When they stand there to talk, you really feel the voice. The pain. The cry. That this is really the victim of what is you know.

Far from non-political, the women's testimonies, grounded in felt and lived experiences, give them a power and an authority that theorising alone could never carry.

Insisting that this is the most important location from which one can know, UAWO challenges what it means to be political, who has the right to speak, when, where and to whom. By giving women the microphone, UAWO empowers women to demand recognition as actors with the ability to speak for themselves. Lauretta explained:

You know how powerful this tool? Somebody to give you a microphone? It's a power ... When you give them that – empower them to meet the public – it's something like integrating. So they begin to open. You know, they begin to feel free.

Crucially, articulating experiences of victimisation, exploitation and abuse for themselves is a display of agency that simultaneously counters the tendency to view these women as backward and voiceless. Using the victimhood narrative as an effective way for women to access the public sphere and highlight inequalities as a public issue requiring policy action, while rejecting the role of passive and vulnerable objects, UAWO performs a tricky but necessary balancing act. As Sassen points out, there is, after all, a distinction between powerlessness and the condition of being an actor even though lacking in power.[12]

CLAIMING VISIBILITY ...

Recognising the connection between visibility and rights, UAWO seeks symbolic gains in order to secure a foothold in public debates from which its members can make claims. In the struggle over what kinds of protests against the prevailing regime of citizenship can be seen and heard, UAWO has identified and mobilised collectively as mothers on behalf of their children, as activists, as 'exotic Others', and as women mobilising international discourses of equality and women's rights.[13] The following subsections discuss these four, sometimes overlapping, examples of 'acts of citizenship'.

... as mothers: 'No to Racism from the Baby's Cradle'

UAWO launched its first campaign in late November 2005, entitled 'No to Racism from the Baby's Cradle', with a demonstration in central Athens (Figure 2.1). Posters were prepared appropriating the well-known Benetton advertisements that depicted a group of babies of different skin colour (Figure 2.2), and leaflets were handed out demanding legalisation, the right to birth certificates and citizenship rights for children born in Greece to migrant parents.

Figure 2.1   Members of UAWO take part in a workshop activity
Photo credit: Zaphiriou-Zarifi.

Conceived by individual mothers contesting policies harmful to their children, the campaign proved to be an extremely effective way to mobilise women. Hana's response was fairly typical. Tired of 'facing this discrimination' at her children's school alone, she immediately understood that 'I cannot fight alone. It's something we have to come together, bring this out because maybe there are things some people take advantage because it's not known.'

Mobilising the mother stereotype as a way to demand recognition and respect for themselves as well as papers and citizenship rights for their children was a clever political move. Starting with an issue that was shared by all migrant parents not only provided a solid ground on which to build strategic alliances with other migrant groups, it also invoked a narrative that Greek parents and those sympathetic to children could be moved by. Strategically, this was a relatively unthreatening way for women who had been constructed as Other to announce their arrival on the

Figure 2.2 Campaign poster for 'No to Racism from the Baby's cradle'
The text reads: 'We return with the demand 'NO to racism from the cradle'. Birth certificates should be issued to migrants' children born in Greece and (they should be registered with the municipality.
Photo credit: Zaphiriou-Zarifi.

political scene without provoking a backlash. By politicising the mother stereotype, they were able to push the political agenda while simultaneously validating their claims for respect and understanding, and justifying their reasons for migrating to Greece in the first place.[14] African women were also reminding Greek society that they are more than domestic workers, prostitutes, victims of trafficking and exotic Others; that they are worthy mothers struggling to feed, clothe and educate their children, just like 'us'.

The 'No to Racism from the Baby's Cradle' campaign also marked a significant departure from the way things had previously been done on the Athenian activist scene.[15] Instead of Greek activists taking leadership roles with migrant groups in support, this campaign was initiated, orchestrated and organised by the women themselves.[16] Moreover, because previous demonstrations were usually dominated by Greek activists and migrant men, the presence of African women and their children at the front of these demonstrations was, at the time, a novel sight.[17]

Understanding the power of their collective presence and visibility on the streets of Athens, the children of women from different African countries were instructed to sing Greek Christmas songs. Bringing together linguistic and religious signifiers in this way was a powerful statement of belonging.

In a context in which certain bodies being seen as political is a display of power and agency that can provoke anxiety, fear and resistance from some quarters, politically 'coming out' as mothers in this way proved to be an extremely effective strategy.

Figure 2.3 UAWO pose for journalists with then Minister for Immigration, Tasia Christodoulopoulou, at a rally for 'second-generation' rights outside parliament on the eve of a vote on changes to citizenship law, 24 June 2015
Photo credit: Zaphiriou-Zarifi.

Though it may appear to reinforce stereotypes, the women adopted the pre-written scripts according to which they are normally 'read' in Greece in order to subvert such representations. By speaking in public spaces for the first time 'as mothers' they were able to voice their own claims in ways that contrasted with prevailing representations of victimhood and backwardness and marked the emergence of new political subjectivities and discourses.[18] As Zavos observes, 'Identifying migrant women's agency in such acts of performative appropriation of available discourses and terms of address is important for recognising the different ways in which they actively wield power and recast national and political imaginaries.[19] Constituting themselves as the mothers of those with 'the right to claim rights', they were speaking to the norms within which they lived, rather than operating outside them.[20] Acting as citizens by proxy on behalf of their children they were thus able to claim social intelligibility within common and culturally legible discourses.

UAWO thus entered the political landscape with a multi-layered strategy that mobilised important forms of embodied resistance as a way to call attention to the unjust effects of precarity. By using already legible cultural codes surrounding motherhood they were able to cross other racialised and gendered boundaries and so enter the political field. Using new forms of embodied political interventions, they engaged a vocabulary that breaks with masculinist models of autonomy because they showed that vulnerability is part of resistance and that modes of alliance are characterised by interdependency and public action.[21]

... as anti-austerity activists

Alongside the narrative of financial crisis and social anomie, there has also been a more positive commentary on the crisis in Greece pointing to a shift in values towards a more democratic and inclusive form of politics. Protest, dissent, non-compliance and outrage have been expressed on the streets by increasing numbers of people demanding to be heard. Quick to recognise an opportunity for visibility of a more positive, agential nature, UAWO has taken its place in the endless demonstrations, occupations, festivals, performances, solidarity meetings and events taking place across the city.[22] The crisis has thus brought UAWO not only increased publicity and greater recognition but also opportunities for members to articulate their grievances and demands alongside those of others and to form new alliances in broader struggles for social justice.

This growing movement has included anti-austerity protests and rallies, politically themed festivals (most notably the Anti-Racist Festival) and a proliferation of 'international' days (such as International Refugee Day). The displays of diversity at such events, even if they are somewhat transient and do not extend to other areas of the women's lives, are nevertheless important and mark a significant and positive change in Greek society. Tsilimpounidi argues that 'diversity is one of the strong elements

Figure 2.4   UAWO attends an anti-racism demonstration, Syntagma Square, 21 March 2015

Photo credit: Zaphiriou-Zarifi.

of the Greek social milieu since 2008: such protests had created a faceless, borderless, multicultural and polyvocal movement'.[23] This 'facelessness' is an invisibility of an altogether more positive kind for African women. For many, being part of a multitude collectively mobilised in resistance is both empowering and liberating. In these spaces of protest citizens stand alongside non-citizens, sometimes even identifying with them to claim rights they now feel they too are being denied.

Interestingly, as these women (and men) enact citizenship thus, some more radical citizens have been claiming the migrant label to highlight their experiences of marginalisation. In Exarchia, the traditional anarchist stronghold neighbourhood of central Athens, street art with faceless figures and the tagline 'we are all immigrants' began to appear in 2011.[24] While this was a powerful statement of solidarity, it was primarily about highlighting the marginalisation and feelings of non-belonging among citizens during the crisis. The positioning (in terms of experience, needs, relation to the state and so on) of a marginalised Greek citizen is qualitatively different from that of a non-citizen migrant, and invoking similarities is in danger of unintentionally obscuring this fact. This is a constant struggle for UAWO and its members: how to form allegiances with others and still be seen and heard.

It remains an open question how far these seemingly inclusive spaces will sustain solidarity with African women's interests and activisms, and whether they will extend to, and bring greater recognition and rights in, other areas of their lives.[25] Nevertheless, taking up space in the city, being part of performances of solidarity and becoming visible as political agents alongside others is an important way for women to 'talk back' to modes of inferiorisation.[26] In these acts of citizenship, women are fighting for a democratic transformation from below; they are actors rather than subjects, which is a powerful statement of belonging.[27] In contrast to their everyday experiences on the streets of Athens, within these transient spaces women appropriate social narratives of difference in ways in which they are celebrated for their non-Greekness. The hope is that, over time, through regular visibility and presence of this kind, women will carve out more space for themselves in Athens and become recognised as subjects that count in other areas of their lives also.

... exotic Others: detoxified difference/eating the Other

Amidst the growing anti-austerity movement, women have been creating new pathways to greater liveability not only in terms of social intelligibility but also in material terms. They have organised and taken part in events where they assert their 'African-ness' on their own terms and as something to be celebrated. By taking ownership of the 'African women' identity thus, UAWO uses it as a way to build a common bond, to counter prevailing notions of them as negative Other, and to earn some income. Identifying an appetite for 'exotic' cuisine and handicrafts, women use their skills and creativity to earn both money and positive recognition as 'exotic' Others.

As bell hooks writes in her chapter 'eating the other', through the commodification of Otherness 'ethnicity becomes spice, seasoning that can liven up the dull dish that is mainstream white culture'.[28] Women would dance at events (Figure 2.6), turn up in full eye-catching 'traditional' dress (Figure 2.5), and sell their 'exotic' food and handicrafts. In these spaces, women are finding ways to be appreciated for that which they are, rather than being defined – and feared – according to that which they are not (non-Greek, non-citizen, non-white and so on).

Figure 2.5   Members of UAWO attending a fundraising event for Sierra Leone
Photo credit: Zaphiriou-Zarifi.

The paparazzi-like attention they received when they wore their African dress, though superficial, raised women's profiles and gave them a chance to articulate their concerns to journalists, TV channels and so on. Nevertheless, the contrast between these events and the exclusion women experienced in their everyday lives remains troubling. The problem perhaps lies with the reduction of the stranger to the level of 'being'. By emphasising the association of being with the body through food, dance and dress in these limited spaces, the African woman stranger comes to be assumed to be knowable.[29]

Rather than being 'Different to the point of being unknowable', visibility of this kind allows for the perception of being 'known' as exotic Other and creates a distance that makes proximity less threatening.[30] The 'detoxification of one's neighbour', Žižek has argued, suggests a 'clear passage from direct barbarism to barbarism with a human face'.[31] Difference thus 'decaffeinated', to borrow Žižek's phrase, is safe for appropriation and consumption, along with other products stripped of their malignant qualities (such as cream without fat, coffee without caffeine and beer without alcohol).[32] It is also far less threatening than claims to equality, similarity and/or co-presence on the buses, in the workplace and in the neighbourhood. In contrast to the dangerous stranger who

Figure 2.6   UAWO dance group performs at a fundraising event for Sierra Leone
Photo credit: Zaphiriou-Zarifi.

transgresses boundaries by wearing the same clothes, shopping in the same places and eating the same food (signs that she may even be seeking to become 'one of us'), in the alternative spaces of festivals, bazaars and cultural events the Other is made known in specific ways that ultimately operate to maintain both her marginalisation and the status quo.[33] Reinforcing her position as temporary guest, Greek culture is (re)constructed as dominant and the Greek tradition of hospitality acts as a form of defence, enabling both fears of loss of 'purity' as well as demands for recognition to be temporarily ignored.[34]

… as women: International Women's Day

In 2015, UAWO marked International Women's Day (IWD) with a photography project in which four African and four Greek women wore each other's traditional dress. Together symbolising 8 March (IWD) and female solidarity, UAWO called upon a discourse of 'women's rights' and used the platform of the much publicised IWD in order to align themselves with feminist organisations in Greece and beyond.

According to Butler, one way for those who are deemed illegible and unrecognisable to resist normative constructions and hierarchies is to insist on being 'like you', and to speak 'in the terms of the "human".'[35]

The IWD project was very much about this – about talking back to discriminatory binaries to emphasise commonality and humanity over stereotypes and dehumanisation. As Lauretta explained:

> It's something that is a symbolic something to gain public opinion that they can see that no matter the difference between us, we can fit in the same clothes or shoes or whatever it is so that we can fit in the society, you understand. That I can fit in your clothes and you can fit in my clothes so we have to work together to make a better society.

Simultaneously a proclamation of presence, commonality *and* difference, the project was intended to remind the Greek public that 'we' are 'like you' and that we can work together, across differences, for the good of all. The project was thus also a manifestation of UAWO's aim to work 'hand in hand' and 'create mutual bonds of solidarity between Africans and our host the Greeks'.[36] In this way, strategic alliances were formed not only with other Others who occupy similar positions of disadvantage but also with Greek women.

By leveraging the modes of recognition available to members in order to assert their humanity through commonality, UAWO was doing more than claiming public recognition as being 'like us'. Also inverting expectations by putting a Black woman in a Greek costume and a white woman in an African one, they were fighting the misrecognition, stereotyping and dehumanisation that permit all kinds of violence towards them. Ruth, who is from Nigeria and has lived in Greece for over 20 years, explained how the project challenged racist inferiorisation:

> It looked strange to them, but a lot of them can get the message that we are sending message that everybody we are one. There's no difference – the colour, no matter where you come from, no matter the colour you have – we are all the same thing. We think the same way. There's nothing different from us as a human being. So they have to learn that. It's very, very important for them to know that one and change their ways of treating people.

The assertion of equal humanity – that 'there's nothing different from us as a human being' – is crucial because, as Athanasiou points out, when a life that does not figure as normatively human is violated, this violation remains unrecognised, misrecognised or recognised in an injurious way, through terms that enable derealising violence.[37]

The technique of unsettling the order of things by juxtaposing things not usually found together (here, an African woman in an Ipirot costume), is one UAWO has employed before. Putting on short theatrical performances in which 'the Greeks play the African – the immigrants – and we play the Greek' to show 'how they treated us in the office – bureaucratically', UAWO has made powerful statements about prejudice and inequality.[38]

Figure 2.7 International Women's Day project, 8 March 2015
Photo credit: Zaphiriou-Zarifi.

Role reversal disrupts expectation within the realm of the familiar, thereby shedding light on women's experiences in ways that make it harder for others to turn away. Thus employing modes of representation that deliberately confuse, the opportunity is created for women to behave in ways not prescribed, and perhaps not always sanctioned, by dominant norms.[39] By challenging dominant ways of being, the IWD project created 'a space of illusion' that highlighted the constructed nature of national identity, thereby exposing every real space of assumed national belonging as 'still more illusory'.[40] Without offering resolution or consolation, these tactics disrupt and test our customary notions of ourselves – and, in doing so, those of others. Thus, UAWO is widening the possibilities and creating a little more space for their members.[41]

As with many UAWO actions, the IWD project operated at multiple levels. On the surface, it was presented as the opportunity to exchange cultural traditions (which remains one of the organisation's specified aims and objectives) and as such, was a very positive experience for all the women who took part. Ruth beamed as she described how happy it made her when the Greek participants enjoyed wearing her daughter's clothes. Despite being looked at strangely by some members of the public, the visibility she experienced gave her a sense of belonging.

> For me yesterday I feel belong, you know? In a positive way yesterday I feel. Because they looks at me ... what are they going to say about me? I'm just a Greek woman. Normally, without the dress, I feel I'm a foreigner. Yesterday I don't feel that ... I feel like them [the Greeks], you know? It make me feel belong.

Lauretta agreed: 'it make me feel I belong more'. Though this was soon undercut by sadness at her lack of citizenship, which even after 32 years living in Greece remains elusive to her.

This more formal dimension of belonging was emphasised by setting the photographs in front of parliament – a potent symbol of the Greek nation-state from which these women are, on the whole, politically excluded (Figure 2.8). Appearing so publicly in Syntagma Square amongst the hordes of passers-by, and by taking control of their image themselves, the African participants experienced a feeling of hyper-visibility in ways that contrasted dramatically to their everyday experiences of 'visible invisibility' as Other.[42] In a context in which even everyday routine activities like travelling on buses, working or living in the city are transformed into forbidden and illegal acts, it is not difficult to see why, in Lauretta's words, 'The pictures says a lot ... it has a lot of meaning to us.'[43]

The location also signals another, considerably more controversial, level at which the project acquired meaning both vis-à-vis Greek society and for those taking part. Remaining within the bounds of gendered constructions of women as bearers of tradition and reproducers of the nation, the project deliberately subverted national and national*ist* symbols.[44]

Figure 2.8 Women pose outside parliament for the International Women's Day project, 8 March 2015

Photo credit: Zaphiriou-Zarifi.

The traditional Greek costumes the African participants (from Sierra Leone, Ghana and Nigeria) wore represented three regions that are part of the narrative of Greek national identity and the formation of Modern Greece. By dressing in costumes from Thrace (Figure 2.9), Asia Minor and the island of Ios, they were claiming – albeit temporarily – an identity they are told daily, both implicitly and explicitly, can never be theirs. By deliberately transgressing normative notions of 'Greekness' in this way, the women mounted a new means of resistance to dominant, seemingly natural forms of identity and belonging.

Rewriting the script of what it is to be an African woman in Athens they had, for a time, unsettled definitions provided by Greek socio-political discourses and widely propagated as truth.[45] By appearing as Greeks in front of one of the main symbols of state power alongside white Greek

Figure 2.9   A member of UAWO in a traditional
Thracian costume

Photo credit: Zaphiriou-Zarifi.

women in their own traditional dress (a 'version' of themselves widely
accepted and even celebrated), the women disrupted 'what has become
settled knowledge and knowable reality' and used, as it were, their
'unreality to make an otherwise impossible or illegible claim'.[46] Far from
being intended as 'passing as white' (which would support the national
desire to assimilate difference), this was a deliberate disruption of the
'face of the nation'.[47] By subversively appropriating tradition – by fusing
and *con*fusing the difference between traditional images of Greek and
African femininity – the women were presenting a challenge to established norms and concepts. Highlighting the constructedness of identity
and national belonging denaturalises 'fixed' social categories. After all,
as history tells us and the 'Greek' costume from Asia Minor illustrates,
there is nothing fixed, given or natural about the boundaries of the
nation-state.

In these cracks, openings begin to appear and new lines of alliances and
solidarity emerge. For when African women demand to be recognised as

equal to Greek women, even if this effort fails again and again, there is value in the calling into question 'the normative horizon in which recognition takes place'.[48] This crisis puts the current norms of recognition into question, establishes a critical point of departure for the interrogation of available norms and sets up the possibility that a new set might be developed.[49] This is perhaps what gave Ruth, Lauretta and others such a boost that day – the feeling that they had rattled the norms they were so often excluded by and hope at the possibility of alternatives.

CONCLUDING REMARKS

Recognising that change can only be worked out or negotiated on the basis of the given order – that there is little to be gained by indulging in the 'fantasy of godlike power' in which they can remake the world – UAWO works towards improving the situation of African women in Athens incrementally.[50] As this chapter has shown, UAWO works within dominant scripts – it appropriates available modes of recognition, even sometimes using gendered and racialised stereotypes as resources, in order to present its members in recognisable ways. Thus appearing to stick (more or less) to the categories available to them, women are able to articulate their own claims and perform acts of citizenship in ways that present themselves as lives worthy of public recognition and of protection. Using their bodies to claim presence and a more positive visibility in the media, on the internet and on the streets, women are constituting themselves as citizens – as those with 'the right to claim rights'.[51] This is about more than symbolic forms of representation; it is about using common narratives to disrupt the reproduction of both symbolic and material hierarchies that regulate access to resources.[52]

Though social intelligibility is crucial to living a liveable life, recognition does not in and of itself lead to a redistribution of rights and resources. As several of the examples discussed in this chapter illustrate, hierarchical binaries of difference may be reinforced even as a more positive recognition and sense of belonging are attained. By conforming to the notions Greeks may already have about 'Africans' and 'Africa', the danger is that stereotypical representations confirm that these women are of 'another place' such that they remain strange (and estranged) yet become familiar in their unfamiliarity. Hence, whether women's efforts to unsettle norms that construct them as 'ungrievable' or 'out of place' bodies to be feared will also lead to more rights and resources in the longer term remains an open question.

Nevertheless, when women constituted by that which is 'before and outside' themselves in ways that often deny them a voice take control of their image to represent themselves as actors, an altogether different kind of visibility is made possible.[53] Attempts to restore the African identity on a more positive footing, through their own initiatives and with pride, are, at the very least, a form of self-representation that contributes to the empowerment of women who are all too often ignored, inferiorised and excluded in many areas of their daily lives. The hope remains, therefore, that by continuing to provide counter-narratives to their 'out of placeness',[54] these women will achieve a more positive and, gradually, a less stereotypical visibility that will lead to their wider acceptance in Greece's changing socio-political landscape.

NOTES

1. Akwugo Emejulu and Leah Bassel, 2017. 'Whose crisis counts? Minority women, austerity and activism in France and Britain'. In J. Kantola and E. Lombardo (eds), *Gender and the Economic Crisis in Europe*. Springer International Publishing, Cham, pp. 185–208.
2. Engin F. Isin and Greg M. Nielsen (eds), 2008. *Acts of Citizenship*. Zed Books, London; New York.
3. Engin F. Isin, 2009. 'Citizenship in flux: The figure of the activist citizen'. *Subjectivity* 29, pp. 367–88 (p. 371).
4. Ibid. Isin argues that Arendt's 'the right to have rights' is too passive and possessive to capture the activist figure of citizenship.
5. Ibid.
6. Alexandra Zavos, Penny Koutrolikou and Dimitra Siatitsa, 2017. 'Changing landscapes of urban citizenship: Southern Europe in times of crisis'. *Citizenship Studies* 21, pp. 379–92.
7. Fatima El-Tayeb, 2011. *European Others*. University of Minnesota Press, Minneapolis.
8. bell hooks, 1991. 'Homeplace: A site of resistance'. In *Yearning: Race, Gender, and Cultural Politics*. Turnaround, London, pp. 385, 389.
9. Teresa Piacentini, 2014. 'Everyday acts of resistance: The precarious lives of asylum seekers in Glasgow'. In Katarzyna Marciniak and Imogen Tyler (eds), *Immigrant Protest: Politics, Aesthetics, and Everyday Dissent, Praxis: Theory in Action*. SUNY Press, Albany, NY, p. 174.
10. bell hooks, 1994. *Teaching to Transgress: Education as the Practice of Freedom*. Routledge, New York, p. 91.
11. Ibid.

12. Saskia Sassen, 2002. 'The repositioning of citizenship: Emergent subjects and spaces for politics'. *Berkeley Journal of Sociology* 46, pp. 4–26.
13. Imogen Tyler, 2013. *Revolting Subjects: Social Abjection and Resistance in Neoliberal Britain*. Zed Books, London.
14. Alexandra Zavos, 2012. 'Building alliances: Greek and migrant women in the anti-racist movement in Athens'. In Glenda Tibe Bonifacio (ed.), *Feminism and Migration*. Springer Netherlands, Dordrecht, pp. 227–42.
15. For further discussion on how things were previously done, see Alexandra Zavos, 2010. 'Gender, migration and anti-racist politics in the continued project of the nation'. In I. Palmary, E. Burman, K. Chantler and P. Kiguwa (eds), *Gender and Migration: Feminist Interventions*. Zed Books, distributed in the USA exclusively by Palgrave Macmillan, London; New York, pp. 15–30. See also Alexandra Zavos, 2014. 'Gender and the politics of immigrant protest in Greece'. In Katarzyna Marciniak and Imogen Tyler (eds), *Immigrant Protest: Politics, Aesthetics, and Everyday Dissent, Praxis: Theory in Action*. SUNY, Albany, NY, pp. 225–41.
16. Zavos, 'Gender and the politics of immigrant protest in Greece'.
17. Ibid.
18. Ibid.
19. Ibid., p. 232.
20. Isin, 'Citizenship in flux'.
21. Judith Butler, Zeynep Gambetti and Leticia Sabsay (eds), 2016. *Vulnerability in Resistance*. Duke University Press, Durham.
22. Alexandra Zavos, 2012. 'Building alliances'.
23. Myrto Tsilimpounidi, 2012. 'Athens 2012: Performances "in crisis" or what happens when a city goes soft?' *City* 16, pp. 546–56 (p. 549).
24. See ibid. for further comment on this.
25. Akwugo Emejulu and Leah Bassel, 2015. 'Minority women, austerity and activism'. *Race & Class* 57, pp. 86–95 (p. 93). Emejulu and Bassel raise similar concerns in their study on minority women's rights in Scotland, England and France.
26. bell hooks, 1989. *Talking Back: Thinking Feminist, Thinking Black*. South End Press, Boston, MA.
27. Tsilimpounidi, 'Athens 2012'.
28. bell hooks, 1992. *Black Looks: Race and Representation*. South End Press, Boston, MA, p. 21.
29. Sara Ahmed, 2000. *Strange Encounters: Embodied Others in Post-Coloniality*. Routledge, London; New York.
30. John Berger, 1975. *A Seventh Man*. 1st edition. Viking, New York, p. 254.
31. Slavoj Žižek, 2010. 'Liberal multiculturalism masks an old barbarism with a human face'. *Guardian*.
32. Ibid.
33. Gabriella Lazaridis and Eugenia Wickens, 1999. '"Us" and the "others"'. *Annals of Tourism Research* 26, pp. 632–55.
34. Mariangela Veikou, 2016. 'Economic crisis and migration: Visual representations of difference in Greece'. *Cultural Studies* 30, pp. 147–72.

35. Judith Butler, 2004. *Undoing Gender*. Routledge, New York; London, p. 14.

36. This quote is taken from the UAWO's aims and objectives.

37. Judith Butler and Athena Athanasiou, 2013. *Dispossession: The Performative in the Political*. 1st edition. Polity Press, Malden, MA.

38. In one theatrical performance a white Greek was shown struggling with African office workers at a local authority/bureaucratic institution.

39. Kevin Hetherington, 1998. *Expressions of Identity: Space, Performance, Politics*. Sage, London.

40. Michel Foucault (Jay Miskowiec, trans.), 1986. 'Of other spaces'. *Diacritics* 16, pp. 22–7 (p. 27).

41. Peter Johnson, 2006. 'Unravelling Foucault's "different spaces"'. *History of the Human Sciences* 19, pp. 75–90.

42. George Kandylis, 2017. 'Urban scenes of citizenship: Inventing the possibility of immigrants' citizenship in Athens'. *Citizenship Studies* 21, pp. 468–82 (p. 478).

43. Olga Lafazani, 2013. 'A border within a border: The migrants' squatter settlement in Patras as a heterotopia'. *Journal of Borderlands Studies* 28, pp. 1–13.

44. Nira Yuval-Davis and Floya Anthias, 1989. *Woman-Nation-State*. Palgrave Macmillan, Basingstoke.

45. B. Wearing, 1998. *Leisure and Feminist Theory*. Sage, London.

46. Butler, *Undoing Gender*, p. 27.

47. Ahmed, *Strange Encounters*.

48. Judith Butler, 2005. *Giving an Account of Oneself*. 1st edition. Fordham University Press, New York, p. 24.

49. Ibid.

50. Butler, *Undoing Gender*, p. 3.

51. Isin, 'Citizenship in flux'.

52. Tyler, *Revolting Subjects*.

53. Butler, *Undoing Gender*, p. 3.

54. Piacentini, 'Everyday acts of resistance'.

3

Making Space: Black and Womxn of Colour Feminist Activism in Madrid

Nadia Nadesan

The central question posed by different social movements in Madrid and across Spain has been how to create radical democracy under austerity. However, the demand for greater accountability and justice focused exclusively on class oftentimes obscures the long histories of exclusion from political processes and full citizenship based on gender and race. Concurrent with the rise of different citizen platforms for democracy and participatory processes, there has also been the creation of a queer Black feminist community struggling for recognition, justice and equality.

The defining moment in public memory around Madrid's activist culture in the past decade has been the 15M movement and encampment in Plaza del Sol. Sparked by the 2008 economic crisis and subsequent austerity measures imposed on Spain by the European Union, the European Central Bank and the International Monetary Fund, the 15M movement takes its name from the mass demonstrations that began on 15 May 2011. Plaza del Sol is the literal centre of the capital city of Madrid and symbolises Spain's national identity. The occupying of Plaza del Sol represented to the entire country a symbolic reclaiming of the city.[1]

For activists writing about their experience of 15M, taking Plaza del Sol served as a critique of the public sphere as white and male.[2] Maria PTQK, an activist and writer, asserted that the critique and challenge posed by 15M to the traditional public sphere was not necessarily in the messages and wide-ranging content produced, but rather in the praxis of the protest. Without the overarching banner of a single message, the lack of hierarchy and abstract political desires invited the enormous level of participation in the square.[3] Rather than constructing a coherent political message, 15M became defined more by the process and practice of placemaking for a new kind of city and coexistence reflected in activist spaces that followed, as well as in Spain's *okupa* (squatting) tradition seen in spaces such as EVA (Espacio Vecinal Argunzuela), Este es un Plaza and Ingobernable.[4] The resounding outcome and nature of this practice has been the 'thousands of networked micro-utopian prototypes characterised as collective, open, and process-based'.[5]

15M set a precedent in shaping placemaking and social movements in the city. However, at the time it did not include a utopian ideal for a world that accounted for racism that encompassed the demands and desires of Black and People of Colour (BPoC). From 2012 Madrid has been the beginning of that endeavour to make space for BPoC as well as create and include BPoC communities and perspectives as part of the wider narrative of a progressive social movement. More specifically, within BPoC communities, Black and womxn[6] of colour have initiated processes of incorporating feminism into their communities as well as pushing the feminist movement to take racism into account. Looking at the composition of the left-wing spaces as they stand now, Black and womxn of colour are few in number or absent – despite the fact that Madrid is witnessing flourishing Afrofeminist activism in this political moment. In this chapter, I will examine the gap between the rhetoric of justice and the inclusion of Afrofeminist activists in supposedly liberatory spaces, as well as the space and placemaking practices of Black and womxn of colour as a part of a larger social praxis in the city. By examining various political moments and events, I will highlight the nature of collective placemaking practices within Black and womxn of colour communities and spaces and how they disrupt and respond to social movements around the city.

BLACK WOMEN, INTERNATIONAL WOMEN'S DAY AND THE WOMEN'S STRIKE

Since 2012, Madrid has seen a new wave of Afrofeminist activism. In addition to broader afrodescendente civil society organisations and networks in Madrid, there exists an array of organisations led by Black womxn, most of which have also appeared during this time. One of the principal organisations is Empoderamiento Femenino Afrodescendiente en España (EFAE), which was founded in 2016.[7] The organisation focuses solely on Black women of African descent and arose out of the need to both represent womxn in spaces of Afro empowerment as well as Black womxn in feminist spaces. The founders were friends who were motivated to bring a more nuanced practice of care and intersectionality into feminist politics. Their aims were twofold: to support their own community and to grow the Afrofeminist movement in feminist politics to encompass more than just lip service to the images and idea of intersectional practices. Other organisations such as Kwanzaa, a student organisation with similar political leanings, began in 2015.[8] Both organisations have assumed a cornerstone role and work in creating space for Black womxn as well as learning for and by Black womxn for themselves and others. Some of the work they did in 2017 included hosting open workshops and talks in Matadero[9] on cultural appropriation, the historical memory of Blackness, colourism, as well as generally participating in other panels and events as teachers.[10] Their work pushes forward their agenda of not just creating space for Black womxn and representation in political spaces but also valorising and recognising the work of Black womxn as integral to the fabric of social movements. Although relatively young organisations, EFAE and Kwanzaa regularly host events throughout the year and also collaborate to create events, at times spontaneously to respond to current events happening in the city of Madrid. However, despite the creative work that EFAE, Kwanzaa and other Afrofeminist organisations are undertaking, they are often invisibilised or met with hostility in mainstream activist spaces.

During the *huelga* or the women's strike on International Women's Day demonstrations on 8 March 2018, womxn of colour were often invisibilised in terms of presence and discourse in the events leading up to and during the *huelga*. While activists carried placards and posters with images of brown and Black women such as Angela Davis and Audre Lorde, there were actually very few Black and womxn of colour participating in the demonstration and speaking at the protest. Although white women were shouting that 'care work is work', there was little recognition that Spain's care system is made possible by domestic workers who are more often than not womxn of colour and migrant women.[11] Images such as Figure 3.1 were prevalent on social media.

These satirical invoices monetarily quantify the unpaid labour of care work such as cooking, cleaning, looking after children and older relatives, and companionship. However, there were no infographics demanding a living wage and secure employment for precarious care workers, many of whom are womxn of colour. While a popular rallying cry was that the women who marched would 'march for all those absent', there was no critical reflection or debate about who was absent and why. When the domestic workers came out to demonstrate on International Care Worker

NÓMINA MENSUAL POR EL TRABAJO DIARIO

Empresa: La Sociedad Capitalista   Trabajadora: Mujeres

Periodo de liquidación del 1 de cualquier mes al 28/30/31 de cualquier mes de 2018

DEVENGOS

Salario Base... (mínimo por 8 horas de trabajo)..................735,90

Complementos:

- Planchar..........................100
- Cocinar..........................300
- Limpieza extraordinarias..........300
- Cuidados de niños, mayores, enfermos, mascotas........50
- Nocturnidad.......................100
- Acompañamiento....................100
- Gestión y organización............100
- Compras...........................100
- Consejera.........................100

******Total Devengado...............1985,9

RETENCIONES

Retención a cuenta IRPF 5,73%.........114,19
Cotización a la Seguridad Social 4,7%....93,34
Cotización D+F+P 1.65%................32,77

*******Total retenciones..............240,29

Total devengado	Total retenciones	Total a percibir	Total que percibe
1.985,9	240,29	1.745.6	0

DERECHOS ADQUIRIDOS PARA SU JUBILACIÓN "0"

Asturies Feminista 8M   @Asturies8M   @Asturies8M   asturies8m@gmail.com

Figure 3.1   asturies femenista 8M
Source: www.facebook.com/Gafasmoradas/photos/a.18184045783
85858/2296435307249447/?type=3&theater

Day on 25 March 2018,[12] the demonstration was much smaller than the 8 March protest. Barely a fraction of the 6,000[13] women who went on strike for 8M were at this demonstration. This lack of solidarity from white women was criticised in the Afrofemininas blog.[14] The post explained that in part the lack of participation from some Black womxn during the *huelga* comes from the lack of solidarity from white women. The blog also criticised the non-presence of white feminists during the International Day Against Racism on 21 March 2017. Days before the march, EFAE answered this need by creating a space for Black womxn, and more broadly womxn of colour who were going to march. EFAE set up meeting points in the city for womxn of colour to meet and create a unified bloc in the march. Womxn from these organisations have taken up the very necessary work of creating points of encounter and care in broader left-wing politics.

LA CANCHA AS A RESPONSE TO 8M

One of the events following the *huelga* was *La Cancha es Nuestra* (The Court is Ours). The event was named after the section of the public park, Casino de La Reina, reserved for basketball and football. The event organisers were from the community centre in the Casino de la Reina park, EFAE, Kwanzaa and Migrantes Trangresorxs.[15] Along one of the walls of the court hung huge canvases of a photo exhibition showing different people of colour in Madrid with statements about their lived experience and philosophies of life. *La Cancha* was a day that consisted of art, sport, music and food created by and for Black and womxn of colour. Unlike the *huelga*, *La Cancha* sought to take seriously and interrogate how activists come together, inhabit a space and build community across difference.

One of the events during *La Cancha* was a photoshoot. Womxn from EFAE brought clothes, makeup, backdrops and cameras to photograph Black and womxn of colour. During that process the womxn of EFAE dressed and applied makeup to a variety of womxn. Each stage of being photographed required different degrees of bodily care from dressing someone in clothes that would flatter them to understanding different skin tones and touching the faces of friends and strangers and wanting them to feel confident and beautiful as they took their photos. These acts of care brought to the fore the importance of care work as a means to building relationships and sustaining the importance of care across the intersections of different identities. *La Cancha* manifested 'a theory in flesh ... where the physical realities of our lives – our skin colour, the land or concrete we grew up on, our sexual longings – all fuse to create a politic born out of necessity'.[16] As a space it embodied the following sentiment from Genny Lim's 'Theory in Flesh' from *This Bridge Called My Back*:

> We are the Coloured [womxn] in a white feminist movement
> We are the feminists among the people of our culture
> We are often the lesbians among the straight
> We do this bridging by naming ourselves and telling our stories in our own words

It is important to address the legacy and continuing role that white feminism has played in excluding different kinds of women from the wider feminist movement. Within the white, Eurocentric context of Madrid, there's a sense of wariness of being invisibilised, tokenised, outright talked down to, insulted and ignored because of an 'emotional disconnect'[17] to identities that exist outside of white womanhood. However, *La Cancha* presented a different premise to a feminist space. As a place for and by womxn of colour the presence, respect and participation of a diversity of womxn was expected. Moreover, it allowed for a reversal of the power dynamic between white women and womxn of colour. The new question for white feminists became how can they support, learn, cohabitate in the space rather than the usual exclusionary dynamics of how can 'we' be more inclusive of 'them'.

EBANFEST: ICTS IN THE MOVEMENT

Nearly two months after the *huelga*, the first Ebanfest was held in Matadero. Ebanfest is an exclusive festival centred around celebrating queer Black and womxn of colour. The festival was founded by two young Black womxn, @itswinnie and @corneliaham, in collaboration with the artist activist collective, Ayllu.[18]

One of the significant aspects of Ebanfest was that information about and entry to the festival was solely available through Instagram. Within the larger tapestry of social movements and social transformation, Ebanfest has followed in line with the recent turn towards ICTs becoming a core instrument of communication, community making and organising. The Instagram community that participated in Ebanfest demonstrated similar characteristics observed by other scholars studying activist and movement-oriented communities on social media. For example, integral to participating in the community is 'continuous, communicative engagement'.[19] Finding out about Ebanfest required following those who would at least in part be coordinating the effort or being connected to someone who may have similar interests and share them with you via Instagram. Exclusivity was enforced through filtering in only those who knew who to follow and who could also get permission to be followers. The two separate processes on Instagram allow one to be part of the BPoC Instagram community: having an interest in BPoC communities shaping what you see and who you follow, as well as possibly demonstrating that interest in one's own posts. Being accepted as a participant required both processes in tandem.

Moreover, Instagram's introduction of stories to the app also meant that information about the festival was at times only available temporarily in 24-hour story cycles. Ebanfest publicly made their speakers available on their Instagram through posts, but the practices, participants, time and place were only available on stories, which meant that one had to check in regularly for these pieces of information that were only temporarily available. Therefore, in part, one of the conditions of even being able to attend the festival was continuing dedication to checking in with this online community.

However, more than just a space for organising the festival, Instagram served as a space for participants to initiate informal acquaintances and friendships that, in turn, could be manifested in the physical space of the festival. Some of the participants at the festival had 'seen' each other on Instagram and were able to later initiate real world contact and dialogue at the festival. Through their Instagram profile, Ebanfest gathered a spatially dispersed community and were able to facilitate that localisation in the real world of the Matadero.

Because the medium for communication and organisation has been Instagram, this online community has taken a distinct departure from Twitter and Facebook, two social networks that have received far more attention from the academic community. One explanation for this difference might be in part explained by the social, cultural image production that Instagram enables. As a space of individual production of visual media, language and culture, it has become a space, in the case of Ebanfest, for Black and womxn of colour participants to bring their own histories and text to the images that they and their communities consume. As such, these Instagram communities create practices of cultural production and 'willfully looking' at images that centre on this community, whose aesthetics and values are re-affirmed and validated by participation in physical spaces such as Ebanfest.[20]

The festival covered three topics: Black hair care, creating radical spaces for children and motherhood within the context of race and migration, and the relationship between sex and colonial histories. Each panel had the purpose of public consciousness-raising within this community, creating a collective narrative of personal oppressions.[21] However, because the festival was organised by two Black womxn and the first talk centred on Black body politics through speaking about

Black hair, the experience of Black womxn was central to learning and discussing practices of care and political awareness. While terms such as 'people of colour' are often used to create an umbrella for solidarity, the people under this umbrella are diverse, different, and not immune to racism amongst each other and harbouring sentiments of anti-Blackness. Centring Black womxn's experiences established an explicitly Black space within the festival as well as what other participants might learn and understand to practise solidarity and care.

Striving towards a liberatory space, seeking to be freer from different forms of oppression is communal and complicated. This effort requires mutual understanding about how systems of oppression function and what requires priority in terms of care and attention. The exclusivity of Ebanfest enabled womxn to talk and express needs in terms of care and anger unapologetically. Within white or whiter activist spaces this expression is misread, debated and tiresome for Black and womxn of colour.[22] Therefore, having an exclusive space freed the participants to break from certain limiting norms and expectations of navigating the white gaze and privilege and respectability politics.

One method to frame this space might be as a counterpublic, which Nancy Fraser defined as space created in response to exclusionary politics of the public (sphere) by and for subordinated peoples that allows its members to freely 'speak in their own voice'.[23] In her work on counterpublics, Fraser ultimately proposes that a realistic conception of a more egalitarian society looks like a plurality of counterpublics rather than the elusive public sphere in which participatory parity exists. Fraser posits that counterpublics enable participants not only to speak to each other, but that they might speak with greater clarity and force outside of the counterpublic. The comfort and freedom facilitated by Ebanfest thus serves more than just to demarcate a time and space for practising greater freedom and voice. Feeling greater freedom and acceptance provides a new lens with which participants may evaluate the other life worlds around them as well as re-affirm their own feelings and position in their day-to-day interactions. As such, a counterpublic created by Ebanfest adds to and expands the fabric of 'micro utopias' around the city. Within the greater expanse of the left-wing movement, there remains much work to do in creating the links between the politics and spaces such as Ebanfest and other left-wing spaces. One significant space in creating new networks has been the organisation around Pride in Madrid in 2017.

MAKING SPACE: MADRID PRIDE

In the summer of 2017, Madrid hosted World Pride. However, the pride celebration was felt by various observers and participants to be dominated by white gay men. As a response to the feeling that the original radical politics of pride had been lost in this white consumerist extravaganza, *Orgullo Crítico* (Critical Pride) was organised.[24] The march was an attempt to critique the politics of World Pride and demand for re-politicisation of the LGBTQI+ movement.

Ironically for an event seeking to re-radicalise pride, the organising body of the *Orgullo Crítico* did not include any BPoC. However, Entre Lineas: Migrantes Transgresorxs (Between the Lines: Transgressive Migrants) took up the mantle in creating a space for queer BPoC in *Orgullo Critico*. Migrantes Transgresorxs is a LGBTQQI+ BPoC-led organisation. While the organisation is a mixture of people, womxn of colour provide much of the needed labour to make events happen. For *Orgullo Crítico*, they organised events exclusively for BPoC including a poster making session. Womxn of colour easily made up the majority of the people within the poster making session. This session was a space for queer BPoC to socialise and devise a collective statement to read at the end of the *Orgullo Crítico*. Much like *La Cancha*, the poster making session involved a mixture of a political agenda along with everyday practices of hanging out and making space for the process of a group of people being together. These sessions highlight the importance of informal relationships and friendships within activist circles. Demonstrations are made possible, safer and even more bearable by connecting with familiar faces on the streets.

In June 2017, around 5,000 people filled the Nelson Mandela Plaza and spilled into the surrounding streets to gather the *Orgullo Crítico*.[25] The march was made up of several different gay and queer communities. The BPoC bloc numbered less than 100 people in the march. However, this small bloc of BPoC became an important rallying space for the queer community of colour to have a voice as well as feel a sense of belonging to an LGBTQI+ community that is almost exclusively white.[26] It was perhaps the only time there was any public demonstration that attempted to make space for queer people of colour during World Pride.

Migrantes Transgresorxs was the first organisation to make political participation of a community of queer BPoC in Madrid possible. It provided a necessary link and participation with the wider activist community and BPoC communities. Given the growth and exclusivity of different BPoC counterpublic communities, the organisation with *Orgullo Crítico* demonstrated the means through which a network to the larger activist community can be connected where the BPoC queer community was both a part of another and within their own space. The organising and collaboration with *Orgullo Crítico* became important because as a stepping stone it provided an amplified point of interaction to recreate the LGBTQI+ community and disrupt consumerist, white normative narratives.[27]

CONCLUSION

In this chapter, I have attempted to explore Black and womxn of colour activism in Madrid and put this creative activism in the context of the broader social movements and struggles within the city. In doing so, I sought to illuminate the different strands of activism and cultural production that shape the environment in which the BPoC community finds both its resources and antagonisms.

The history and creation of an open, plural and collaborative BPoC community committed to anti-racist feminist activism has only manifested in the last few years. However, the momentum and speed of the production of texts, resources and collectives have demonstrated a shift in Spanish activism. Race and ethnicity are important sites of struggle for realising democracy and parity in participation. This chapter has sought to look at activism within the city relationally to demonstrate the networks and processes necessary for communities to be created as well as the gaps that the BPoC community has filled. Within the plurality of organising in Madrid, there is a constant and necessary tension in the interdependence of different movements. However, Black feminist activism in Madrid has arisen to make spaces for conversation, care and engagement even in the absence of solidarity and empathy among fellow white activists. They have shifted the feminist discourse and activism in Madrid by sheer force and belief in the value of their work and importance of their own space. Their new urban activism brings to the fore lived experiences and radically transformative politics that give necessary depth and dimension to social justice mobilisations in the city.

NOTES

Websites last accessed 31 January 2017.

1. A. Walliser, 2013. 'New urban activisms in Spain: Reclaiming public space in the face of crises'. *Policy & Politics* 41(3), pp. 329–50.
2. www.mariaptqk.net/macho-alfa-y-acampads-en-beta/
3. A. Fernández-Savater, 2011. 'Apuntes de acampadasol'. *Diario Público*. http://blogs.publico.es/fueradelugar/a partir del 20/5/2011
4. S. Gonick, 2016. 'Indignation and inclusion: Activism, difference, and emergent urban politics in postcrash Madrid'. *Environment and Planning D: Society and Space* 34(2), pp. 209–26.
5. M. García-Lamarca, 2017. 'From occupying plazas to recuperating housing: Insurgent practices in Spain'. *International Journal of Urban and Regional Research*, 41(1), pp. 37–53 (p. 38).
6. The spelling of womxn serves to disrupt normative notions of cis womanhood and allude to an expanded identity or notion of women.
7. https://femiagenda.org/portfolio/efae-empoderamiento-femenino-afro descendiente-en-espana/
8. https://twitter.com/afroKwanzaa?lang=en
9. Matadero Madrid itself is the product of the progressive Department of Culture within the city that has had a high degree of autonomy in the last decade. Created in 2006 by the Madrid city council it was given the mandate to 'promote research, production, training, and dissemination of creation and contemporary thinking' through a multidisciplinary approach in arts, design, literature and urbanism. However, perhaps what has made Matadero so central as an institutional resource in the BPoC community has been the fact that it allows residents without residential papers to apply for and fill positions for research and art residencies and programmes. Moreover, it allows the space to be exclusively BPoC. www.mataderomadrid.org/que-es-matadero.html
10. https://twitter.com/colectivoefae?lang=en
11. M. León, 2010. 'Migration and care work in Spain: The domestic sector revisited'. *Social Policy and Society* 9(3), pp. 409–18.
12. International Domestic Worker day is on 30 March, however, the day of the demonstration in Madrid took place days earlier.
13. www.lavanguardia.com/economia/20180308/441354667931/dia-mujer-8m-huelga-feminista-manifestaciones.html
14. https://afrofeminas.com/acerca-de/
15. https://twitter.com/mohagerehou/status/977195349273169922
16. C. Moraga and G. Anzaldúa (eds), 2015. *This Bridge Called My Back: Writings by Radical Women of Colour*. SUNY Press, Albany, NY, p. 82.
17. www.theguardian.com/world/2017/may/30/why-im-no-longer-talking-to-white-people-about-race
18. Ayllu is an artistic and political collective in Matadero that aims to recognise and reify colonial histories and create a space that is critical of and dismantles

white supremacy. www.mataderomadrid.org/ficha/9094/en-residencia:-ayllu. html

19. P. Gerbaudo, 2018. *Tweets and the Streets: Social Media and Contemporary Activism*. Pluto Press, London.

20. R. Wanzo, 2015. 'Pop culture/visual culture'. In Lisa Disch and Mary Hawkesworth (eds), *The Oxford Handbook of Feminist Theory*. Oxford University Press, Oxford, p. 652.

21. R. Heberle, 2015. 'The personal is political'. In *The Oxford Handbook of Feminist Theory*, pp. 593–609 (p. 600).

22. www.theguardian.com/commentisfree/2018/may/08/how-white-women-use-strategic-tears-to-avoid-accountability

23. N. Fraser, 1990. 'Rethinking the public sphere: A contribution to the critique of actually existing democracy'. *Social Text* 25/26, pp. 56–80 (p. 66).

24. https://orgullocritico.wordpress.com/

25. R. Iverson, August 2017. Interview.

26. F. El-Tayeb, 2011. *European Others: Queering Ethnicity in Postnational Europe*. University of Minnesota Press, Minneapolis.

27. S. Donaldson, 2013. 'European Others: Queering Ethnicity in Postnational Europe by Fatima El-Tayeb'. *Callaloo* 36(2), pp. 485–7.

4

Those Who Fight For Us Without Us Are Against Us: Afrofeminist Activism in France

Cyn Awori Othieno and Annette Davis
on behalf of Mwasi Collectif

If one didn't know better, one would think that Afrofeminism in France started with us, the Mwasi Collective. However, the tradition of Afrofeminist thought and organising in France dates back to the beginning of the twentieth century. When two sisters, Paulette and Jeanne Nardal, started a literary club in their apartment in Clamart, Paris, it quickly became a hub for Black intellectual thought to flourish in the 1920s. The Nardal sisters focused on creating a safe space to discuss Black literature way before the language surrounding safe spaces was even uttered. They provided an environment where Black minds were free to critique their reality without boundaries.

In this chapter we talk about the movements and individuals that followed in the Nardal sisters' footsteps. Be it via Twitter, academic institutions or occupying public space, Afrofeminists in France have been building resistance against patriarchal, racist, capitalist, ableist, colonial French society by any and every means necessary. The legacy of Black migrant women-led organisations such as la Coordination des Femmes Noires (1976–80) and le Mouvement pour la Défense des Femmes Noires (MODEFEN, 1981–94) laid the foundation for the activism we claim today. One can't speak of Afrofeminism and other forms of Black feminism without mentioning an essential factor: safe spaces or non-mixed environments. One of our biggest obstacles as Afrofeminists is having our spaces and right to meet privately respected, not questioned or attacked as reverse racism. As we near the 100-year mark between the Nardal sisters' arrival in France and our own movement, we gravely realise that little has changed in 100 years. Anti-Blackness still fuels state racism in France: Makomé M'bowole, Bouna Traoré, Luwam

Beyene, Lamine Dieng, Adama Traoré, Marie-Reine are just a few of the names of the victims of French police brutality over the last century.[1] Archiving our movements is as political today as it was back then. We do so as a testament to our history of Afrofeminist existence, resistance and brilliance.

PAULETTE AND JEANNE NARDAL

The origins of Afrofeminism in France can be traced back to the Nardal sisters in the 1920s. Upon their arrival in France from Martinique, Jeanne Nardal and her sister Paulette Nardal (1896–1985)[2] started a weekly literary salon in their apartment to encourage critical Black thought. At the time, Paulette was a writer, a journalist and the first Black woman to study at La Sorbonne. Her sister Jeanne was also a writer, philosopher and political essayist. Together they carved out a space where the Black intellectual elite, such as Aimé Césaire, Nicolas Guillen, Léopold Senghor, Langston Hughes, met to think about and debate Black French identities.

In doing so, the Nardal sisters both facilitated and contributed to the theorisation of Blackness or *La Négritude*. Together the Nardal sisters produced reviews, books, studies on Blackness like *Le Revue du Monde Noir* and argued why Blackness should be understood as a global, diasporic phenomena. In our own tribute to the Nardal sisters, Mwasi created *les cafés afrofem*, an ephemeral brave space where we meet and discuss topics that affect our day-to-day lives as Black women and femmes in France.

LA COORDINATION DES FEMMES NOIRES (1976–81)

In May 1976, a group of African and Caribbean women created la Coordination des Femmes Noires (or le Mouvement des Femmes Noires) in Paris (Figure 4.1). This activist group brought together African and Caribbean women, most of whom were university students and young intellectuals to fight against female genital mutilation (FGM), polygamy, racism, neocolonialism, exotic or miserabilist representations of Black women and women's rights in general.

In July 1978, they argued:

From the confrontation of our experience as women and as Blacks, we have realised that the history of our struggles, in our countries and in

Figure 4.1 Coordination femmes noires, date created: 1978
Source: Coll. Génériques/Odysséo.

our migration, is a history in which we are denied and falsified. This is why our struggle as women is above all autonomous because we fight against the capitalist system that oppresses us and in the same breath, we fight the contradictions from activists who pretend to fight for socialism yet still perpetuate in their practice, a domination with regards to women that they would typically denounce in other areas.[3]

This analysis of left-wing politics, in which Black women experience racism and sexism in supposedly liberatory spaces, remains as true today as it was almost 40 years ago. Also noteworthy is the necessity of organising autonomously – in non-mixed spaces – in order for Black women to authorise ourselves. Mwasi takes inspiration from this autonomous organising in our work today.

La Coordination des femmes noires also participated in anti-Apartheid initiatives in solidarity with their South African siblings. The group disappeared at the beginning of the 1980s but they paved the way for other organisations of Black women in France to exist after their time.[4] Gerty Dambury, one of the then members still lives and works in Paris today and continues artistic and activist work individually as well as part of 30 Nuances de Noires, a Black feminist marching band.

LE MOUVEMENT POUR LA DÉFENSE DES DROITS DE LA FEMME NOIRE (MODEFEN, 1981–94)

Cameroon-born journalist and writer Lydie Dooh-Bunya created le Mouvement pour la Défense des Droits de la Femme Noire (MODEFEN) in 1981 (Figure 4.2). The movement opposed racism and sexism while promoting the emancipation of Black women.[5] In an interview on the condition of Black women in France, Dooh-Bunya denounces the lack of space for her and her Black sisters in the white-dominated feminist movements, where issues such as polygamy, FGM, forced marriages or racism weren't included on the agenda:

> Our [white] French feminist comrades showed us that they were capable of being in solidarity; their solidarity was crucial to us, and even flawless, with regards to FGM. That being said, we had other issues that were specific to Black women to discuss with them: racism at work, racism for

Figure 4.2   Lydie Dooh-Bunya
Photo credit: Maswi.

housing, at school, when our children are excluded or killed; because it is common that a child is killed for being African or Arab. We regret that more [white] women aren't more solidaristic pertaining to these human rights violations; or at the very least, that they don't show their solidarity by various actions. This is why it is essential that we, Black women, do not become wagons for others struggles, but that we too say out loud what oppresses us and what we expect from others.[6]

The organisation ceased to exist in 1994 but the impact of its members' struggles continues with the grassroots organising against police violence against Black and brown French people.

ROKHAYA DIALLO

Rokhaya Diallo is a French-Senegalese journalist, writer and activist. As a Black French Muslim woman and public figure, there's no denying what her presence and visibility on television and in the media mean to Blacks and Muslims in France; namely, through her role as a host on Black Entertainment Television France (BET) and during her various appearances on national French television networks. She's also the author of several books that discuss race and racism in France such as *France Belongs To Us* (2012), *How To Talk To Kids About Racism* (2013) and *Afro!* (2015),[7] a collection of photographic portraits of Afro-Parisians with natural hair.

At the end of 2017, she was appointed to the CNNum, the national digital council; an unpaid position as part of an advisory board for the French government. When Diallo's appointment was made public, controversy was sparked due to her views on institutional racism in France and *Charlie Hebdo*.[8] Following the growing media attention against Diallo, the head of the council resigned, so did all other members appointed except one. The French government then succumbed under pressure and removed Diallo from the board.

In an interview with Al Jazeera, she observed:

The government was asked by people who disagree with my views to evict me from the council. The fact that I was tackling racism, systemic racism, that I was supporting Muslim women who wanted to wear the hijab ... basically it was those views and the way I frame my views on racism in France [which led to the removal].[9]

After the attacks on the *Charlie Hebdo* headquarters in 2015, some argued that their Islamophobic, racist and xenophobic representations were to be tolerated as they were part of their expression of freedom of speech. Today, it's easy to see that freedom of speech is not absolute and that it is only tolerated for some while others, such as Diallo, are silenced.

AMANDINE GAY

Gay is a French Afrofeminist filmmaker, activist, researcher and journalist. After graduating from the Institute of Political Sciences in Lyon with a Masters in Communication, she joined the Conservatory of Dramatic Art and began performing in theatre, film and television. In 2012, Amandine Gay directed a feature-length documentary, *Ouvrir La Voix* (Speak Up/Make Your Way),[10] which documents conversations with 24 Black women living in France and Belgium. The documentary highlights the diversity of European Black francophone women while exploring the various forms of discriminations they experience in Western countries.

Gay's film not only gave visibility to francophone Black women, it allowed them spaces to meet and confront experiences thanks to screenings held across Europe and North America. In France, the film was received by white moviegoers as marking the beginning of Afrofeminism. Media outlets nationwide gained interest in the movement and all of a sudden, French Afrofeminists were being interviewed and interrogated about Afrofeminism as if it were a fashion trend they had just invented. The idea that this movement is 'new' denotes the erasure of Black women's long history of activism and theorising in France. The assumption that Afrofeminism is a millennial occurrence is an insult to the intellectual labour of our foremothers, from the Nardal sisters to MODEFEN. This enthusiasm can be linked to the film's nationwide commercial success: a documentary about Black French women's experiences is less threatening than those same women, most of whom are Afrofeminists, organising in real life and disturbing the status quo.

That being said, it is undeniable that Amandine Gay's work has been essential to the recognition of the movement today. She has been close to Mwasi for years and many outspoken Afrofeminists in France consider her work influential; indeed, after meeting at an *Ouvrir La Voix* screening in 2016, a handful of African and Caribbean women created a Black feminist collective named *Sawtche*[11] in Lyon.

FANIA NOËL

Fania Noël is a Haïtian-born activist, writer and community organiser. She focuses her activism on anti-Blackness, Afrofeminism and the racialisation of gender from a Marxist and Pan-African perspective. She also works on climate justice. In 2015, she founded *AssiégéEs*,[12] a radical intersectional review, by women, queer and trans people of colour. In her commitment against racism she co-created and co-organised the Decolonial Summer Camp,[13] a five-day grassroots summer camp for people of colour with seminars and workshops about anti-racism in France.

ATOUBAA (2016–PRESENT)

Atoubaa, is a blog by and for Black French women, created by Rhoda Tchokokam. On their platform, they write:

> Atoubaa was born out of the desire to see and observe ourselves and document existences that are continuously ignored. This blog, named after our editor-in-chief's mother, is a tribute to the experiences that made our own possible, but it's also an exploration of Black women's creativity. How do they express themselves? How do they represent themselves? Who are the subjects of their artwork? In an attempt to answer those questions, we turned to visual art. The answer(s) we found were quickly dismissed as incomplete. Our creativity cannot be limited to a digital, visual experience. It manifests itself in poetry, music, physical space and defines the way we view the world. We encourage these different forms of expression by creating a platform that understands the importance of legacy, a space that acts like an intersection of [our] past, present and future. What motivates us is providing space for the women whose voices we refuse to listen to. Atoubaa aims to act as a digital gallery where Black women combine art, culture and well-being.

Atoubaa has contributed to the positive representation of Black women since its inception, promoting art by Black teenagers who wouldn't be recognised as 'artists' in the white-dominated art world. Their contribution is essential in the decolonisation of the internet from whiteness and the English language. Indeed, creating space for Black French women to speak about themselves and their peers in their own vernacular, thereby bypassing the omnipresence of hegemonic North American Blackness is an inherently political act. The possibility of Black narratives not merely existing but being amplified in other territories than the United States is crucial to the future of Black representation. The acknowledgement of nuance, context and our respective colonial legacies is a revolutionary goal if we wish to value all Black narratives across the diaspora.

SCIENCESCURLS (2016–PRESENT)

Higher education has always been a space of oppression and mis-representation not only for people of colour, but for Black women in particular. The lack of representation in curricula as well as tutors and professors are some of the reasons that most Black women students feel neither valued nor wanted in academic spaces.

In 2016, Black and brown students at the Paris Institute of Political Studies, Sciences-Po, created SciencesCurls. Their association aims to raise awareness about 'textured hair' in order to call out and challenge offensive stereotypes in academic contexts.

In spring 2017, only eight months after the collective was founded, the Faculty of Political Sciences tweeted about the student initiative using a sheep emoji to address them.

The group took to Twitter to confront their faculty and launched the #NousNeSommesPasVosMoutons ('we are not your sheep') hashtag to spread the word and demand an official apology from the school. The backtracking that followed (the tweet was deleted from the faculty's account) and reluctance to issue an official apology (instead, they issued a Facebook status) reflect the yawning gap that exists between white French academic institutions and their non-white students.

FRENCH TWITTER'S AFROFEMINISTS

France's 'Black Twitter' is very active and fruitful. Self-identified twitter-afrofems have become known for their witty and insightful com-mentary on society and culture. Economiss, Kiyemis, La toile d'Alma, Mrs Roots, Colonel Nass, Many Chroniques, Le blog d'Elawan, Keyholes and Snapshots, Naya la Ringarde are part of a growing online community who carry the voices of Black French women. Some are artists and writers, others are school teachers, students, entrepreneurs. They share their analysis of pop culture, literature, racism, sexism, misogynoir, neo-colonialism, classism, fatphobia, police violence and Islamophobia and promote more nuanced representations of Black French women which break with exotic and racist stereotypes.

30 NUANCES DE NOIRES (2016–PRESENT)

30 Nuances de Noires is a choreographic marching band which aims to question the occupation of public space by Black feminine bodies (Figure 4.3). The decision to combine dancers and musicians is a nod to marching bands in New Orleans, USA. The marching band was founded by Sandra Sainte Rose Franchine, an Afro-Caribbean choreographer and dancer. When speaking about the marching band, she says: 'Dance becomes political when the stakes, on top of being unifying, question the spectator's gaze and viewpoint.'

Beyond being a symbol of resilience, her goal is for 30 Nuances de Noires to be a space of self-(re)affirmation. Historically, Black communities have always shared their musical and dance culture and practice in places of socialisation such as clubs, cabarets, battles and, naturally, in the streets. In communities across the Black diaspora, music, dance and

Figure 4.3   A 30 Nuances de Noires performance at Horizons Nécessaires Festival, Paris, 18 June 2017

Photo credit: Seka Ledoux.

customs contribute not only to the memory and maintenance of African heritage but also to its reinvention through spaces of resistance like these.

Flamboyance, strength, re-appropriation of one's body and politics in the streets and in public parks allow these women to imagine a world in which they are more visible and less monolithic; an ode to the plurality of Black feminine existence not merely through but beyond their performance.

MWASI COLLECTIF (2014–PRESENT)

Mwasi[14] is an Afrofeminist collective actively involved in the fight for Black liberation in France (Figure 4.4). The collective was founded in 2014 by Sharone Omankoy. We work in a non-mixed environment, exclusively open to Black and mixed-race women and femmes. Our political manifesto states:

> Our Black Feminism is a political and collective response to a racist, sexist, hetero-patriarchal and capitalist system, and founded in the history of women and Black Feminists who have organised and participated in the fight for freedom and emancipation while contributing to the construction of feminist thought in France, Africa, the Caribbean and throughout the Black diaspora.

Figure 4.4   Mwasi marching at the 2015 MAFED (*Marche des Femmes Pour la Dignité*) Women's March for Dignity, Paris, October 2015

Photo credit: Mwasi.

In July 2017, Mwasi launched the first Afrofeminist European festival, *Nyansapo*, named after the Adinkra symbol of wisdom (Figures 4.5 to 4.9).[15]

Figure 4.5   Nyansapo festival goers exit an afternoon workshop, Paris, July 2017
Photo credit: Elsa Rakoto.

Figure 4.6   Nyansapo festival goers sit on the curb in front of *La Générale*, Paris, July 2017
Photo credit: Elsa Rakoto.

Figure 4.7   An attentive audience listens to a roundtable talk on day 2 of the festival, Paris, July 2017

Photo credit: Elsa Rakoto.

Figure 4.8   Festival goers chat in the foyer of *La Générale* decorated with Mwasi fabrics and memorabilia, Paris, July 2017

Photo credit: Elsa Rakoto.

In the months leading up to the festival, the Parti Socialist Paris mayor, Anne Hidalgo, called for its banning due to its 'reverse racism' allegedly because of our commitment to Black and/or people of colour-only workshops. Establishment French anti-racist organisations like Ligue Internationale Contre le Racisme et L'Antisemitisme (LICRA) and SOS Racisme also condemned Nyansapo for its exclusion of white people.

In an excerpt from our statement, *The Audacity Of Being an Autonomous Political Black Organisation*, published on our website a week after a coordinated campaign of the cyberharassment that ensued, we stated (trigger warning, mention of rape, physical assault):

Last week, we were called racist countless times. They accused us of promoting racial segregation and discrimination. They compared our association to the Ku Klux Klan. They told us to stop with our stories. They told us to stop 'pretending to be Americans'. They told us we were colourist and that we were going to sort people according to their melanin count. They told us that it was actions like ours that led to genocide, to the Holocaust. They told us we'd be better off in South Africa. They told us to go live in 'Black-only places'. They told us to go back to Africa. They told us that we declared war against white people, against white men, against white women (who were now sad because of us), against white people in relationships with black people, against white people who had mixed-race children, against white people who had black friends. They told us we wanted to destroy the nation, the Republic, humanism, universalism. They told us we were stupid, idiots, useless. They told us we were whores. They told us we were sluts. They told us we were stupid bitches. They told us to go take one up the ass (several dozen times), to go get excised (4 times), to go get sodomised by various animals (3 times). They told us they were going to 'smash our faces in' (twice), 'beat us to a pulp', 'skin us' (once). They called us monkeys (3 times), mules (once), little shits (twice). The defenders of white feminism, lacking visibility, want to build their careers off our backs, all the while criticising us for not co-signing their anti-blackness.

As a reminder, all we're doing is organising workshops for black and mixed-race women about racism, hetero-patriarchy and capitalism. Bear this in mind as you re-read the first paragraph and sigh, loudly.

Apparently, in 2017, in France, the idea of people of African descent organising politically and autonomously is so intolerable that it warrants an online harassment campaign and threats from the authorities to cancel the event. Actually, that's not completely accurate. In 2017, in France, you can have gender/self-segregated feminist gatherings amongst women. There is a risk of some criticism from men who don't understand why they can't come and share their invaluable opinion on the status of women, but you can still get subsidies from Paris City Hall, as is the case for *La Maison Des Femmes*, where men aren't allowed. One can organise feminist festivals reserved for women, such as *Cineffable*, and get funding from Paris City Hall.

Oddly enough, as soon as a certain criteria is added, i.e. the racial one, the idea of safe spaces becomes unbearable and one must push back from the highest levels of office. You know, those spheres of power where non-white people are so rare that when you have one, you're sure to put them front row and center in all the pictures.

Of course, we want Black women to discreetly clean our offices and watch the kids while we put in these high-powered executive hours. But Black women organising themselves politically, coming together and sitting down to define agendas and strategies of struggle and resistance – is much less pleasing.

In spite of the audit issued by the Défenseur des Droits, an independent body of the state that fights racism inflicted on individuals by

Figure 4.9   Mwasi collective and volunteers pose at the end of the Nyansapo Festival, Paris, July 2017

Photo credit: Mwasi.

institutions, the festival took place and successfully brought together Afrofeminists from Spain (Afrofeminas), the Netherlands (The Glo-Up), Belgium (Mwanamke) and the United Kingdom (Black Lives Matter UK) to name just a few.

In reality, this victory cannot be dissociated from the online and offline presence of Afrofeminists across France and the rest of Europe. Their rapid analyses in the form of newspaper articles and artwork were a true testament to the political power of Black sisterhood and its intolerance of Black women erasure.

One of the factors that separates our activism from that of our predecessors is the internet. Black activism in 2018 is closely entwined with technology and art. With the rise of social media and the virality of Black content, meme and gif culture are as present in our timelines as they are in our activism. And rightfully so, since Black people are at the source of this imagery. The internet has been a powerful tool in the planning, organising and resisting of Black feminine, LGBTQIA+-led activism: it allows us to connect with other Afrofeminists despite being geographically distanced. It allows us to reach out to siblings who are isolated in communities with little to no presence of their culture and people, it has allowed us to seek and give international support in moments of national or international Black grief.

In the same vein, one must note that the 'safety' (or the illusion of it) that the internet provides is both ephemeral and conditional. As a collective that mainly works in non-mixed spaces, we're hyper aware of the dangers of the internet and how that danger can translate from being a virtual one to a tangible one. On 17 February 2018, we planned a non-mixed outing for Black folks and teens to go see the blockbuster superhero film, *Black Panther*. The night before, LICRA, the same anti-racist group that attempted to get Nyansapo closed down, shared screenshots of emails we'd sent to participants on Twitter, thus revealing details of the screening and private roundtable discussion to the whole world.

The LICRA tweets stirred up a frenzy on French Twitter and MK2 *Quai de Loire*, the cinema where we had reserved seats, cancelled our booking and made a public statement about our supposedly 'discriminatory practice'. Far right groups jumped on the LICRA bandwagon and proceeded to harass, insult and threaten us for wanting to give 100 Black people a little joy and representation. We write this chapter as we await a hearing date from French police for the crime of being Black and celebrating Black representation in the Seventh Art.

CONCLUSIONS

Many of the women in this chapter call themselves *Afroféministes*. A new term for historical struggle for justice and liberation. Women of the African diaspora have carried Black feminism(s) everywhere colonialism and patriarchy have operated. France is no exception to the rule. Its colonial past and its current neocolonial policies have been denounced and challenged by generations of militant Black women; alongside their non-Black comrades, among men or as part of non-mixed organisations. As children of the digital era, today's Afrofeminists use new technologies to continue our elders' militant work. The internet has turned out to be a precious tool in the connection of Black stories of resistance across the diaspora. Online platforms are crucial tools to amplify the suppressed voices of Black women in France. Black women are carving out spaces on the web to bring their struggles to the front line, where white feminism and/or patriarchal anti-racism have failed them.

However, this outspokenness isn't welcomed by everyone. The media attention and subsequent backlash that Afrofeminism attracts in France perfectly encapsulates the asymmetrical balance between the hyper-visibility and simultaneous invisibility of Black women, their labour and their voices. Suddenly, French media can't get enough of us, and yet we wonder where these people disappear to once it's time to march in the street in protest of the death of another Black man at the hands of the police. Where are they to demand higher wages for Black domestic workers who are often women?

Celleux qui se battent pour nous, sans nous, sont contre nous. Those who fight for us without us are against us. The necessity to write our own stories and create our own archives, like we have done with this chapter, is precisely for this reason: to make sure history doesn't get told by anyone other than those who lived it. We, members of the Afrofeminist collective Mwasi, wish to honour and transmit the memory of our sisters' resistance as we follow in their footsteps and pursue their work. We, the daughters and children of our mothers and grandmothers who fought for Black people and women's rights, vow to inspire our communities with positive images and stories of our strength, resilience and sisterhood. For us, by us.

NOTES

Websites accessed 19 September 2017.

1. Collectif Cases Rebelles, 2017. '100 Portraits contre l'Etat Policier'. Editions Syllepses.
2. E.M. Church, 2013. 'In search of seven sisters: A biography of the nardal sisters of Martinique'. *Callaloo* 36(2), pp. 375–90. *Project MUSE.*
3. Nadia Châabane, 2008. 'Diversité des mouvements de "femmes dans l'immigration"'. *Les cahiers du CEDREF* 16, pp. 231–50.
4. Coordination des Femmes Noires, Juillet 1978, p. 2. https://drive.google.com/file/d/0B9hpOdso-6vyTVlMTmsyZow5LWc/view
5. Philippe Dewitte, 2005. 'La condition des femmes noires en France. Un entretien avec Lydie Dooh-Bunya'. *Revue Hommes et migrations* no. 1257, septembre–octobre.
6. Ibid, p. 82.
7. *France Belongs To Us*, 2012. Michel Lafon, Paris. *How To Talk To Kids About Racism*, 2013. Le Baron Perché, Paris. *Afro!*, 2015. Les Arènes, Paris, 2015.
8. *Charlie Hebdo* is a satirical weekly French magazine whose headquarters were attacked in 2015 after publishing Islamophobic content. Twelve people were killed.
9. www.aljazeera.com/programmes/talktojazeera/2018/02/rokhaya-diallo-race-religion-feminism-france-180214065524123.html
10. https://ouvrirlavoixlefilm.fr/
11. https://sawtchecollectif.wordpress.com
12. www.assiégé-e-s.com
13. https://ce-decolonial.org/
14. Mwasi means 'woman' in Lingala.
15. https://mwasicollectif.com/

5

Afro Women's Activism in Belgium: Questioning Diversity and Solidarity

Nicole Grégoire and Modi Ntambwe

SOME EVENINGS, BLACK WOMEN GO BACK TO BEING BLACK

Name yourself! Call yourself an Afrofeminist, an Afrodescendent, an Afropean, an Afropunk, a Queer, an Artivist ...With or without capital letters, give yourself a name! Not for the sake of putting yourself in a box, or in a cage, but for the rage. The rage to exist. To get out of the shade. To stand back up. To make yourself, make them, make us visible. Be proud of your journey, of your colour, of your origins! Speak from where you stand, of who you are, of who you aspire to be. Be proud of everything: of your doubts, of your ambivalences, of your backwashes, and of your mistakes! Do not apologise for anything! Never accept to have your activism accused of dividing women! Who can contest your strategies, your actions, your sweat, your homemade sauce to create a more egalitarian and more united world? Who has a right to define the respectable feminists, the good, the true, the noble ones, and the others? Who has a right to speak of non-mixed spaces for some, and of communitarianism for the others?

Never accept to be called paranoid when you denounce structural racism, based on your own daily experience ... Acknowledging yourself as a victim is not making yourself a victim! ... Cultivate your radical nature as you see fit: firmly at the margins, in decision-making centres, or tightrope walking above bridges between two banks. Do not feel guilty about criticising so-called 'mainstream' feminist movements on the one hand while on the other, applauding all the rights we gained thanks to this institutionally rooted struggle! Head held high in front of private turfs and of privilege denials! Keep being a spur!

When will a colonial history of white feminism be written? When will the obsolete men/women binary be behind us? When will women of colour hold leading positions? Trust your intuitions to guide your collaborations! Refuse, when you feel instrumentalised, essentialised, called not as an expert but only as the expert of your personal history; when you are an alibi, a colour quota, an exotic word. Accept, light-hearted, when you feel respected and at your right place! Get rid of your inhibitions with money and get remunerated for your work! Pull yourself out of precarity and wish for the many to attain this unprecedented height! Undertake, build, network, federate! Get inspiration from the ones who have walked these stony pathways before us, from those sisters who became icons, and from those that are not much cited, not much read, not much translated. Always be ready to put your own house in order. Self-criticism. Humility. You are part of the intellectual elite, you are probably a city-dweller and you have at your command an important symbolic, if not economic, capital. Self-segregation is close ... Be creative in order to widen your circle! That blinker does not befit your open mind. Look at these wonderful allies, friends, supporters! You are not alone. We are not alone.

Chase away the jargon, make sure all your sisters understand you when you speak of intersectionality, whiteness, colourism, racialised women! Love your own, but with lucidity. For some of your brothers, you remain a 'horizontal'. For some of your brothers, you are sick, contaminated by white feminism. Do not fantasise about Africa from a distance! Do not heed the siren's calls that are promising you a mythical land! Learn about the history of the struggles, go drink at the source of Black feminism, of the fight for civil rights, of Black Lives Matter, to strengthen yourself in our own pathway to decolonisation! Learn languages and look at your family growing! Remember that everything is political, including hair, but that nothing is political, including hair! Do not judge the ones that are not joining in your dance. Take action, denounce, transgress, claim, suggest! May your individual fulfilment go with collective emancipation! Turn your back on toxic people!

Take care of your inner fire, of your breath of life and of your health! Spare your forces to make your way. To make ways. Surround yourself with people who are ready to face the harshness of life and to fight on your side! The circle gets narrower, that is true, but in this new space bodies and hearts get closer to the poetic ember ... Never forget who you are, who we are! We are from all ends, from all winds. We are female griots, dressed in Black skins; we are Black women winged with indomitable feathers. (Lisette Lombé, Afro Manifesto (excerpt), January 2018)[1]

Lisette Lombé is a Belgian-Congolese writer, poet, artist and a feminist. She previously had a long career in mainstream Belgian feminist movements. After experiencing burnout, she dramatically changed her career plans. She became a full-time artist and she now uses her talents to give motivational talks and training on team building.[2] The text above, written as a poetic manifesto to call out to our Afro sisters[3] for the new year, condenses important thoughts about a new generation of Afro women's activists in Belgium. Based on the themes it highlights, this chapter addresses several issues at stake within this new generation – self-determination, controversies, postcoloniality and intersectional limitations – while questioning its (dis)continuities with previous generations of Afro women's activism.

The herstory of Afro women's activism in Belgium still has to be written. We, the authors of this text, are two Belgian women of Congolese (Democratic Republic of Congo) origin, with different backgrounds and careers but connected by our involvement and/or our interest in Afro, women's and Afro women's solidarity movements. Nicole Grégoire is a social scientist who studies black solidarity movements in Europe and in the United States. Modi Ntambwe has a long activist career in Congolese, Pan-African and women's organisations. As we are currently witnessing an Afrofeminist resurgence in Belgium, we came together to reflect upon its development and (dis)continuities with previous Afro women's movements.

DIVERSITY AND SOLIDARITY: A DIACHRONIC PERSPECTIVE

Contemporary African diasporas in Belgium are mostly made of migrants coming from sub-Saharan Africa who settled in Belgium from the 1960s onwards, and of their descendants. They were first male students coming from the former colony (Congo, now the DRC) and trusteeships (Ruanda-Urundi, now Rwanda and Burundi) in order to be trained as the administrative elite of their newly independent countries.[4] Student migrations later developed from other sub-Saharan countries as well, such as Cameroon, Senegal and Nigeria.[5] Women first came as students' spouses – who often had to work petty and undeclared[6] jobs to provide for the family while their husbands were studying.[7] Then, as they obtained greater access to higher education in their countries, they came as students themselves. Some also came as spouses of white Belgian men who had migrated to sub-Saharan African countries and were returning to Belgium, with a diplomatic status, or to work as civil servants in African institutions.[8]

In 1980–90, precarious migratory profiles multiplied, due to (1) students encountering difficulties in converting their student visas into resident permits that would allow them to stay and work in Belgium and (2) a growing number of asylum seekers, men and women, fleeing political turmoil in sub-Saharan African countries.[9] For a lot of migrants, the difficult access to long-stay residence permits, the non-recognition of diplomas for those holding higher education training from their countries of origin, structural racism and the ethno-stratification of the employment market lead to social and economic downgrading. A significant degree of brain waste is being observed: African diasporic communities in Belgium tend to combine higher levels of education with higher levels of unemployment than the average white Belgian population. When African diasporic migrants do work, they are often underemployed and underpaid. Women, in particular, show a higher degree of underemployment than men. However, some women have 'made it' in higher status occupations.[10] Hence, a variety of profiles coexist in terms of national origins, legal, social and economic status.

Sub-Saharan African migrant women of all status and backgrounds have organised women's solidarity, mostly on an ethnic or national basis, through informal self-help associations like *tontines*[11] or other support groups that allow them to exchange survival and/or emancipation strategies.[12] In that sense, Afro women's activism in Belgium is as old as (or even older than) sub-Saharan African women's immigration. However, and as in other European countries, it is the educated women who played a leading role in formalising Afro women's activism and rendering it visible in the wider Belgian society.[13] During the 1990s, as formal ethnic organisations were blooming, stimulated by new integration policies and related funding, a formal 'African' associational milieu developed in Belgium.[14] Afro women also founded and/or led gendered and non-gendered 'Pan-African' organisations dedicated to the African diasporas as a whole. For example, the Council for African Communities in Europe and in Belgium (CCAEB) and the RVDAGE/VL,[15] two major

Pan-African organisations that emerged in the 1990s as advocates of the 'African community', were initiated and led by Afro women. Moreover, the Union des Femmes Africaines (African Women's League (UFA), the first major Pan-African women's organisation, was founded in 1998 by and for immigrant women coming from various sub-Saharan African countries. Pan-African organisations like the UFA, the CCAEB and the RVDAGE/VL worked as interest or lobby groups for Afro women in Belgium and 'at home' through their female leaders, who were involved in mainstream feminist/women's Belgian and European organisations that they could use as a springboard to lobby in political circles.[16]

As a founder of UFA explained:

> The creation of this association was responding to a need, women were asking for it. When we started, we had about 100 members ... There are problems that are typically women's issues, upon which women have to reflect, to find solutions, problems that men do not necessarily experience ... Listen, men are not going to go mobilise for excision [female genital mutilation] issues! It is the women that are circumcised ... it is the little girls that are traumatised. The social pressure is exerted on women ... In most African countries, a woman who wishes to travel needs her husband's official authorisation. For such issues, only women would do something to push for change. (Interview, 26 December 2008, our translation)[17]

Parallel to a political context focused on immigrants' integration and stimulating immigrants' participation in the Belgian civil society, mainstream feminist/women's organisations developed an interest in immigrant women in the 1990s and opened forums for discussion with them.[18] For a lot of immigrant women, this was an opportunity to get out of the shadows and to work their way out of precarity. Thanks to its connections with mainstream feminist/women's organisations that had some of their members in key political positions, UFA played a major role in helping Afro women with precarious or undocumented residency status to regularise their legal status. It also worked as a lobby group to bring political attention to the situation of women and children in war and conflict zones in the home countries and to influence Belgium's foreign policy in these countries. It is important to note that the political agenda of UFA and other Afro women's organisations that became involved in Belgian feminism in the 1990s did not (or at least not openly) disrupt those of mainstream feminism. In particular, the focus on 'harmful traditional practices'[19] and on the violence against women followed the white feminists' classical view on 'Third World' women (and by extension of migrant women from the 'Third World') as women needing to be saved from the barbaric traditional customs of their own societies.

In general, the first 'African' organisations rather adopted an accommodating approach[20] when dealing with the host society. Mostly created by first generation immigrants born in the 1960s or before and trying to foster their inclusion in the Belgian society, these organisations focused their work on securing the basics for survival: residency status, the right to work and the ability to enrol the children at school. In other words, advocacy for 'the community' focused on negotiating within the existing consultative frameworks and using the institutional discursive registers of 'integration' as regards immigrant politics, and of 'development' as regards homeland politics.[21] During the 2010s, however, a younger generation – both in terms of age and activism – started to take over the 'African' associational milieu and to develop new, often more subversive forms of activism. This younger generation is mostly made up of individuals born in the 1970s and after who are often children of immigrants and do not experience a precarious residency status and, hence, feel more entitled to challenge the system.

Along with adopting new Afro identities that assert the permanence of the Black presence in Europe (Afro-Belgian, Afrodescendant, Afro-European, Afropean, Afropolitan, Afrofeminist), they have developed new organisations that focus on Black or Pan-African solidarity in Belgium, Europe and the rest of the world, rather than on 'homeland'-related activities. Making extensive use of social media, they are building movements that eschew the old integrationist approach and talk back to the system. For example, Collectif Mémoire Coloniale et Lutte contre les Discriminations (Collective for Colonial Memory and Fight Against Discrimination, CMCLCD) was founded in 2012 and launched a large decolonial movement in Belgium that is challenging Belgium's colonial legacies and silencing about its colonial past and racial politics.[22] Mostly male led, the CMCLD gathers several generations of immigrant and Belgian-born Pan-African activists. Women have participated in that movement, but more recently, women have started creating their own organisations in order to counter male patriarchy in the decolonisation movement and to voice their own postcolonial critique.

As a founder of the Afrodescendant women's anti-racist committee BAMKO,[23] created in 2015, puts it: 'Men were monopolising the mic ... What can you do to get the mic, to be heard? Well, you need not to be in the same structure, you need indeed a structure that is not led by a man' (interview, 29 January 2018, our translation). Some of these young Afro women's organisations have launched a new women's movement in Belgium: Afrofeminism, which is addressing women's oppression and emancipation from an intersectional perspective largely inspired by Black American feminism. Lisette Lombé's 'Afro Manifesto' above highlights this emergence of new political identifications and 'ways of being'[24] among a new generation of Afro activist women.

AFRO WOMEN'S ACTIVISM 2.0: AFROFEMINISM, RENEWED SELF-DETERMINATION AND CONTROVERSIES

Afrofeminism is quite young in Belgium. However, it is quickly developing and gaining attention inside and outside activist circles, so quickly that some activists now scathingly call it a trend. Social media is playing an important role in increasing the movement's visibility and appeal.[25] The non-mixed Afrofeminist collective Mwanamke (i.e. 'woman' in Swahili) was created in 2015 with the aim of gathering Afrodescendant women in Belgium in order 'to struggle for self-determination within our communities and within the patriarchal and capitalist Western society'.[26] Its activities are multifarious: Mwanamke has organised and participated in various anti-racist protests, showing solidarity with brutalised Afrodescendant women – and men – across the globe; it also provides psychological and organisational support to Afrodescendant women facing gendered racist harassment and violence – helping them to file complaints, for example; it creates non-mixed safe spaces where Afrodescendant women share their experience and strategies about their racialised and gendered condition; it organises events showcasing professional Afrodescendant women in order to promote role models; and it participates in various events with the idea of having more Afrodescendant women visible in the public space.[27]

The young Belgian Afrofeminist movement is mainly francophone,[28] and closely tied to neighbouring France where the Afrofeminist collective Mwasi was born in 2014 and became famous in 2017 for organising the Nyansapo Festival in Paris, an Afrofeminist festival that was strongly criticised by the far right but also by the socialist and social democratic left and by establishment anti-racist organisations who wrongly inter-preted its Black-only spaces policy in most of the workshops it offered as an example of 'anti-white racism'[29] (see Chapter 4, this volume). Afro-feminism redefines and explores the experience of women of African descent in Europe in terms clearly articulating class, race and gender.

In Belgium, 2017 was a landmark year for Afrofeminism. French filmmaker Amandine Gay's documentary *Ouvrir la voix* (Speak Up/ Make Your Way) was released and a series of screenings and debates took place in Brussels with the filmmaker. *Ouvrir la voix* was shot in France and in Belgium; it showcases 24 French-speaking Afro women sharing their experiences as Black women belonging to these countries where most of them grew up and revealing the complexities of intersectional oppressions in their daily life. The film was released to widespread critical acclaim in Belgium and covered by the mainstream French-speaking press.[30] The film coincided with a number of events that Afro-Belgian organisations like Mwanamke, BAMKO and CMCLCD's recently created cellule *afroféminine* (Afrofeminine cell) organised with prominent cultural institutions in Brussels like ERG Art School and the Bozar Centre for Fine Arts; and with well-established predominately white LGBTQI, feminist, anti-racist and intercultural organisations like Coordination Holebi, Vie Féminine, BePax and Centre Bruxellois d'Action Interculturelle.

Although this sudden interest for Afrofeminism in the wider cultural and activist arenas obviously represents a discursive opportunity for Afrofeminist claims and concepts to be heard, these developments cannot obliterate the fact that the Afrofeminist movement's legitimacy and relevance keep being contested, at different levels. First, many Afro women activists, although they might mobilise in various ways for women's rights, would not necessarily adopt the feminist label with which they do not identify because they associate it with white feminism, that is, with white female domination, for example. Moreover, the Afro-feminist movement is bringing in new understandings of Afro women's oppression in Belgium by developing a 'new' subversive vocabulary[31] to articulate Afro women's daily lived experience of gendered racism: Afrofeminists denounce structural racism, white supremacy, colonial legacies, negrophobia, misogynoir, whitemensplaining, whitewomans-plaining, male privilege, white privilege, using theories and interpretive frameworks with which previous Afro women's movements did not identify, or even connect.

In a politically raceless context,[32] a political agenda framed in terms clearly linking postcoloniality, race and patriarchy, including a critique of heteronormativity, and drawing major inspiration from Black American feminism, might appear too radical to older, more accommodating, generations of Afro women activists. Second, the mainstream, predominately white Belgian feminist movement, although showing a courteous, 'politically correct' interest for 'other' feminisms, as explained by a founder of Mwanamke below, tends to consider that Afrofeminists are breaking down the supposed universality of the movement and does not participate in Afrofeminist mobilisations:

It is a constant critique [that we are facing that Afrofeminists are dividing the feminist movement]. But it will not be said up-front actually. However, we encounter a lot of difficulties in debates, even with people that are supposedly anti-racist activists, it is always very hard for us to convey our message because people find us really, and that is omnipresent, they find us too radical. Always! ... People say: 'Yes, but after all we have to stay united, we are all women anyhow. We all experience patriarchy.' And we always have to explain: 'Yes indeed, but we do not experience it in the same way', you see, so we have to explain that over and over again ... (Interview, 6 April 2018, our translation)

Third, male-led Afro-Belgian organisations, although some also starting to show some interest in Afrofeminism, do not seem to take its political agenda seriously. Classical critiques about Afrofeminists being black women contaminated by white feminism or dividing the Pan-African decolonial anti-racist movement arose when Mwanamke was created, for example.[33]

SELF-CRITICISM:
QUESTIONING INTERSECTIONAL LIMITATIONS

The use of social media has created a new context where the intensive circulation of Black feminist thought is made possible and defined by Afrofeminists themselves. However, although the Afrofeminist movement recognises the multi-dimensionality and plurality of Afro women's experiences and makes it a point to include Afro women of all status and backgrounds, it has to be noted – as highlighted by Lisette Lombé – that it is mainly carried by an intellectual, settled, urban elite of Afro women.

That leads us to the questions: Who speaks on behalf of whom in the movement? And how to make the voices of the plurality of women that shape the Afro feminine presence in Belgium – especially the ones with lower social, economic, symbolic and citizenship capital – heard? How to leave no one on the silence side? How, as well, can Afro women activism 2.0 trigger a wide and productive intergenerational conversation with previous generations of activists? To enable this, it is time to start researching, archiving and documenting the herstory of Afro women's presence and activism in order to develop a perennial and widely accessible source for understanding the evolution of our condition and struggles. A recent book from the Platform of Women from the Congolese Diaspora in Belgium is an excellent illustration of this much needed effort to document the experience, struggles and achievements of Afro women in Belgium with their own words.[34] At the individual level, Afro women in Belgium, especially artists like Lisette Lombé, Joëlle Sambi, Lindah Nyirenda, Christelle Munganyende and Chika Unigwe, have been writing – both in the French-speaking and Flemish-speaking parts of the country – about the complexities of our condition.

Looking at what could be done collectively – in addition to creating safe spaces where Afro women can exchange, explore their histories and experiences, develop their own narrative, build awareness of a common condition and assert their identities – turning the 'awareness group' into a 'think tank' and setting up a politics of publication[35] about the Afro women's condition in Belgium would certainly help develop and con-solidate a field-based, situated knowledge from and on the very specifics of this condition, which in turn would help strengthen the argumen-tation, standpoint, voice and scope of the movement. Such initiatives have started in France, for example, with the creation of the intersec-tional journal *AssiégéEs*,[36] which counts notable contributions of Belgian Congo-descendent activist Po BK Lomami.[37]

As Bassel and Emejulu put it:

Solidarity requires minority women to resist essentialised notions of race and gender, and to recognise the differentials in power and privilege that exist between different kinds of women ... There is a need for knowledge production about the diverse, contradictory and competing notions of what it might mean to be a minority woman in Europe. There is also a need for dialogue: speaking with and listening to each other – especially to those women who are too often deliberately unheard – in order to develop knowledge and ideas for rethinking equality, freedom and solidarity.[38]

Finally, what does the future hold for Afro women's activism and other feminisms in Belgium? Let us bring utopia in: collaboration should be about moving forward with a movement that is truly self-reflexive, inclusive, decolonial and anti-racist and beyond alliances dynamics. Afrofeminists (intergenerationally and intersectionally) and other feminist movements would in this context be defined as *camarades de lutte* (comrades in struggle).

IN ANY CASE, YOUR SILENCE WILL NOT PROTECT YOU

There is still a long way to go to reach, if ever reachable, what we call an empathetic womanism across feminine/feminist movements. There is no doubt that this cannot be attained without first acknowledging, analysing and working on what divides us as women. It also requires us being able to critically look at the way feminist/feminine movements organise, especially when they reach a certain level of institutionalisation and become at risk of developing an organisational culture that is contradicting their own values. This is why Lisette Lombé's manifesto is first and foremost a call to Black women to speak up for ourselves, to preserve ourselves, to be proud of ourselves, to resist assigned identities and silencing, to develop a new vocabulary, to connect to transnational Afro women's solidarity and, in short, to combat the various pathways of symbolic and epistemic violence. It is also a call to Afrofeminists to teach resistance by example, without judging the women who do not join the movement. A call that beautifully resonates with Audre Lorde's words: 'it is not difference that immobilizes us, it is silence'.[39]

NOTES

1. Lisette Lombé, Manifeste Afro, January 2018 (our translation). Original and full French version available on www.facebook.com/notes/lisette-lombe/certains-soirs-les-femmes-noires-redeviennent-des-noirs/10156085851944706/?fref=mentions (accessed 10 March 2018).
2. http://lisettelombe.com/ (accessed 10 March 2018).

3. The 'Afro' prefix in this text condenses all Afro labels by which we could define ourselves as people of African descent living in Europe: African, Afro-European, Afropean, Afrodescendant, Afro-Belgian etc.

4. Congo was under the Belgian King's and then the Belgian government's rule from 1885 to 1960. Ruanda-Urundi was Belgium's trusteeship from 1919 to 1962. For a better understanding of postcolonial migrations and stakes in Belgium, see Sarah Demart, 2013. 'Congolese migration to Belgium and postcolonial perspectives'. *African Diaspora* 6, pp. 1–20.

5. Nicole Grégoire, 2013. '"Faire avancer la communauté". Diasporas africaines et associationnisme panafricain en Belgique'. Thèse présentée en vue de l'obtention du grade de Docteur en Sciences politiques et sociales. Université Libre de Bruxelles.

6. The immigration status of students' spouses prevented them accessing the official employment market: their residence and working rights were indeed dependent on those of their spouses and until 2003, foreign students' access to employment was made very difficult by the law on working permits. As a consequence, most students' spouses were working undeclared jobs, which at a later stage of their life would have an important impact on their access to retirement benefits. See Frank Caestecker and Andrea Rea, 2012. *Migrer pour un diplôme*. Academia-l'Harmattan, Louvain-la-Neuve.

7. Nadia Ben Mohamed, 2006. Femmes d'origine étrangère dans l'espace public. Dirigeantes d'associations et élues politiques à Bruxelles. Vol. 36, Cahiers Migrations. Academia Bruylant, Louvain-la-Neuve, pp. 93–4.

8. Salimata Kaboré, 2007. *Les femmes d'Afrique subsaharienne en Belgique: participation d'une diaspora*. Centre avec, Bruxelles.

9. Grégoire, '"Faire avancer la communauté", pp. 59–73.

10. Jacinthe Mazzocchetti and Marie-Pierre Nyatanyi Biyiha, 2016. *Plurielles. Femmes de la diaspora africaine*. Karthala, Paris. Suzanne Monkasa, 2017. *Les femmes de la diaspora congolaise en Belgique s'expriment*. Plateforme des femmes de la diaspora congolaise de Belgique, Bruxelles.

11. *Tontine* is a money saving or an economic solidarity system in which a group of women, usually from the same ethnic group or region, pay into a common till on a regular basis. The money so accumulated can be used as a solidarity fund.

12. Kaboré, *Les femmes d'Afrique subsaharienne en Belgique*. Grégoire, '"Faire avancer la communauté". Césarine Sinatu Bolya, Marie Godin and Nicole Grégoire, 2013. '"Le Kivu, c'est notre Alsace-Lorraine, monsieur!" Femmes d'origine congolaise dans l'espace public belge et contraintes de la dénonciation en situation postcoloniale'. *African Diaspora* 6, pp. 97–121.

13. Adelina Miranda, Nouria Ouali and Danièle Kergoat, 2011. 'Les mobilisations des migrantes: un processus d'émancipation invisible?' *Cahiers du Genre* 51, pp. 5–24.

14. Nicole Grégoire, 2010. 'Identity politics, social movement and the state: "Pan-African" associations and the making of an "African community" in Belgium'. *African Diaspora* 3(1), pp. 159–81.

15. Conseil des Communautés Africaines en Europe et e Belgique: the RVDAGE/VL (Raad van Afrikaanse Gemeenschappen in Europe and in Belgium) is the Flemish branch of the CCAEB.
16. Grégoire, '"Faire avancer la communauté"', pp. 196–8, 264–7.
17. Interviews have been conducted in Brussels by Nicole Grégoire.
18. Grégoire, '"Faire avancer la communauté"', p. 264.
19. UFA's official statement, *Annexe du Moniteur Belge*, 07/02/2006, N. 06028911, N. d'entreprise 464.491.329.
20. An accommodating approach can be defined as a strategy opting for negotiation within the frameworks of the dominant group, while a protest approach disrupts these frameworks and aims at transforming them. On an accommodating approach see Gunnar Myrdal, 1996. *An American Dilemma: The Negro Problem and Modern Democracy*. Vol. II. Transaction Publishers, New Jersey. On a protest approach, see Charles Tilly, 1984. 'Les origines du répertoire de l'action collective contemporaine en France et en Grande-Bretagne'. *Vingtième Siècle. Revue d'histoire* 4, pp. 89–108.
21. Grégoire, '"Faire avancer la communauté"', pp. 156–81.
22. www.memoirecoloniale.be/presentation (accessed 10 March 2018).
23. www.bamko.org/ (accessed 21 March 2018).
24. Véronique Clette-Gakuba, 2016. 'Mise en oeuvre de la question postcoloniale en Belgique: les artistes Joëlle Sambi, Pitcho Womba Konga, Mufuki Mukuna et Lisette Lombé'. In Sarah Demart and Gia Abrassart (eds), *Créer en postcolonie 2010–2015. Voix et dissidences belgo-congolaises*. Bozar; Africalia, Bruxelles, pp. 250–9.
25. As creator of the Afrofeminista blog Aïchatou Ouattara explains: 'African and Afrodescendent women have always fought for their freedom and for their emancipation, this is not something new. However, with the multiplication of social networks and of Afrofeminist blogs, Afrofeminism has gained visibility, has allowed numerous black women to express themselves and has freed the word on our histories and experiences' (http://kidjiworld.com/une-femme-un-modele-24/, our translation, accessed 21 March 2018).
26. Rencontre avec le Collectif Mwanamke. www.evensi.com/rencontre-collectif-mwanamke-rue-mons-10-1400-nivelles-belgique/251812908 (our translation).
27. Interview with a founder of Mwanamke, 26 February 2018 (our translation).
28. Belgium has three official linguistic communities: the French-speaking, the Flemish-speaking and the German-speaking.
29. www.huffingtonpost.fr/2017/05/29/comme-au-nyansapo-fest-pourquoi-certaines-associations-pronent_a_22114431/ (our translation). Also see https://nyansapofest.org
30. See, for example, www.rtbf.be/culture/cinema/realisateurs/detail_l-interview-d-amandine-gay-pour-ouvrir-la-voix?id=9777139; http://plus.lesoir.be/126634/article/2017-11-28/ouvrir-la-voix-des-temoignages-purs-et-percutants; www.moustique.be/19741/comment-amandine-gay-ouvre-la-voix-de-afro-feminisme

31. Drawing on transnational Black feminists' knowledge production, that vocabulary is not new per se, but it appears as such in the Belgian context. As Bassel and Emejulu put it: 'We do not seek to represent Black feminist knowledge production or resistance as "new", but it is certainly dangerous and subversive to European modernity'. Leah Bassel and Akwugo Emejulu, 2017. *Minority Women and Austerity: Survival and Resistance in France and Britain.* Policy Press, Bristol, p. 29.

32. Various scholars have highlighted 'the silence about race' in Europe, where an ideology of colour-blindness and an institutionally orchestrated amnesia about colonial history tend to dismiss postcolonial citizens' racial justice claims (starting with the vocabulary used to make these claims). David Theo Goldberg, 2006. 'Racial Europeanization'. *Ethnic and Racial Studies* 29(2), pp. 331–64. Alana Lentin, 2008. 'Europe and the silence about race'. *European Journal of Social Theory* 11(4), pp. 487–503. Bassel and Emejulu, *Minority Women and Austerity.*

33. Interview with a founder of Mwanamke, 6 April 2018.

34. Monkasa, *Les femmes de la diaspora congolaise en Belgique s'expriment.*

35. Elsa Dorlin, 2008. 'Introduction. Black feminism Revolution! La Révolution du féminisme Noir!' In Elsa Dorlin (ed.), *Black Feminism. Anthologie du féminisme africain-américain, 1975–2000.* L'Harmattan, Paris, pp. 9–42 (pp. 24–5).

36. www.assiégé-e-s.com/. Asserting the epistemological centrality of the former colonial subjects' lived experience and using a variety of genres, *AssiégéEs* offers a situated, decolonial and intersectional critique of the school system, the health system, the white-dominated 'revolutionary' movements, the popular culture, and therefore produces and disseminates a knowledge that challenges – and offers room to reinvent – the francophone postcolonial fabric, including academic practices and epistemologies.

37. http://pobklomami.org/index.php/po-b-k-lomami-2/

38. Bassel and Emejulu, *Minority Women and Austerity*, p. 28.

39. Audre Lorde, 2017. *Your Silence Will Not Protect You.* Silver Press, London, p. 6.

6

A Black Feminist's Guide
to Improper Activism

Claire Heuchan

Some things in life are unforgettable, and speaking at a feminist conference for the first time is definitely one of them. I remember being delighted when the Feminism in London team (now FiLiA) got in touch to ask if I'd speak on a panel about online misogyny, and surprised that they considered me a significant enough entity within the movement to extend an invitation. Even early on in my life as a feminist, it became clear that London feminists could do that very London thing of imagining nothing important happened outside of their city – my engagements with the movement took place either in my native Scotland or on digital terrain. More significant still, I was a young Black woman going to address a conference where most of the speakers and many of the attendees were white women whose position enabled them to be more confident in their claim to the feminist movement than me. In the run-up to Feminism in London, the self-doubt I felt can all be traced back to race and place. In retrospect, it seems significant that I questioned my own legitimacy, and not the way belonging acts as an unseen gatekeeper to mainstream feminist spaces.

I remember how I clutched at the podium to stop my hands from shaking during the talk. I remember thinking that I'd better not vomit because Bianca Jagger was sitting directly in front of me, and having her plush fur coat expertly dry cleaned would likely cost more than the meagre contents of my bank account could stretch to. I remember being too nervous to even contemplate making eye-contact with any of the audience as all the public speaking guides recommended. There was an acute tension in me that stemmed from realising that a great many women in the audience not only didn't share my experiences of misogynoir, but could choose not to recognise them as legitimate – whiteness is a shield that protects people from looking at difficult things, even as they benefit from that ugliness.

Communicating digitally had, until this point, enabled me to challenge the racism of feminist women without the embodied discomfort that comes with waiting to see whether your words will be heard and appreciated. Digitally, I could send my ideas out into the world once – perform the intellectual and emotional labour once – and women could engage with it over and over again without further effort on my part. In person, I came to see, it played out differently. There is a certain vulnerability in being a young Black woman voicing her dissent to a crowd of predominantly white women that is partially mitigated when there are screens and screens between us. Restricted to face-to-face communication, it seems unlikely my younger self – filled with shyness and self-doubt – could ever have claimed voice. And yet my message came across and was favourably received if the applause was anything to judge by – that too was a surprise. I remember thinking, as groups of women approached the stage to ask and share things with me, that my being there was legitimate.

But what I remember most about speaking at Feminism in London is the woman who approached me in the corridor between sessions, saying she thought the online misogyny panel was interesting and that she wanted to know more about me. She asked, in a conversational sort of way, 'So, what is it that you do?' Being in my early twenties and halfway through a Master's programme, this was a question not easily answered – I was a touch defensive about my life still very much being in the process of taking shape. Still, there was one concrete thing to be mentioned, highly relevant as it had brought me to the conference in the first place. 'I'm a Black feminist blogger,' I told her. 'I write as Sister Outrider[1] – essays on race in the feminist movement.' She smiled and said 'No, I meant what else do you do? What did you do to be a speaker at Feminism in London?' Questioning can function as a way of challenging belonging. The questioner assumes the authority to demand account from the other person. There are endless questions designed to establish why a brown person is in a mainly white space, the most notable of which is 'Where are you from, originally? No – I meant, where before that?'

On the one hand, there was no detectable malice behind her question. On the other, it was unsettling to have my feminist credentials casually policed by a white woman, discomfiting to have the legitimacy of my speaking at a predominantly white feminist conference questioned. Why did she feel entitled to ask that question in the first place? The short answer: whiteness. The longer answer: being young, Black, rooted in elsewheres that were immaterial to her, I was an easy target for disrespect. And so I resisted answering. I could have told her about any number of the community projects I was involved in at Glasgow Women's Library – perhaps proof that I was part of 'real' feminist spaces would have appeased her, though there is little outward glory in being part of a collective. Instead, I channelled my inner Miranda Priestly,[2] responded 'that's all', and headed to the next session without offering justification.

ON VOICE AND VALUE

This valuing of the physical to the exclusion of the digital was not unfamiliar. There is an expectation that the proper feminism is what happens offline; that it can be complemented but never matched in significance by feminist activism that occurs within digital spaces. This devaluing of the digital typically comes from older white feminists, who did not grow up as the native inhabitants of the internet and have other avenues of voice open to them. Even as digital technology plays an ever-increasing role in our lives and societies, there remains a perception that the work and connections facilitated by digital media are superficial – not productive or meaningful. Some seasoned feminists have even gone so far as to dismiss the practice of activism online as a distraction from 'proper activism',[3] creating a binary of true and false feminist practice that privileges organising in person over organising online. As Sarah J. Jackson observes, there is greater democracy for Black women within digital spaces and more scope for an intersectional approach to politics to be heard.[4]

Patricia Hill Collins and Sirma Bilge argue that 'social media, particularly Twitter and the feminist blogosphere, play an important role by providing platforms for feminists of color who hitherto rarely had access to larger audiences. Gaining popularity on social media can also prompt the careers of these black feminist bloggers, helping them publish in more traditional venues.'[5]

The digital sphere has arguably proven to be more successful than analogue media such as print, television or radio at enabling women of colour to redress the underrepresentation of our voices in public discourse – in particular, within feminist discourse. Women of colour are both producers and users of social media, using 'produsage'[6] as a means of generating self-representation. Self-representation has not always been readily accessible to women of colour, either within social movements or traditional media. The expectation within social movements that women of colour participate in spaces that disregard or even compound a facet of our own oppression has long been documented. Almost half a century ago, Frances Beale wrote of the 'double jeopardy'[7] of racism and misogyny experienced by Black women and Kay Lindsay described the misogynoir of a liberation politics that demands Black women overlook their replication of either racism or misogyny:

> As the movement towards the liberation of women grows, the Black woman will find herself, if she is at all sensitive to the issues of feminism, in a serious dilemma. For the Black movement is primarily concerned with the liberation of Blacks as a class and does not promote women's liberation as a priority. Indeed, the movement is for the most part spearheaded by males. The feminist movement, on the other hand, is concerned with the oppression of women as a class, but is almost totally composed of white females. Thus the Black woman finds herself on the outside of both political entities, in spite of the fact she is the object of both forms of oppression.[8]

As 'producers' of social media, women of colour gain sufficient narrative control to demonstrate that – as Audre Lorde once said – 'There is no thing as a single-issue struggle because we do not live single-issue lives.'[9] We create spaces and build platforms where our participation in feminist discourse is not dependent upon a splitting of the self, but rather enables a holistic approach that will typically (but not always) demonstrate the intersecting[10] nature of oppressions.

Portals into digital space – such as smartphones, tablets and laptops – grow steadily more commonplace although, it is worth noting, not universally affordable. As such, barriers that traditionally kept women of colour from accessing substantial audiences are partially eroded – meaning there is a greater democracy; both regarding who engages in public discourse and, crucially, whose voice gains traction and is heard. In addition, the ways in which Black women employ digital technology to conduct activism can differ significantly from the methods of the wider – and whiter – feminist movement:

> Black cyberfeminism offers a cohesive argument for interrogation and resistance. Black cyberfeminism is attentive to the mechanisms

of political economy in its attention to power relations that define and constrain social mobility: race, class, gender and sexual orientation.[11]

As a consequence of hierarchies such as race, gender and class, white and male and middle class voices were treated as the default and centred by old media, which cannot be imagined as an exception to the normative standards that govern wider society. In certain respects, digital spaces have the potential to contain a more level playing field. Creating a blog is free. Creating a website is free. Creating a video channel is free. Creating social media accounts to share your content is free. Anyone who is able to access the internet can hypothetically broadcast their message to an audience, which women of colour have done to great effect.

Although there is reward, the digital environment is not without risk – in particular for women of colour. Racialised and gendered forms of abuse are endemic, along with abuse relating to any other marginal identities one might occupy. To speak when you are Other results in backlash. Research[12] found that of the 70 million comments that have been left on the *Guardian* news website, the vast majority of abuse was directed towards women and people of colour, women of colour in particular. There is an undeniable mental cost to occupying the digital public sphere as a woman of colour, and not simply the emotional damage done by experiencing overt racism. Women of colour involved in liberation politics, especially Black women, carry a tacit expectation that we will function as learning resources[13] for other people – this emotional and intellectual labour, like all forms of feminised labour, are made invisible and not necessarily recompensed. Trudy highlights the irony of people exploiting Black women as 'activism'[14] while claiming to be anti-capitalist or otherwise invested in liberation politics. A growing selection of crowdfunding platforms such as Patreon, PayPal and Ko-fi enable and encourage the compensation of content or labour, yet the trend towards monetisation of content raises a new set of questions about the balance between complicity in and resistance of a capitalist system. Even as one attempts to dismantle white supremacist capitalist patriarchy, compromise is necessary to survive.

In recent years, Black feminist bloggers such as Reni Eddo-Lodge, Aph Ko and Renina Jarmon have published books that would never have come into being without the success of their blogs, a pattern which the trajectory of my own writing mirrors. Of this connection, Jarmon writes that 'drawing a line from my online work to my print work is important because it demonstrates how new media disruptions are creating space for the creation, publication, and distribution of stories that may not previously have found their audiences'.[15] With digital media, women of colour have made waves with wide-reaching messages that would rarely have been granted a platform by traditional outlets:

> feminist media researchers have identified [blogs] as important spaces for the formation of networks, communities and counterpublics which seek to disrupt hegemonic ideologies about issues such as feminism, sexual assault, and rape culture ... While blogs can be linked to other social media platforms such as Facebook and Twitter, blogging is not inherently about promoting or maintaining social ties. Yet despite this, feminist bloggers have managed to develop communities through blogrolls, re-blogging a post, inviting contributions from other female bloggers, participating on comment boards, and providing links to other feminists' blogs in their own posts.[16]

Cyberfeminist space has also enabled women living with disabilities and chronic illnesses to participate in parts of the movement that would otherwise have remained inaccessible. During my own struggles with mental illness, I have frequently observed that being active within feminist spaces online is possible for me at times when being active within feminist spaces offline is not.

To dismiss the digital as disposable when reflecting upon the contemporary feminist movement is to disregard a wealth of radical discursive opportunities. Feminism is a social movement, and as such cannot afford to remain static by overlooking recent technological developments enabling the formation of community spaces. Although the humans who occupy digital spaces continue to be locked in the matrix of domination,[17] which means the replication of pre-existing hierarchies online is inevitable without a collective conscious resistance, there is also the potential for another path towards freedom.

ON BLACK FEMINIST BLOGGING

Before offering advice on Black feminist discursive activism, I must observe that mine is not the definitive Black female experience and that no such thing exists. These observations are the product of knowledge developed through my time writing as Sister Outrider, and I share them in the hope that they will assist other women of colour in building their own platforms. While I write primarily about blogging, where my own experience lies, I encourage women to apply the underlying principles as creatively as they see fit. Digital media still contains an abundance of unmapped territory, the bulk of which is home to the experiences of marginalised peoples – in particular, women of colour.

I began Sister Outrider in 2015 at a time when I was midway through an MLitt in Gender Studies and just starting to believe that I might have something worth saying. I write primarily about feminism, power, race, identity and sexual politics. Initially, my expectation was maybe a dozen readers, a little engagement, and catharsis through having a creative outlet to channel my thoughts on issues of structural power. The reality, I could not have predicted – my work is translated into French, Spanish, German, Portuguese, Dutch and Korean and read around the world.

Although feminism is an international social movement, it also – from what I have learned – has a distinct character in each country. What I tend to notice first is whether or not a country's feminism, broadly speaking, can comfortably connect race and gender in women's lived experiences. A French feminist collective (predominantly white) wrote to request permission to translate an essay on interracial solidarity between women, a translation which they nearly did not publish because it included a brief quotation from Martin Luther King Jr (who was at points misogynistic). I have cited and acknowledged the work of numerous white feminists, though their racism (e.g. Susan Brownmiller embedding the myth of Black men as hyper-sexual predators into the feminist canon) complicates my relationship with their work – but, rather predictably, no white woman has ever taken issue with me quoting any white feminist who has ever proven problematic. It is French radical feminists who have taken up with my writing, curious about my perspective on the relationship between gender and sexual politics. Last summer I spoke at a French radical feminist conference attended by women from around the world. German interest in my work is foremost a consequence of an Afro-German movement, influenced by Audre Lorde during her time in Berlin. From what I can detect, German readers are predominantly interested in my approach to difference between women and expression of a Black lesbian feminism. In the spring of 2018 I delivered a lecture on those themes in Berlin.

Different facets of my feminism resonate in different ways, and location plays a role in that. Although I find the hyper-visibility overwhelming at times, there is something quite affirming about knowing that one woman will connect with what another doesn't engage with. Nothing ever feels pointless after publishing, on one level because of how women interact with my essays internationally. Part of that success can be attributed to vulnerability. That's not to say there is anything fragile about me, or how I present myself to the world, but rather that I am open to engaging with challenging ideas. Brené Brown describes vulnerability as 'not [about] knowing victory or defeat, it's understanding the necessity of both; it's engaging. It's being all in.'[18] When women of colour practise radical honesty we do two things. The first is to open up the space for social change. The second is to illuminate parts of our lives and perspectives that have for too long been erased. Supressed truths have a way of resonating when they are set free. In that respect, vulnerability is a state of openness that makes meaningful connection possible between author and audience.

The second factor involved is need. I needed to share the ideas that shape the essays of Sister Outrider. Every one of them filled me, consumed me, weighed on my mind in a way that was unsustainable. It was impossible to hold them in, and containing the ideas felt like a repression of sorts. Fanon's *Black Skin, White Masks* is one of the greatest interrogations of how race is constructed, a truly brilliant analysis of how race operates as a hierarchy. The cultural and political significance of this book cannot be overstated. Along with his analysis, what really stood out to me were his words in the preface: 'This book should have been written three years ago ... But these truths were a fire in me then. Now I can tell them without being burned.'[19]

The ideas that burn within you are the ones that it is necessary to act upon and, often, necessary for the world to hear. While those ideas need not be overtly political (although within white supremacist capitalist patriarchy it is inherently political for a woman of colour to claim public space to fill with her voice), you will develop an instinct for communicating what feels urgent. Toni Morrison once said that 'if there's a book that you want to read, but it hasn't been written yet, then you must write it'. The same applies for creating content through any digital medium. I grew up Black in an overwhelmingly white area, and internalised the doubt projected onto my voice in that context. Finding a different setting, a digital location, enabled me to overcome at least some of the challenges that come with occupying a purely physical, analogue Scottish context.

Although digital media has made it easier for women of colour to access means of amplifying our messages, the same structures of power remain in place that discourage women of colour from speaking out. I hesitated to begin blogging, convinced that someone more knowledgeable, more experienced, more intelligent and better at communicating would come along and say everything that I believed needed to be said better than I could ever say it. But the mythical perfect Black feminist never did materialise, and in the meantime the same patterns of racism kept happening in feminist spaces. The first series of essays I published were a critique of racism within the feminist movement. I wrote the series in long-form partly to create a lasting resource, something not ephemeral in the way a tweet is. Having the same basic conversations about race and feminism over and over again was emotionally exhausting, and the medium of microblogging didn't allow for a more efficient use of my energy on its own. My motivation in publishing these essays was mainly because I wanted future generations of Black feminists to have a better experience than me in mixed spaces, and partially because I was done spending my life subtweeting the hell out of racist white women.

Confidence is something of a chicken and egg issue – it comes from publishing your work, but it is necessary to have a degree of confidence in order to publish in the first place. To any woman of colour questioning whether her ideas and projects are worthwhile, doubting that she has anything of value to add to public discourse, I say: do it. Mediocre white men have been sending their work out into the world for centuries without pausing to think about whether their voice is really necessary. And your voice is absolutely necessary.

Engagement with your work can be overwhelming, whether it's positive or negative. You can control what you write or produce, but not the life that content takes on after publication. It's like sending your child out into the world once they're basically an adult. You hope that you've given them the necessary qualities to survive, to do well for themselves, but their life is no longer yours to determine the shape of. People project a lot of power and knowledge onto writers and cultural producers. Very quickly, and without your say-so, you can be elevated to a pedestal. While that might sound good at first, it is really discombobulating. I was 23 and confused about a lot of things when I started writing Sister Outrider, but women more than twice my age would reach out to me like I had all the answers. Like a reverse Jon Snow, I'd panic and tell them 'I know nothing!' Now I'm 25, a little less confused and with a few more answers, but still struggling with having a degree of public profile. White women will project an almost mythical quality of wisdom onto the things you say because a woman of colour said them – they will make you the Morgan Freeman character in the story of their lives.

If your content gains traction, that will start to be on your mind during the creative process. You'll work out what appeals to people and what doesn't, and know you can use that information. Or you can also not use it. It's up to you. I've chosen to walk a middle ground – even when I know there are things that won't be read as much. Partly I publish them because they still kindle a fire in me, but also because they're a useful reminder that I'm a person with my own interests and enthusiasms that extend beyond what my audience thinks I am or should be. As both a cause and consequence of poor mental health, digital space can be draining. I crochet every day as a way to disconnect and be present in my own body. The overwhelming majority of my followers on social media didn't sign up to see pictures of scarves or blankets, but they are what keeps me sane – and it feels important to highlight that tension between the expectations placed upon me and the reality of my life as a Black woman with mental illness.

It would be remiss of me not to mention abuse when encouraging women of colour to enter public discourse. There is no way to prepare or guard against it entirely. I've been told that gays and lesbians are all paedophiles and I should be locked up. I've had death threats, men saying they'd come to my university to pay me a visit, trolled with images of anything from lynchings to gorillas, and if I had a pound for every time I'd been called any kind of racial slur I'd be halfway towards paying off my student debt.

Every time I write about anything relating to race, there is racist abuse. Earlier this year, after publishing an essay on lesbian erasure, I realised it was the first thing I'd put on my site that hadn't got a racist comment – either in the comments or on Twitter. That was a weird moment – happy, but also disconcerting because I realised how habituated I'd grown to getting abuse.

If you receive abuse and threats, report it to the website in question and contact the police. I can't guarantee the case will come to anything, but if you get regular abuse from someone having incidents of it documented makes a difference. The mechanisms in place are imperfect, but the more we make use of them when in need, the more those who control them will be forced to recognise the reality of our situation.

With any form of activism, it's important to take time out – especially with the digital, when it's easy to check your phone first thing in the morning and last thing at night. Don't become so absorbed that you cease doing what you love. Do your nails, go abseiling, play with your pets, have a walk – don't let the intensity of responses to your work keep you away from looking after yourself. Equally, remember: anyone who sends you abuse wants to destabilise you and make you fall silent. Don't give them the satisfaction or the power to push your voice out of public discourse.

Keep your passion for creativity alive by producing things that are just for you. Make space for things that you want to articulate but not necessarily share. Do not bind self-expression to public consumption. I have a purple notebook half full of essays about reading with my grandmother, the grief of losing my grandfather, thoughts after finishing books, quotations that struck a chord, friendships, anxiety – whatever was on my mind. Most of them will never be published. Some of them might, one day – but that's not the point. I wrote them for me. I wrote them because I find joy in writing. Don't lose that.

Lastly, don't lose sight of all the good that your work facilitates – both for you and for others. As Renina Jarmon surmises:

> Blogging on the internet consistently over the last eight years has provided me with the opportunity to find my tribe, claim my voice, and establish my brand. I also pride myself on having a blog that serves as a safe space for men and women to talk about race, gender, sexuality, and patriarchy. By safe space, I don't mean that ideas aren't challenged and contested because they are. What I mean by a safe space is that people disagree with each other without resorting to name calling.[20]

Your work has revolutionary potential – all the more for being an improper form of activism, one which encourages those who engage to scrutinise their pre-existing system of conferring value. It has the power to enable connections, reclaim a narrative and achieve social good. Watch your ideas and principles grow into something that is impossible to anticipate, and savour the joy.

NOTES

Websites accessed 11 March 2018.

1. Sister Outrider. https://sisteroutrider.wordpress.com/
2. See Meryl Streep in *The Devil Wears Prada*.
3. K. Mendez, 2015. *Slutwalk: Feminism, Activism and Media*. Palgrave Macmillan, London.
4. Sarah J. Jackson, 2016. '(Re)imagining intersectional democracy from Black feminism to hashtag activism'. *Women's Studies in Communication* 39(4), pp. 375–9.
5. P. Hill Collins and S. Bilge, 2016. *Intersectionality*. Polity, Cambridge, p. 112.
6. A. Bruns, 2008. *Blogs, Wikipedia, Second Life and Beyond: From Production to Produsage*. Peter Lang Publishing, Bern.
7. F. Beale, 1970. 'Double jeopardy: To be Black and female'. In T. Cade Bambara (ed.), *The Black Woman: An Anthology*. Signet, New York, pp. 90–100.
8. K. Lindsay, 1970. 'The Black woman as a woman'. In T. Cade Bambara (ed.), *The Black Woman: An Anthology*. Signet, New York, p. 85.
9. A. Lorde, 1982. 'Learning from the 60s'. www.blackpast.org/1982-audre-lorde-learning-60s
10. K. Crenshaw, 1991. *Mapping the Margins: Intersectionality, Identity Politics, and Violence Against Women of Color*.
11. T. McMillan Cottom, 2016. 'Black cyberfeminism: Intersectionality, institutions and digital sociology'. In Jessie Daniels, Karen Gregory and Tressie McMillan Cottom (eds), *Digital Sociologies*. Policy Press, Bristol, p. 13.
12. Becky Gardiner, 2016. 'The dark side of Guardian comments'. www.theguardian.com/technology/2016/apr/12/the-dark-side-of-guardian-comments
13. Trudy, 2013. 'Exploitation of Black women's labor … in the name of feminism or justice?' www.gradientlair.com/post/57089878980/black-women-labor-exploitation-by-mainstream-whites
14. Trudy, 2016. 'I am tired of being expected to work for free'. www.thetrudz.com/blog/f-you-pay-me-tired-of-free-labor-requests-bbhmm
15. R. Jarmon, 2013. 'How I used the internet to find my tribe, claim my voice and own my brand'. In *#Blackgirlsarefromthefuture: Essays on Race, Digital Creativity and Pop Culture*. Jarmon Media, Washington DC, p. 54.
16. Mendez, *Slutwalk: Feminism, Activism and Media*, p. 38.
17. P. Hill Collins, 1990. *Black Feminist Thought: Knowledge, Consciousness and the Politics of Empowerment*. Routledge, London.
18. B. Brown, 2012. *Daring Greatly: How the Courage to be Vulnerable Transforms the Way We Live, Love, Parent, and Lead*. Penguin, London, p. 4.
19. F. Fanon, 1952. *Black Skin, White Masks*. Grove Press, New York, p. 2.
20. Jarmon, 'How I used the internet to find my tribe', p. 62.

PART III

Emotions, Affect and Intimate Relations

7

Revisiting the Home as a Site of Freedom and Resistance

Gabriella Beckles-Raymond

In the twentieth-century migratory waves to Britain from across the African diaspora, people left their homelands with their own conceptions of home. These were invariably shaped by traditional African, colonised African and creolised colonial experiences.[1] On account of these colonised experiences across the diaspora, some of these conceptions of home were in many ways similar to English versions of home. For instance, three ceramic birds on the walls, damask tablecloths and doilies on the furniture were as much a feature of Caribbean homes as they were English during that period.[2] However, upon arriving in Britain, in addition to these socio-historical contexts African/Caribbean people experienced, their encounters with the hostilities of British society exposed a tension between core ideas entailed in the Western conception of home: (a) home as a geographical place, (b) home as physical space, and (c) home as feeling of acceptance and belonging, and the conceptions of home that reflect the reality of the lived experiences of people from the African diaspora.[3] What might be conceived as only a cultural clash actually speaks to both (1) a problem with how one particular concept of home is universalised and applied to people whose lived experiences are not reflected within the parameters of that conception and (2) a problem with the conflation of the core ideas entailed in the Western conception of home and the use of one to define the other in ways that negatively impact certain people's experience of home. Consider, for example, the following popular phrases mapped onto the different elements of home identified above and how they conflate the different possible interpretations of home: 'Home (a, b) Sweet Home (c)'; 'An Englishman's Home (b) is His Castle (c)'; 'A Woman's Place (c) is in the Home (b)'. The universalisation and conflation of these different interpretations of home have ramifications for people of the African diaspora living in the British context.

In grappling with these tensions, as an inevitable feature of their experience in Britain, African/Caribbean people revisit, re-imagine and reassert their conceptions of home. A salient example of this reconceptualising of home can be seen in the so-called 'Windrush generation'. The *Empire Windrush* docked in Essex in 1948 with almost 500 passengers on board from the Caribbean who arrived to help rebuild the country after the devastation of the Second World War.[4] In the decades following their arrival, Caribbean people tried to make Britain home and in doing so transformed the dwellings in which they lived. Front rooms became churches, flats became impromptu nightclubs in the form of house parties, and kitchens became beauty salons.[5] In adapting the home to suit these multifarious uses, ever-resourceful Caribbean people redefined the home space in ways unintelligible to conventional Western ideals. And yet, Caribbean people in Britain retained a traditional sensibility. Indeed, as people of the African diaspora, part of what Caribbeans brought with them was a strong sense of dignity and house-pride that manifests in everything from images of Jesus above the doorway to the exclusive front room into which only special guests were permitted to enter.[6] Home, for Caribbean people, reflected their identity, their sense of self-worth, and the one space over which they could have dominion no matter what happened beyond the front door.[7]

As a descendent of the Windrush generation, I want to explore the ways in which twenty-first-century Britons of Caribbean heritage are revisiting the home in attempts to navigate the idea of home as a physical/ geographical space and home as a feeling. I will focus on the role women are playing in this process, first because the home continues to be treated as a primarily female domain, and second, precisely on account of this bias, home for women is a space in which the fight for freedom must crucially be waged.

'HOME, SWEET HOME'

This lyric from John Howard Payne's nineteenth-century classic – 'Home, Sweet Home' – speaks to the joy of returning home as a place of warmth (physically and emotionally) and contentment, uniquely able to provide a place of security, comfort and serenity. 'Home' of this conception offers us stability – a fixed point, a space and place to which

we can return, giving our lives continuity over time and across generations. It speaks to the familiarity of family, the shared experiences, the
emotional commitment and connectedness that together provide a sense
of rootedness and belonging for past, present and future inhabitants of
that abode. However, to contain this sense of comfort solely within the
confines of that single space or continuous geographical location negates
the broader social, historical and cultural contexts that affect whether
we can appeal to such physical and geographical fixity for the feeling of
being truly at home.

For people of Caribbean heritage in Britain, the community and,
indeed, the country in which our homes are located necessarily impacts
our experiences of and our conceptions of home. Britain's treatment of
our homelands historically through systems of colonialism, imperialism
and in their present-day extensions is not lost on those of us who, by
various twists of historical fate, find ourselves born in and/or residing
in Britain. Subscribing to the kind of 'pernicious ignorance'[8] afforded
by the epistemological currency of the racial contract,[9] which would
have us disconnect the affairs and status of modern-day Britain from its
ever-present past, is not a viable option, nor is the racialised nationalism
that is fundamental to British identity.[10]

The experiences of people of Caribbean heritage in Britain automat-
ically trouble the idea of home as fixed, nationalistic, and rooted, both
personally and within a community. For a people with a migratory past,
both forced and voluntary, we must grapple with what that means for our
sense of being at home. It is not by chance, for instance, that references
to home feature heavily in reggae music or that we refer to Jamaica as
'Yaad'.[11] One could say that to be Caribbean is to exist in and of multiple
contexts.[12] So, for people of Caribbean heritage in Britain, even to have
spent life mostly in one accommodation or locale or have never travelled
abroad says nothing about the separations, disconnections, journeys and
reunions that are invariably part of the family experience.[13]

To be racialised as Black is to be excluded from the national narrative
that frames who belongs and who can be viewed as rooted in this culture,
as part of the nation's traditions, especially those pertaining to home.
Picture, for example, the quintessentially English pastoral scene – the
thatched roof cottage in a country village – with a family of Caribbean
heritage planting flowers in the front garden. For some, the image causes
cognitive disruption; 'pastoral' and 'rural' carry very different connotations.[14] Yet the contrasting euphemism, 'urban' belies the preference

many of us have for more pastoral/rural or semi-rural lives and that growing flowers, fruits and vegetables is very commonplace in Caribbean homes. That we tend to live in Britain's major cities is a consequence of other social and economic factors rather than an indication of what our dreams of home might be.[15]

Our experiences of unstable housing conditions here, both in the case of private rental accommodation in the postwar period and social housing today, further challenge the idea of home as fixed and rooted in Britain.[16] A disproportionate number of us are homeless, in care and living in social housing, which means we are disproportionately subjected to the destabilising processes and outcomes that result from that relationship between individuals and state.[17] As the Grenfell Tower 'social murders' show, '[o]ver 170 years after Engels, Britain is still a country that murders its poor'.[18] Alongside the gentrification of areas with high proportions of people racialised as Black, who are disproportionately poor in Britain, the myriad of legislation, processes and practices constitutes a systematic disregard of the very idea of home for racialised people.[19] Britain is, after all, 'the master's house'.[20]

Nevertheless, in resistance to structural forces and through inheritance of our foremothers' conceptions, we understand home as an ever-evolving, fluid space that is at once singular and multiple, individual and communal, actual and virtual. For us, home incorporates our actual residence and so many other spaces that hold significance. For decades, Caribbean people have repatriated for retirement and many other reasons. Some have moved to places other than their home island. Some have acquired second homes or access to another's elsewhere. Interestingly, access to these additional homes is not exclusive to women of a certain economic standing. Direct and/or extended family arrangements, repatriation, inheritance, and the comparative strength of British currency in Caribbean economies enabled access to homes for many, who otherwise would be unable to afford a second home. Some of us are so committed to having another home outside of Britain that we have moved mountains, financial and otherwise, to realise that dream. In doing so, we reject the kind of nationalism that makes traversing the world a politically charged bureaucratic nightmare for those racialised persons who do move and get labelled 'immigrants'.[21]

Similarly, home is not taken simply as an individualistic dwelling or a place where one goes to sleep at night. Home could be or include anywhere from a church or beauty parlour to a panyard. These communal, public spaces provide emotional and cultural elements particularly important to our conception of home.

This desire for a communal life of home also manifests in a large number of online communities of Black women of all sexualities, who are able to connect across time and space.[22] In these virtual communities, one's actual residence or even residential status doesn't matter. They are home because we are connecting with our sisters. Continuity and rootedness become diasporic – a sense of being connected to one's peoples, ancestors physically, historically and spiritually.[23] Thus, the concept of home is never fixed, it must, like the people re-imagining their homes, traverse space, place and time.

AN ENGLISHMAN'S HOME IS HIS CASTLE

This idea dates back to a seventeenth-century English common law, designed to prohibit strangers from entering another's home.[24] Later it came to signify the idea that a person, as the ruling power in their home, can do as they please within that domain. Traced through Western thought, this posits home as a private space where one can function as separate from the legal and political spheres which constitute public space.

The structural and domestic arrangements that existed during Caribbean/Atlantic slavery and their enduring legacies in the British context directly contradict the idea of the home as a truly private space.[25] Enslaved people had no right to privacy of any kind, including control over their own bodies, dominion in the home or anywhere else. Similarly, the history of enslaved people housed in their enslavers' homes also rendered this idea of privacy meaningless.

These features of enslavement highlight the difficulty of making distinctions about what rightly constitutes 'the privacy of one's home'. Interestingly, in twentieth-century Britain, in contrast to slavery, women of Caribbean heritage were excluded from 'private' domestic work and instead deemed suitable only for 'menial and dirty' domestic work in public spaces.[26] These employment patterns of Black women over-concentrated in low skilled, low paid work continue today and reflect the precarious position of women racialised as Black in public spaces.[27]

Moreover, the rights of women of Caribbean heritage to treat their own homes as genuinely private spaces where they have the right to refuse entry to outsiders have not been the experience of many individuals. People racialised as Black are more likely than their white counterparts to live in rented accommodation, either private or social housing.[28] In both circumstances, as tenants we are subject to the whims of landlords who often impose a hyper-intrusive oversight of their properties when leased to persons racialised as Black and the vicissitudes of public policy.

Domestic work and state intrusions aside, women of Caribbean heritage preserve customs and ways of living that are inconsistent with the idea of home as a private space. It is common in the Caribbean for access paths to one home to run through the borders of another. Many Caribbean homes have verandas, which blurs the line between inside and outside the home; people pick fruit from their neighbour's trees; kitchens can extend into the yard, where food is cultivated and prepared in the open and becomes a forum for social interaction; and the communal use of standpipes for bathing and collecting water all defy the framing of the home as the sole domain of one's private life.[29] This is not to suggest that people of Caribbean heritage do not value privacy, but rather that the way the home is conceived is inconsistent with the idea of the home as a private space, nor is this particular construction of private space an ideal to pursue.

In contemporary Britain, the privacy of the home has been taken to such individualistic extremes that people expect to be completely cocooned from the outside world once they enter their front door. Moreover, the British imaginary on intrusion is indelibly racialised such that fears have mutated from plausible threats of someone breaking into the home and conflated with 'foreigners' taking over whole communities, contaminating what it means to be British. The break-in that many feel at risk of is cultural, social and racial.[30]

Women of Caribbean heritage tend not to share this exclusionary sensibility. This is partly due to being connected to cultural contexts, mores and customs born out of a more communal philosophy and also because we are acutely aware of the negative consequences of adopting this fear-driven mentality.[31] It is actually women racialised as Black who have a very real need to protect ourselves from social and cultural erasure and from non-consensual or coerced intrusion into our bodies.[32] We challenge the private/public distinction by using our homes in communal, social and political ways; rejecting the excessive urge to keep others out, while simultaneously giving our own bodies the privacy, regard and love so often withheld or denied by others. In addition, more of us are choosing to work from home, whether self-employed or otherwise, often with a focus on promoting health, wellbeing and self-care – nourishing the body physically, mentally and spiritually.[33] These reflect the ever-present need to protect one's body as one would one's home and further underscore the inadequacy of dichotomous framing of private/public as an interpretive lens for discussing the lives of women of Caribbean heritage in Britain.

A WOMAN'S PLACE IS IN THE HOME

Today, not many people would proclaim their support for this antiquated expression. While few would say it publicly, it remains a fact that our society is fundamentally patriarchal and heterosexist.[34] Women racialised as Black, especially lesbian, are supposed to know their 'place', where place means their position in a gendered hierarchy, not the physical location 'home'. Our 'place' is to have our needs unseen and unheard, even as we are viewed as a dominating force, hence the conundrum of hyper-visibility/silencing women racialised as Black consistently describe.[35] The heterosexist patriarchy that underpins these phenomena is compounded by the cultural hybridity of our existence, meaning we also grapple with Caribbean versions of patriarchy.

Women of Caribbean heritage often encounter both versions of patriarchy most acutely in the home, partly because men of Caribbean heritage, subjected to anti-Black racism, lack structural power in other spaces, giving rise to a 'frustrated masculinity' that expresses itself at home.[36] I recently attended a reggae concert where a Jamaican artist did a predictable heteronormative shout out to the crowd to big up women who know how to please their man in the kitchen and the bedroom. It fell on deaf ears to those of us who are financially independent and have no intention of being anyone's domestic or sexual object. Many people (especially men) did respond as the artist intended but there was a palpable disconnect between the patriarchal sentiments and certain members of the audience even as the love of the music brought us together. Given male prowess in the kitchen is highly valued among men and women of Caribbean heritage, the tensions and contradictions within patriarchal forms emerge as they encounter different sexual attitudes and cultural practices.

Stereotypes of Black women as 'controlling' and 'emasculating' continue to exert their force in Britain. The contradictory portrayal of Caribbean women as desexualised mammies and overbearing matriarchs endures, often unmatched by self-affirming power.[37] If 'granny', like 'big momma', is so loving and supportive, how do we understand her apparent acceptance and promotion of patriarchal relationships and parenting styles that are detrimental to both women and men?[38] Moreover, if she is so beloved and respected, how do we reconcile that with the fact that she is so often isolated physically and emotionally and her needs viewed as secondary to everyone else's? Similarly, if the matriarch or 'independent Black woman' is so strong and masculine, how do we make sense of her vulnerabilities? How do we understand the rates of physical, sexual and psychological abuse so many women and girls experience in the home? Additionally, what of those family members who live outside the home, for example, fathers who are separated from their children's mother, but nevertheless exert patriarchal influence, even in their absence?

An irony exists within parenting whereby many practices that twenty-first-century Britons of Caribbean heritage deem facets of 'Caribbean culture' – giving your child 'licks' and other manifestations of autocratic discipline – and therefore uphold as elements of their heritage are actually colonial legacies more akin to historical practices by British enslavers and traditions of British boarding school.[39] They are neither 'Black' nor Caribbean in the sense invoked or misremembered. Still, insofar as patriarchy is systemic, women of Caribbean heritage in Britain must balance maintaining the relationships that matter most with our desire to transcend heterosexist, patriarchal values and cultural practices that are incompatible with our vision for our lives.

In this vein, women of Caribbean heritage in Britain are revisiting our homes, lifestyles and parenting. First, we exist beyond the narrow confines of the hegemonic British conceptions of the 'home'. We are present, transformative and valuable to every aspect of British life, impacting media, culture, politics, academia, sport, science, industry and beyond. Rejecting the idea that the home is the primary place women can be of use, especially as child-bearers, has been fundamental to women of Caribbean heritage's advancement in Britain. However, we have not necessarily embraced mainstream feminist approaches to women working outside the home.[40] In light of capitalistic exploitations of women racialised as Black's labour and cultural traditions throughout the African diaspora, it is unsurprising that we tend to value the opportunity to stay at home when we become mothers.[41] This is not to deny the reality that for many the choice to stay at home to parent is often either necessary or impossible because of restrictive familial and/or employment circumstances. Nevertheless, women of Caribbean heritage in Britain are developing support groups, online communities and a range of creative strategies to manage balancing life as mothers with work and home.

Part of the importance of home, for women of Caribbean heritage in Britain, comes from it being where mothering most substantively occurs. Women, regardless of sexuality, typically experience a reckoning upon becoming a parent that reasserts the place of the home. This is particularly significant for mothers of Caribbean heritage because of our dual responsibilities for, on the one hand, protecting our children from heterosexism, patriarchy and anti-Black racism in British society, while, on the other, equipping them with tools to flourish in often hostile settings beyond the home.[42] In the home, we are drawing on creolised life experiences, creating spaces that enrich our children intellectually, culturally and spiritually. Here we exert our power to redefine the ideals of home, rejecting anti-Black, heterosexist, patriarchal domestic mores to create a place and space that provides the foundations for freedom for ourselves and our families. The home, then, is not a woman's place insofar as that idea seeks to exclude women from public and political affairs. Rather, it is where women can make a most profound political contribution – raising their children to respect and value women, and indeed all people.[43]

CONCLUSION: HOME IS WHERE THE HEART IS

My intent for this chapter was to revisit the concept of 'home' and consider how our lived experiences enable us to re-imagine this idea. This is crucial for having happier homes in the personal sense and ensuring that attempts to consider our human problems include the home; the place that matters most in our lives. The Western conception of home as rooted, private and patriarchal is untenable for women of Caribbean heritage in Britain. We are challenging the home as merely another site of systemic domination and revisiting it as a space of freedom. We demonstrate that the home, rather than rooted and private, is relational,[44] both in terms of its connectedness to all other aspects of the lived experience and also insofar as relationships with others are what actually gives the home meaning. Home is the connections between people that offer safety, security, belonging, love, respect and acceptance. Home then as both an ideal and as a living entity cannot be a place where a person's spirit is crushed and scarred by the impacts of patriarchal, heterosexist or anti-Black domination, whether those forces are viewed as private, personal or socially acceptable. Home is a sacred, emotionally enriching space. It is a dynamic place where our agency and creativity can be expressed. In valuing the home as a place where dominating frameworks are resisted, the political is re-imagined, rootedness redefined as the content and calibre of our connections both within and beyond our physical and geographical homes. Women of Caribbean heritage in Britain are offering a conception of home as a place where we learn what it means to be free and to embody that freedom.

NOTES

1. Beverley Bryan, Stella Dadzie and Suzanne Scafe, 1985. *The Heart of the Race: Black Women's Lives in Britain*. Virago Press, London, pp. 183–5. Kamau Braithwaite, 2006. *The Development of Creole Society in Jamaica, 1770–1820*. Ian Randall, Kingston.
2. Michael McMillan, 2003. 'The "West Indian" front room in the African diaspora'. *Fashion Theory: The Journal of Dress, Body and Culture* 7(3/4), 1–18. Wendy Webster, 2003. *Imagining Home: Gender, 'Race' and National Identity, 1945–64*. Routledge, London, p. 155.
3. Wendy Webster, *Imagining Home*, p. 150.
4. The arrival of Windrush marks the beginning of large-scale migration of Caribbean people to Britain. It is important to note that these people arrived as British citizens.
5. Bryan et al., *The Heart of the Race*, p. 132.
6. McMillan, 'The "West Indian" front room in the African diaspora', pp. 44, 61.
7. Ibid., p.51. Barry Chevannes, 2001. 'Jamaican diasporic identity: The metaphor of Yaad'. In Patrick Taylor (ed.), *Nation Dance: Religion, Identity, and Cultural Difference in the Caribbean*. Indiana University Press, Bloomington, pp. 129–31.
8. Kristie Dotson, 2011. 'Tracking epistemic violence, tracking practices of silencing'. *Hypatia* 26(2), pp. 236–57.
9. Charles W. Mills, 1999. *The Racial Contract*. Cornel University Press, Ithaca, NY.
10. Paul Gilroy, 2010. *There Ain't No Black in the Union Jack: The Cultural Politics of Race and Nation*. Routledge, London, see chapter 2.
11. Chevannes, 'Jamaican diasporic identity', pp. 129–30.
12. Paul Gilroy, 1993. *The Black Atlantic: Modernity and Double Consciousness*. Verso, London, p. 3.
13. Elaine Arnold, 2012. *Working with Families of African-Caribbean Origin: Understanding Issues Around Immigration and Attachment*. Jessica Kingsley, London.
14. Wendy Webster, *Imagining Home*, p. 91.

15. Ibid., p. 172.
16. Ibid., pp. 172–8. Kevin Gulliver, 2016. *Forty Years of Struggle: A Window on Race and Housing, Disadvantage and Exclusion*. The Human City Institute, Birmingham.
17. Gulliver, *Forty Years of Struggle*, see section 6.
18. Aditya Chakrabortty, 2017. 'Over 170 years after Engels, Britain is still a country that murders its poor'. *Guardian*, 20 June.
19. Rajeev Syal, 2017. 'Grenfell Tower victims "murdered by political decisions" – John McDonnell'. *Guardian*, 25 June.
20. Audre Lorde, 2007. *Sister Outsider: Essays and Speeches*. Crossing Press, Berkeley, p. 112.
21. Susan Hayward, 1997. 'Blacks in Britain: Racial discourse in UK politics and media'. *Jump Cut*, No. 41, May, pp. 49–58. Joanna Parkin, 2013. *The Criminalisation of Migration in Europe: A State-of-the-Art of the Academic Literature and Research*. CEPS Paper in Liberty and Security in Europe No. 61, October.
22. Kelly Macias, 2015. 'Tweeting away our blues: An interpretative phenomeno-logical approach to exploring Black women's use of social media to combat misogynoir'. PhD dissertation, Nova Southeastern University.
23. Chevannes, 'Jamaican diasporic identity', p. 130.
24. Edward Coke and Thomas Littleton, 1628. *The First Part of the Institutes of the Lawes of England*. Printed by Adam Islip for the Societie of Stationers, London.
25. Hilary Beckles, 1999. *Centering Women: Gender Discourses in Caribbean Slave Society*. Ian Randal, Kingston, see chapter 8.
26. Webster, *Imagining Home*, p. 158.
27. Office of National Statistics, 2011. *Census Analysis: Ethnicity and the Labour Market, England and Wales*.
28. Gulliver, *Forty Years of Struggle*, p. 21.
29. Chevannes, 'Jamaican diasporic identity', p. 131.
30. NatCen Social Research, 2013. *British Social Attitudes: Attitudes to Immigration*. NatCen, London.
31. Valerie Amos and Pratibha Parmar, 2004. 'Challenging imperial feminism'. In Heidi Mirza (ed.), *Black British Feminism*. Routledge, London, pp. 54–8.
32. Joint Committee on Human Rights, 2015. *Violence Against Women and Girls*. HC 594, Stationery Office, London.
33. Office of National Statistics, *Census Analysis*.
34. Radhika Sanghani, 2014. 'UN: Britain's sexism more "pervasive" than any other country'. *Telegraph*, 15 April.
35. Linda Martín Alcoff, 2006. *Visible Identities: Race, Gender, and the Self*. Oxford University Press, Oxford. Dotson, 'Tracking epistemic violence'. Audre Lorde, 2017, pp. 40–4. 'The transformation of silence into language and action'. In *Sister Outsider: Essays and Speeches*. Crossing Press, Berkeley.
36. bell hooks, 2015. *Feminist Theory: From Margin to Center*. New York: Routledge, pp. 120–3.

37. Patricia Hill Collins, 2000. *Black Feminist Thought: Knowledge, Consciousness, and the Politics of Empowerment*. Routledge, New York, chapter 4. Tracey Reynolds, '(Mis) representing the black (super) woman'. In Heidi Mirza (ed.), *Black British Feminism: A Reader*. Routledge, London, pp. 97–112.

38. hooks, *Feminist Theory*, p. 131; see also 'Revolutionary parenting', chapter 10.

39. UNICEF, Maria Conde and Daniel O'Donnell, 2005. *The Convention on the Rights of the Child and Law Reform in the Caribbean: Fifteen Years Later*. UNICEF TACRO, Panama, p. 16. Joy Schaverien, 2015. *Boarding School Syndrome: The Psychological Trauma of the 'Privileged' Child*. Routledge, London, p. 17.

40. hooks, *Feminist Theory*, p. 134.

41. Ibid., pp. 132–4.

42. Chevannes, 'Jamaican diasporic identity', p. 132. E. Renée Sanders-Lawson and Bill E. Lawson, 2013. 'Trayvon Martin, racism, and the dilemma of the African-American parent'. In George Yancy and Janine Jones (eds), *Pursuing Trayvon Martin: Historical Contexts and Contemporary Manifestations of Racial Dynamics*. Lexington Books, Lanham, pp. 183–92.

43. Chevannes, 'Jamaican diasporic identity', pp. 130–1.

44. Lewis R. Gordon, 2012. 'Essentialist anti-essentialism, with considerations from other sides of modernity'. *Quaderna* 1. https://quaderna.org/essentialist-anti-essentialism-with-considerations-from-other-sides-of-modernity/ (accessed February 2019).

8

Uses of Black/African Literature and Afrofeminist Literary Spaces by Women of Colour in French-Speaking Switzerland

Pamela Ohene-Nyako

This chapter explores the uses of Black literature and literary spaces by contemporary women of colour in French-speaking Switzerland as resources of resistance in the context of experienced white-Swiss and Western cultural hegemony.

Black literature and literary spaces have emerged in French-speaking Switzerland since at least the 1950s and 1960s as a result of Black and migrant experiences, on the one hand, and because of the limited literature on offer, on the other hand. James Baldwin's *Stranger in the Village*, first published in English in *Harper's Magazine* in 1953 and recited in French by Baldwin himself in 1962 in a documentary carrying the same name, is still to this day a relatively known account of an African-American male experience in Loèche-les-Bains, a thermal station in the Swiss Alps.[1] Less known is Vincent O. Carter's *The Bern Book* published in English in 1973, which mentions the racialised experiences faced by this Black American author.[2] Regarding literature written in French, Swiss-based authors such as Théophile Nouatin, originally from Benin, or Rwandan Maggy Corrêa, to name just a few, had their works published in Switzerland, respectively, in 1993 and 1998.[3] More recently, Tchadian Nétonon Noël Ndjékéry and especially Cameroonian Max Lobe are contemporary francophone Black-Swiss authors who are more likely to be known than the latter because of their relative popularity. In addition to Afro-Swiss literary productions, literary gatherings took place from the 1960s onwards amongst African students at the universities of Lausanne and Geneva, for example.

In a post-1968 context and ongoing liberation struggles in Portugal and Southern Africa, discussions focused on Black liberation writings such as those by Amilcar Cabral or Frantz Fanon.[4] These radical socialist and decolonial students' study groups continued in the 1980s – as two participants stated – until the present, in normative academic contexts but not only there. For instance, what became the Université Populaire africaine (African People's University or UPAF) in 2008 stemmed from the African cultural association Regards Africains, founded in Geneva in 1982 and which launched a journal in 1986.[5] The UPAF offers courses, conferences and book launches in the pursuit of intercultural exchanges and in a Black studies perspective. With regards to more cultural nationalist initiatives, one can cite the Afrocentric associations K-neter in Geneva and Nsanda and Sous l'Arbre à Palabres (SAP) in Lausanne, all three founded in recent years by young Afro-Swiss men.

With regards to Black libraries, Zenoo was established in 2007 in Geneva but is no longer functional, and Nsanda as well as SAP are more or less informal platforms that distribute Black and African literature. In this regard, the African Book Fair is to this day the most important venue for bookworms seeking Black and African literature and it has been taking place yearly since 2004 during the Geneva International Book and Press Fair. Its programmers are literary critic Boniface Mongo-Mboussa and novelist Pascal Kramer who organise literary conversations with Black and African authors, as well as rich displays of works of literature from the African continent and its diaspora inclusive of non-Western publishing houses. Another important literary initiative based in Geneva is the literary platform *La Cene Littéraire* founded by Flore Agnès Nda Zoa, which promotes politically engaged literature and awards authors yearly with its literary prize. *La Cene* and Afrolitt' are the only formal and relatively known literary platforms founded and run by Black women, and this chapter focuses on Afrolitt'. Afrolitt' is a literary platform founded in May 2016 in Lausanne; its mission is to use Black/African literature to foster critical knowledge and sharing in an openly Afrofeminist and inclusive approach. As its founder and director, I moderate the Afrolitt' meetings, which are open to all. These mixed group discussions are scheduled every nine weeks, in Lausanne and Geneva, and revolve around a particular book that is announced previously.

Almost unexpectedly, at each Afrolitt' meeting, I started hearing noteworthy feedback from participants and sensing the specific needs and expectations of women of colour – and mostly women of African descent. For example, in April 2017 an Afrolitt' meeting was organised in Lausanne around the novel *On Beauty* by Zadie Smith, and about ten people attended: a very large majority of them were women of African descent. These proportions had become a feature of the meetings: from inception, Afrolitt' has been a platform mostly engaged with by Black women and women of colour. Before the start of the meeting in Lausanne, a white man came in; his unease conveyed his internal questioning of whether he was in the right place. A few of the women present seemed to be wondering the same thing. When we reached the end of the session, a Black woman who is a frequent attendant of the meetings openly declared that she needed such a space as a Black woman, and so had been sceptical upon first seeing the white man (who was still among us) but later relaxed because she felt that he had the right attitude throughout the discussion. Her unabashed statement and voicing of a need for safe spaces stayed with me for months, along with the observation that most meeting participants were women of African descent and women of colour.

In this chapter, I seek to explore (1) the uses of and relationships to Black/African literature by Black women and women of colour and (2) why they attend literary spaces such as Afrolitt'. While acknowledging the importance of analysis and self-definition evident during the discussions held by the participants, my aim is to consider how reading practices and participation in mixed Afrofeminist literary spaces are ways of resisting white cultural hegemony and patriarchy. This, in turn, gives information on white cultural hegemony as it pertains to literature and literary spaces from the point of view of women of colour in Switzerland.

Since Afrolitt' gatherings are conducted in the form of group discussion, I thought it was pertinent to keep the same structure when conducting my study. As a result, I decided to apply a focus group methodology: focus groups entail group discussions guided by a certain set of questions that enable participants to interact and build on each other's replies and reactions.[6] To select my participants for the focus group, I contacted the women of colour who had attended Afrolitt' meetings or events in Lausanne and Geneva at least twice in the twelve months prior to the study. Ten women were available on the selected dates and both focus groups comprised five participants each. The women who participated are of diverse backgrounds. Some notable elements for context are that eight out of ten were women of African descent. In the Geneva group, two were women from North Africa and the Middle East. A majority of the participants are aged between 26 and 37 years old, aside from one woman in her fifties. Although all live currently in Switzerland, their places of birth differ: out of ten, five were born in sub-Saharan African countries, and the other five in Switzerland and France to parents who migrated from Africa and the Middle East. Additionally, among those who were born in Africa, three schooled there; among those born in Switzerland, one schooled in Eastern Africa. In terms of higher education and professional activities, all participants have at least completed a Master's degree and all work in licensed professions. Finally, half of them are engaged in anti-racist and feminist collectives and initiatives. All discussions were held in French and all translations of quotations are my own.

I begin first with the definitions and diverse understandings that participants had of African or Black literature. This is followed by a section analysing matters of exposure to and visibility of literature, which in turn enables us to delve into the uses of and relationships to Black/African literature by Black women and women of colour. My final section will focus on presenting the reasons and needs that motivate Black women and women of colour to attend Afrofeminist literary spaces such as Afrolitt'.

'BLACK', 'AFRICAN', 'AFRO', 'LITERATURE OF AFRICAN DESCENT': WHAT NAMES AND DEFINITIONS?

The discussions held in Lausanne and Geneva revealed that there are different understandings of what Black and/or African literature encompass. This being said, there is more or less a consensus among participants whereby both fiction and non-fiction works are considered to be literature, and African literature is distinguished from Black literature with regards to the origin and skin colour of the authors. A large majority of the participants defined African literature as literature written by authors living on the African continent but not necessarily by Black authors; this definition included white South Africans and North Africans, for example. As for Black literature – or 'afro literature' as one participant suggested – it is mostly understood to be written by Black authors of African descent, both those living in the African continent and members of the African diaspora, including mixed people if they identify as Black.

One participant suggested the definition 'literature of African descent' as a category of Black literature that features and relates specifically to diasporic experiences and themes. This led to the question of whether Black/African literature has any specificity content wise that would set it apart from other types of literatures. On this point, a majority of participants felt that the centrality of oppression, struggle, emancipation and liberation were particular features of Black/African literature due to the urgency of resistance and lack of privilege Black authors have to escape from socio-political writing. When asked if they read depoliticised or solely entertaining works of Black/African literature, all participants answered that they either didn't know of any or that these genres were less available; instead of going through the effort of research, they would either read fiction written by white authors or go for other cultural productions such as Black TV series, for example. But if entertaining Black literature was made visible, they would read it. This answer is revealing of the lack of easily available information on the diversity within Black/African literature. Crime novels or soaps do exist but are not as well known or promoted as socially conscious works of literature.

Finally, when it comes to literature written on Africa by non-African writers, most participants could mention a few works that they enjoy, but they also stated that they were nonetheless conscious of the recurrent tendency of non-African authors to exotify or stereotype the continent, its societies and culture.

MATTERS OF EXPOSURE AND VISIBILITY

A large majority of the participants have not been exposed to Black/African literature in school, whether they were in Switzerland or in Africa. When they did encounter works by Black/African authors, the participants recalled this as exceptional and worth rejoicing to some extent. On the other hand, many participants mentioned the role family members, friends and activist student groups played when they were young adults; either in sharing names of authors/books to read and family oral histories, in acting as reading and discussion partners or, in the case of one participant, in encouraging her to read African authors at a young age. This indicates that exposure to Black/African literature for almost all participants improved mainly during and after their adolescence due to Black, private and alternative spaces outside of state and mainstream institutions.

Most participants consider that access to diverse and non-mainstream works of literature by Black and/or African authors is still restricted especially in the main Swiss bookstores. The African Book Fair – the only platform mentioned by the participants who did not speak about SAP or Nsanda – is thus seen as useful in compensating for gaps in access. But it only takes place once a year and participants still feel that Black/African literature is difficult to reach in comparison to Western/white literature. Based on their replies, I argue that more than a question of access in terms of availability and affordability, the issue lies in the fact that African/Black literature is not as visible and promoted as Western/white literature. As a matter of fact, no participant mentioned any economic constraint for buying books, implying no financial barrier exists for them to access the literature. Additionally, even if Black/African authors are not displayed on shelves, ordering online is always possible. So, the issue is more about knowing which books and authors to read, being more broadly exposed, easily finding a large diversity in genres, and not having to go through the hassle of research. Indeed, apart from a few Black authors who have been mediatised and thus put on the front shelf in libraries, such as Nigerian novelist Chimamanda Adichie or more recently Ghanaian-American writer Yaa Gyasi and Franco-Burundian musician and author Gaël Faye, finding and knowing about Black/African authors still requires effort. In contrast, finding white literature, crime and soap authors such as Marc Levy requires almost no effort since they are available in any kiosk in addition to mainstream libraries. This relatively limited exposure is proven by the participants' mentioning of authors who remain relatively well known in the francophone and/or anglophone spheres: Angela Davis, Mariama Ba, Amadou Hampâté Bâ, Toni Morrison, Maryse Condé, Maya Angelou, Aimé Césaire, Yaa Gyasi, Alex Haley, Cheikh Anta Diop and Malcom X, amongst others.

The issue of visibility and promotion of Black/African literature partly explains, in my opinion, why the African Book Fair, the UPAF and Afrolitt' are felt like facilitators by the participants: they inform on the books that can be read and inform on where they can be found, and thus act as alternative promotion channels in a hegemonic white culture. The fact that no participant mentioned *La Cene* that fulfils similar goals is revealing of the limited circulation of information on literary initiatives in French-speaking Switzerland.

BLACK/AFRICAN LITERATURE AND RACIALISED IDENTITIES

The question of identity came up early in both discussions and was relatively central to the conversations. As previously mentioned, most participants grew up without reading works that featured people and cultures they could directly identify with. As a result of their increased exposure to Black/African literature after adolescence, many of them are now conscious of how they had internalised the fact that they were not represented in what they read. The fact that characters were often depicted as white and from Western cultures was not something that consciously affected their understanding of identity, as many recall being more captured by the plots. It is only later on in their lives, after they encountered more works by Black authors that featured people and cultures they could more directly identify with in a liberating way, that they realised they hadn't been represented in their previous readings:

> I think that the discovery of 'African literature', put in as many quotation marks as possible, is something that suddenly speaks to you specifically. Suddenly ... well, it's the same as [hair] tutorials indeed, when suddenly one speaks about *your* hair, and not just *any* hair. Before that, you didn't really ask 'are they talking about my hair?' And at some point, people start taking care of your hair, and that is when you realize that your hair hadn't been spoken about previously. (Participant in her thirties, born and schooled in Switzerland and of East African origin)

The participants' understanding of their own identities when they first encountered Black/African literature, as well as the impact on their identities after reading Black literature are different and various. Whereas some consciously and actively seek Black/African literature as a means of identity affirmation and validation, others might not as actively use literature in this way. The latter will nonetheless relate to and identify more with the stories when reading such works because the topics and characters share their experiences and look similar to them.[7] For those who actively read African/Black literature as a means of identity affirmation, an outcome of such a process is the empowering feeling due to having one's experiences echoed and thus validated:

Because of what I experienced, I found answers in literature. I was conscious of the system of oppression, and thought I was alone in my corner, because in Switzerland we don't necessarily have links to other Black People ... and so it is through reading these books that I told myself 'ah there you go', [Black literature] is a bit universal because it concerns all Black People actually. (Participant in her late twenties, born in Central Africa and schooled in Switzerland)

For this participant, reading Black/African literature enables her to tackle a feeling of isolation in her racialised experience through understanding that her experiences are not just individual and exceptional, but concern many other Black people. This reveals the use of transnational Black and African resources where the need is not necessarily to read authors sharing the same origin or location, but the fact that their stories feature narratives of oppression, struggle and liberation from a Black/African perspective which participants identify with.[8] In fact, no participant mentioned any of the Afro-Swiss authors mentioned above in the introduction, and most read francophone and anglophone authors alike since they can rely on translations.

While the Black participants identify directly with works where Black characters and experiences relative to Black people are featured, the North African and Middle Eastern participants identify indirectly. As people who are not Black but who face racial discrimination,[9] they use Black literature, more than Arab or Middle Eastern literature, as a way to deal with their difference because they consider it more available and liberating. Thus, they reach for works by Black Americans in particular, but also to some African authors, who remain relatively more known and therefore serve as resources tackling alterity:

... I read many books by Toni Morrison, but with long gaps in between so it wasn't really intense, but this was in contrast to the fact that Arab literature is more difficult to access. So, if I wanted, if I wanted to deal with my own alterity, the literature that was available either in French or in English, was often Black literature .... (Participant in her thirties, born and schooled in Switzerland and of North African origin)

Can I react to that? ... For me too, [Middle Eastern] literature was quite inaccessible ... and so I asked myself what could I ... what could I relate to? Well sub-Saharan Africa .... (Participant in her late twenties, born and schooled in Switzerland and of Middle Eastern origin)

Another noteworthy aspect is that what seems to count at first for most participants actively seeking Black/African literature as identity affirmation is the ability to find relatable racialised and racist experiences and identities in the texts, more obviously than gender or sexuality-related issues. Indeed, very few participants indicated that they were consciously looking for gendered identity affirmation: the majority of responses could lead one to believe that finding authors or themes to relate to as people of colour was the salient goal. Nonetheless, when pushed to reflect upon the matter, some admitted that they did feel a difference, and identified even more strongly with a story, when reading Black female authors after having read only works by men. But since they were more exposed to Black/African literature by men, those are the works they mostly use(d) for their identity affirmation. This finding also stands for other intersecting identities such as class, religion and so on.

It's more that I came across [Black female literature] and told myself 'Oh, well this is very interesting, it speaks to me more, it tackles issues that concern me more.' But before that, it's as if I didn't realize. I didn't have that consciousness that only men were writing, that I read only men. I wasn't conscious of that. (Participant in her thirties, born in West Africa and schooled there)

Finally, using Black/African literature as a means of identity affirmation seems to be intertwined with practices of learning alternative histories and seeking responses to questions about one's identity and culture outside of a white hegemony. Historical fiction or novels relating to experienced historical events become means for learning about the history of people of colour, which was not generally taught in schools:

Suddenly I discovered that indeed, I have a history. I personally had always thought that there wasn't any, that things were the way they were, that we had always been dominated, that Whites were better, and that it had always been so ... And then I read books that talk about that, the origins [of a particular ethnicity], works by Hampâté Bâ, Camara Laye and all that. (Participant in her thirties, born and schooled in France and of West African origin)

Not only does this reveal the negation of Black/African history in white/ Western hegemonic spaces, but it also emphasises the need for Black/ African narratives and stories in the participant's identity affirmation and personal growth. Indeed, this 'discovery of one's history' of achievement and resistance is felt by the participant as liberating because it counters a negative and racist discourse of underachievement and submission of Africans and their descendants. As a result, it opens up her imagination on past and future possibilities, develops a critical consciousness tackling white hegemonic culture, and is felt like a mental liberation.[10]

AFROFEMINIST LITERARY SPACES

While reading is mostly undertaken as an individual activity, sharing and discussing books are practices that half of the participants undertake frequently. Although Afrolitt' is not the sole platform hosting meetings to discuss books, it is nonetheless worthwhile to understand the uses and expectations of such a space by frequent attendants.

Both focus groups and their resulting discussions reveal that many Black women and women of colour in Switzerland sense the need to gather together in spaces where they feel at ease to express themselves about their racialised and gendered experiences. Black literary spaces such as Afrolitt' are therefore not only attended as spaces to discuss a shared passion – Black/African literature – but also to meet women who share similar views and experiences, even if they all have different opinions on the book read/being discussed.

> It's just that for once it feels good to not have to give explanation, to not have to set the context, to not need to … you start on the same footing. It's a bit like the feminists who feel good amongst themselves. In our case, we are women and Black, so we feel good being amongst Black women. And this space adds to … well you're speaking about literature, so it means … it means that we are Black women who like literature and so we have a space in which we can discuss it with mutual kindness. (Participant in her late thirties, born and schooled in Switzerland and of Central African origin)

In cases where Black women or women of colour were not the sole attendants or even a majority, participants expressed the need for the gatherings to feel safe and to be attended by open-minded – that is, non-racist and non-sexist – people.

Nonetheless, one principal limitation was expressed in both groups: the fact that literary spaces generally attract people who like literature and have a certain class background. Given a general perception of literature and reading as relatively elitist activities and/or opportunities seized by some people to show off their knowledge, this in turn could discourage some women without higher education from joining such groups.

> What I feel is missing a bit in these spaces is a more multidisciplinary approach. Because the thing is that books are things that interest those of us who are here. They interest a certain amount of people, but there is still a privileged access for people from a certain education background, a certain class ... For example, my mother wouldn't have come to a reading group, and my mother is as legitimate as anybody else. And in her way of being and doing many things ... she was ... she would have needed this kind of space as much as me or anyone else. But maybe she would have come if it had instead been a space where she could take a sewing class with her friends. (Participant in her late thirties, born and schooled in Switzerland and of North African origin)

As a result, Black literary spaces represent an opportunity for Black women and women of colour to interact, but other spaces based on other activities should also be imagined. This observation led participants in both groups to emphasise the need for more spaces for Black women and women of colour to be created in order for them to discuss their lived experiences of exclusion and difference in Switzerland.

CONCLUSION

The discussions conducted in both Lausanne and Geneva show that Black women and women of colour relate to and/or make use of Black/ African literature in ways that are identity affirming. Participants also make use of Black/African literature to learn about varied histories. The experiences and outcomes of this process vary between participants, but the practices nonetheless reveal that they face racialised and sexualised oppressions in a white patriarchal society. It is worth noting that if Black/

African literature serves as a resource for identity affirmation, and as a means to learn alternative narratives, participants also mentioned that it could be a means of escape into another reality, a source of entertainment, a way to be fully invested in something, or a source of inspiration for those who write. Additionally, with regards to identity affirmation and learning, participants do not solely rely on literature. Black TV or (web) series, video tutorials, social media, Black cultural events and so on help to achieve similar goals.

Concerning Black literary spaces, participants mentioned that attending such gatherings allow them to meet other Black women and women of colour to exchange ideas about their experiences of discrimination, on top of sharing a passion for books and reading and sharing ideas. Such spaces don't necessarily have to be exclusive, but should nonetheless enable open-minded, non-sexist and non-racist behaviours.

Given the limitations of this research, more could be undertaken to find out why only a few Black men or men of colour frequent spaces such as the Afrolitt' meetings, and to understand how gendered these literary and safe spaces are. Finally, this research was limited to the particular space of Afrolitt' and the women who attend its meetings and events more frequently. Other spaces and geographies, whether in Switzerland or other European countries, should also be explored to broaden our understandings of these dynamics.

NOTES

1. *Un étranger dans le village* by Pierre Koralnik, 1962 © Télévision suisse romande. www.rts.ch/archives/tv/divers/documentaires/8565837-un-etranger-dans-le-village.html (accessed 14 May 2018).
2. V.O. Carter, 1973. *The Bern Book: A Record of a Voyage of the Mind.* John Day Company, New York.
3. C. Batumike, 2006. *Etre noir africain en Suisse. Intégration, identité, perception et perspectives d'avenir d'une minorité visible.* L'Harmattan, Paris, pp. 122, 126.
4. N. Pereira, 2009. Le movement suisse de 68 et le Portugal: de la dictature à la révolution (1962–1975). In J.M. Schaufelbuehl (ed.), *1968–1978. Ein bewegtes Jahrzehnt in der Schweiz/Une décennie mouvementée en Suisse.* Chronos, Zurich, pp. 147–60.
5. UPAF official presentation. www.upaf.ch (accessed 14 May 2018).
6. M.D. Kaplowitz and J.P. Hoehn, 2001. 'Do focus groups and individual interviews reveal the same information for natural resource valuation?' *Ecological Economics* 36, pp. 237–47. J. Kitzinger, 1994. 'The methodology of

focus groups: The importance of interaction between research participants'. *Sociology of Health & Illness* 16(1), pp. 103–21. R. Krueger and M.A. Casey, 2008. 'A basic guide for focus group interviewing'. https://richardakrueger. com/focus-group-interviewing/ (accessed 14 May 2018).

7. On the liberating aspect of reading literature that features characters and cultures of colour, see C. Acosta, 2007. 'Developing critical consciousness: Resistance literature in a Chicano literature class'. *The English Journal* 97(2), pp. 36–42.

8. I extend Jaqueline N. Brown's notion of 'diasporic resources' – Afro-American political and cultural references used as inspiration by other Black people from the diaspora – to include the fact that African influences also play an influential role. See J. Brown, 1998. 'Black Liverpool, Black America, and the gendering of diasporic space'. *Cultural Anthropology* 13(3), pp. 291–325.

9. Political Blackness such as in the United Kingdom does not translate in a contemporary Swiss context.

10. The affirmation that knowing one's past and history is a liberating tool has been claimed by numerous Black intellectuals, activists and writers. See, for example, C. Woodson, 2017 (originally published 1933). *The Miseducation of the Negro.* 12th Media Service, Suwanee. L. Miano, 2012. *Habiter la frontière.* L'Arche, Paris.

9

'Blackness Disrupts My Germanness.' On Embodiment and Questions of Identity and Belonging Among Women of Colour in Germany

Johanna Melissa Lukate

In postwar Germany, the terminology around *Rasse* and race was expunged from Germans' vocabulary and public discourse.[1] This is perhaps most visible in the absence of any racial or ethnic classification schema in the German census, which differentiates between Germans, Germans with a migrant background[2] and foreigners. In contrast, in the United States, Canada and the United Kingdom, the census brings together questions of race, nationality, belonging and citizenship, which 'demand that policy-makers negotiate between technical requirements and the politics of recognition.'[3] In this chapter, I use women of colour's[4] talk about hair to examine the tension between the notion of 'race as a taboo' and the women's experience of their bodies and identities as being positioned within hegemonic – racialised – regimes of normativity that exclude them from a concept of Germanness that is conflated with whiteness.[5] In doing so, I am particularly interested in the ways in which women of colour's aesthetic body work in the form of hairstyling underpins the practice and navigation of citizenship and spurs different modes of being and belonging.

The presence of people of colour in Germany is often portrayed as exceptional and insignificant, limited to two important moments in history: the *Rheinlandbastarde* as a consequence of the deployment of African troops after the First World War[6] and *Besatzungskinder* as a result of the presence of African-American troops during the US occupation after the Second World War.[7] In working with German family photographs dating back to the early twentieth century, Tina Campt, however, points us towards the possibility and necessity to see black Germans as central to the landscape of everyday life in Germany: to recognise them as deeply internal rather than marginal or exceptional; to understand their community as present rather than absent in earlier historical periods; and to perceive them as constituent of Germanness in ways that force us to reimagine German identity itself.[8]

But have we been able to re/imagine German identity in such a way that we recognise 'Black Germans' as German(s)? And if not, how do women of colour make sense of their place within German society? How do they craft spaces of belonging?

METHODOLOGY

The aim of this chapter is to explore the hair politics of women of colour in Germany and their understandings of being and belonging in Germany. I thus draw on 21 interviews with 22[9] women of colour about their life story told as a 'hair story': narratives that reflect the women's coming of age through changes in their hair care and styling routine. These 'hair stories' form an archive[10] through which I theorise and explore the meaning of the women's intersectionally gendered and raced body in Germany.[11] Although the women were not explicitly asked about identity, many women spoke about questions of identity and belonging when asked how their hair (and skin colour) relate to their origins and family background.

The women were recruited through snowballing sampling techniques. Interviews took place in Berlin, which has few people with a migrant background, the Cologne-Bonn Area including Düsseldorf, which is among the regions with the highest rate of people with a migrant background, and finally the Rhine-Neckar Triangle, which is between these two extremes in terms of population diversity.[12]

The women's ages ranged from 22 to 37, and included university and occupational students in subjects ranging from African Studies to Medical Engineering, social and IT workers, office administrators, designers, journalists, an actress and a medical laboratory assistant. Three women were natural hair bloggers and one woman owned an online web shop for hair products. For seven women, one or both parents were from either the Democratic Republic of Congo (thereafter, the Congo) or Ghana. Additionally, women had parents from Gambia (1), Nigeria (2), South

Africa (1), Togo (1), Uganda (1) and the United States (1). Nine women had one white German parent. To preserve anonymity, I have assigned the women pseudonyms and where possible, names were chosen that reflect the women's individual cultural and ethnic roots.

As the daughter of a white German mother and Congolese immigrant father, I was born and raised in Germany and educated in England. My own embodied intersectionality and sense of being German was in continuous dialogue with the women who participated in this project. This dialogical work included a critical interrogation of the fact that being 'Black is not enough';[13] as a biracial woman, I was at times positioned as a light-skinned woman with 'good hair', who never (had to) chemically relax her hair for reasons of practicality, manageability or social acceptability. However, my natural hair complicated my relationship with women who were aware of or had, for example, been subjected to online shaming by members of the natural hair community. In accepting that some women felt apprehensive about being interviewed by me, a social scientist and prominent political activist, well known within African diasporic communities for having chemically straightened her hair, conducted four interviews with women who chemically straightened their hair or wore weaves and wigs.

AM I GERMAN?

'Gehst du mal später zurück in deine Heimat?'
Wohin? nach Heidelberg? wo ich ein Heim hab? (Advanced Chemistry, 'Fremd im eigenen Land')[14]

On paper, citizenship status in Germany is regulated by two legal principles: *ius solis* (right of the soil or birth right citizenship) and *ius sanguinis* (right of the blood). In everyday encounters, however, bodies are visually recognised as raced, gendered and classed; as 'belonging' to a particular space or as 'being from somewhere'. Many women in this study thus struggled with the possibility to position themselves in relation to an unspoken paradigm that equates Germanness with whiteness, citizenship and nation.

Nia: It was always like straightaway like 'I am African', even though I was born in Germany, for me it was always like, yeah, 'I am African'. But also, because people said to me, you could not say,

> because even if you said you were German, for them it would
> have been – except if they asked you: 'Where were you born?'

J: Mhm

Nia: That's when you said: 'In Germany.' I remember, once there was
      a man who said, because he asked me: 'Where are you from?'
      And then I said: 'From Ghana', 'But where were you born?'
      That's when I said: 'yeah, so like Germany.' Then he said: 'Yeah,
      so then you aren't from Ghana, but you are from Germany.
      Your parents are from Ghana.' And that was the first time I
      (clicks her fingers), 'ah, right, like' I must have been 14 or so,
      that's when I realised for the first time 'yeah, it's actually true.
      You are German!' Because you studied here, you were raised
      here, you were born here …

Nia is a 23-year-old university student in Berlin whose parents are both
from Ghana. In this excerpt, she explores her understanding of the
embodiment of identities – 'German', 'Ghanaian' and 'African' – and
how this understanding influenced the practice of naming and positioning herself in conversations and interactions. Nia discusses how she
perceives her body as excluding her from 'being German', prompting
her to identify as 'African'. It is through negotiating her identity and citizenship status with others that she becomes aware of her Germanness
vis-à-vis the realisation that her African/Ghanaian self is void of cultural
knowledge and experience: 'What do you actually know about your
culture?', Nia asks herself, and concludes that she 'couldn't even answer
the question'. Nia's sense of being and belonging is then marked by an
'orphan consciousness'[15] that arises from a lack of experientially lived
knowledge of the Ghanaian culture. In addressing this absence, Nia,
like other women in this project who were born and raised in Germany,
eventually travels to Ghana.[16] My interview with Nia then highlights how
'being' German is an ambivalent and contradictory experience for most
women, which requires constant re/negotiation because citizenship and
identity are intersubjective, dialogical phenomena.[17] As Duveen argues,
identity is 'as much about the process of being identified as it is about the
process of identification'.[18]

To what extent then is 'being German' an embodied experience? What
is the role of hair and/or skin colour in underpinning these women's
practices and understanding of place and belonging in Germany?

... because I grew up with my family, that is with my White family I actually had, like, except for one book I had only children's books with blonde girls or with straight hair, they had long, straight hair and it basically suggests that you do not fit into this and you want to look like them and then you realise somehow that you don't belong, well, you simply don't look like your girlfriends. (Susanne, 36)

In the absence of her father, Susanne, who works in education, was raised by her maternal family in East Germany. The excerpt emphasises how modes of belonging and 'fitting in' are experientially lived through and within intersectionally raced and gendered bodies. Susanne develops an understanding of her own *embodied* difference by comparing herself to characters in children's books 'with blonde ... long, straight hair', and to her 'girlfriends'. In doing so, Susanne represents Germanness as associated with whiteness, which prevents her from being recognised as German: 'I feel German ... but I am not recognised as German. I am always asked where I am from, what I am doing or why I am here, why it is that I speak German so well ...'. The experience of Blackness as a boundary to being recognised as German is consistent with Linke's observation that in postwar Germany 'whiteness has been reclaimed as an unmarked signifier of race and citizenship'.[19] Psychologically, Susanne's struggle for recognition highlights the emotional pain and injury that stem from the denial of recognition. As Honneth notes:

Because the normative self-image of each and every individual human being ... is dependent on the possibility of being continually backed up by others, the experiences of being disrespected carries with it the danger of an injury that can bring the identity of the person as a whole to the point of collapse.[20]

The threat of afro-textured hair as placing the women outside of normative conceptions of not just Germanness but beauty was also addressed by Laurie, who works as an actress. The daughter of an afro shop owner, Laurie is socialised into the Black hair and beauty culture and recalls changing her hairstyle every two months from the age of four.

You know, here in Germany you always felt very much ashamed of this kinky hair. Because everyone was like blonde and straight and amazing hair, and the media and celebrities, straight hair, even

Beyoncé, straight hair. And, of course, you then wanted to look similar to that, this Western image. (Laurie, 28)

The evocation of blonde in both Laurie's and Susanne's narratives emphasises 'how the Aryan aesthetics ... implanted its trace'[21] within the German body memory. Notably, the embodiment of alterity was for many women located in 'this kinky hair' rather than the colour of their skin. As a malleable bodily characteristic,[22] the women acknowledged their hair as a means to performatively re/negotiate their place and identity within the German society. Below I discuss how hairstyling was tied into the practice and navigation of citizenship and created the possibility for performative acts of 'becoming' German.

MASKING BLACKNESS, MAKING GERMANS

My best friend, Natalie, I know her since I was two years old, her hair is much kinkier than mine like, she had a lot more problems with it ... And to this day she wears straightened hair, definitively, because it is also really important to her identity as a German. And then she said it works and ... we like did it together, and we said like, 'now we are going to straighten our hair!' ... It is not only this peer pressure but also this identity crisis of mine, the fact that I did not have a single Black person in my family, not at all, I am the only one. And because of that, em, to also emphasise my Germanness like 'Hey! I am also a part of it.' Like straight hair ... yeah. (Dina, 26)

In this excerpt, Dina, a university student in Düsseldorf, recounts how she first started to chemically straighten her hair. Her narrative exposes multiple factors that contributed to her yearning for straight hair from 'belonging to a group, and they all have straight hair' to the isolation she experienced from being the only Black person in her family. Being born and raised in Germany by her white German mother, Dina, who never met her father, develops a strong German identity that is challenged by her continued sense of Otherness. Like other women she struggles with the denial of recognition: 'What then should I say, where am I from', Dina wonders, 'I am from Germany', ... 'what is your culture?' 'Well, I am German.' Her narrative takes here the form of a 'self-reflective ... dialogue with absent others' (p. 682)[23] through which Dina is able to take the perspective of the other towards herself in such a way that she recognises how 'Blackness was disrupting my Germanness'. In managing her identity, Dina, like her friend Natalie, uses hair straightening as a means to performatively 'emphasise my Germanness'.

The role of friendship groups as the first context in which these women have to negotiate their place and identity in the German society is also central to the narrative of Judith, a 27-year-old Berlin-based designer:

> Judith: I would straighten them every three to six months … It was around that time when I was part of this clique, with these two blonde girls … And you totally had this feeling, you wanted to be part of it, we always determined who was the prettiest of the evening, before we went out, right? And it was never me! So yes, and because of that, and my hair would always drive me mad, always drive me mad, it was such a huge part of who I am.
>
> …
>
> Judith: And … for a long time, I could not identify with my African side. Like, I always said, very clearly said 'I am German, I am German, I am German', and, em, like I did not feel African[24] at all. So, em, that would be the connection that I would draw.
>
> J: So are you feeling African now?
>
> Judith: I feel exactly half-half … Am proud of both sides.

Bringing these two passages from Judith's narrative together allows us to understand how the discomfort and sense of hate that Judith experienced as a teenager towards her hair were tied into her understanding of being German. The two excerpts then represent different stages in Judith's life and hair story. In the first excerpt, Judith talks about her adolescence and how the desire to be 'part of this clique' and to be recognised as pretty motivated her to not only chemically straighten her hair but to wear weaves and blue or green contact lenses as performative strategies that allowed her to pass as white and, by extension, German. The second excerpt explores Judith's identity after her recent transition from chemically relaxed hair to natural hair as shifting from 'I am German' to being 'proud of both sides'.

In retrospect, women like Judith often described relaxing and the wearing of weaves as an attempt to ignore and hide, that is, mask their 'African side'. As Yamada notes: 'My mask is control/concealment/endurance/my mask is escape/from my/self.'[25] Psychologically, the transition process, which is commonly labelled as 'going natural', can be understood as a process of (self-)acceptance and a site of recovery.[26] It is a process of unlearning and breaking free from internalised regimes of normativity and oppression, which construe afro-textured hair as 'bad', 'ugly' and 'inferior' compared to long, straight, Caucasian hair.[27] For Judith, going natural enables her to reconcile her me-as-German with her me-as-African in a way that allows her 'to sometimes really feel like a Queen' and to accept her hair and body as beautiful. In my interview with Judith, identity is thus a dynamic process; identities change and evolve over time, they are 'a matter of "becoming" as well as of "being"'.[28]

DIASPORA'S DAUGHTERS, AFRICA'S DAUGHTERS?[29]

The duality and multiplicity of the women's heritages and identities point towards the complex and at times conflicting web of historical and contemporary processes, formed across imaginative and actual geographic places and spaces, which inform questions of identity and belonging. Within this web, being German is only one of multiple identity positions taken on and open to women of colour.

Manu is a 23-year-old university student, who maintained a strong sense of 'being from the Congo' after migrating to Germany with her family as a child. Confronted with extreme hair loss, she seeks to understand the relationship between hair and 'my identity as a Black woman' in the diaspora.

Manu: mhm so three years ago my hair em started falling out … And so in that year … I spent a lot of time dealing with myself … what are my strengths em very much confronted em where I come from, and like for the first time somehow consciously sought and confronted my identity

J: Identity as a search for your Congolese origins?

Manu: em, no, origins and the like that was always clear because of my parents, they always like, no, but like identity as a Black woman … and so with my hair breaking and I somehow started to question myself: why … why am I doing this? Like why am I straightening my hair? Em, why is it that other women are doing it … and like, what would happen if I were to no longer do it.

As the daughter of a university professor, Manu grew up in a predominately white upper middle class environment while her family
maintained close ties to African diaspora communities. In this context,
relaxing her hair for over ten years was not just about assimilation – the
fact that 'with relaxed hair you looked similar to [the white girls]' – but
about being socialised into a Black beauty paradigm that privileges
'good hair'.[30] People within the African diaspora, Manu is told by her
mother during her transition, 'don't think [natural hair] is beautiful, and
therefore you should not wear it that way'. My interview with Manu thus
emphasises 'the hold that hair straightening has on the collective black
consciousness'.[31] For Manu, this hold renders her natural hair, which she
wears in an afro, a political statement; a performative negotiation of her
identity as a Black woman in the diaspora.

In contrast, 32-year-old Ejo talks about her search for an 'African
identity'. Her story provides a particularly interesting perspective because
it emphasises how women of colour performatively weave 'a mosaic of
cultures and histories'[32] into their identities to craft places of belonging.

Ejo: I wear a lot of African clothing or African jewellery and I very
      much identify with it; like I have a gigantic Africa tattoo on my
      back and like it is to me ... as much home as Germany is my
      home and to me hair also connects to this.
J: Okay, so would you say that you have more of an African
      identity?
Ejo: No, I certainly grew up here, I think [in] German, I was raised
      German by my German mother, like, em, but, em, yeah, I always
      very much sought this African identity.

Like most women with a white German mother, Ejo has a strong sense
of 'being' German rooted in her upbringing, language and familiarity
with the German culture. However, for Ejo, this sense of belonging and
being, of Germany as 'my home', is fully compatible with seeking out and
performatively enacting an African identity through clothing, jewellery
and hair. In other words, she resists the idea of singular identity affil-
iations[33] to fully explore the complex and contradictory ways of being
in the social world. Nevertheless, Ejo struggles with the realisation that
in both Germany and Ghana her dreadlocks are read as a problematic
aspect of identity: 'It is a dirty image of, if you wear dreadlocks it is
straightaway, "Okay, you are wearing dreadlocks, you are a Rasta, you

smoke Marihuana, you are a criminal.'" For Ejo, who now wears her hair natural, the decision to cut her dreadlocks off is thus about the possibility of occupying space in the German society and of fully participating within that space.

Ejo: I started, I would say, a whole new, new life … I started my new degree

J: Mhm

Ejo: And I knew that if I want to work in this area at some point, it would be difficult with dreadlocks … and so, it was in the course of this … I simply cut them off.

Taken together, Manu's and Ejo's narratives illustrate how hairstyling engages these women in a 'critical dialogue'[34] with multiple societies and groups to which the women lay claim. Within these dialogues, hairstyling is both a strategic effort at resistance and at conformity. Far from being fixed, however, these dialogues change over time and across contexts. They are as much a reflection of the women's coming of age as of shifting historical and socio-political processes that shape how we read and understand particular hairstyles and textures.

CONCLUSION

Through women of colour's talk about hair, this chapter has shown how the discourse around 'Blackness' and 'African identity' linguistically masks[35] and simultaneously points towards a racialised identity discourse in Germany that operates along the notion of a binary 'color-line'.[36] Moreover, this discourse is tied into a concept of 'Germanness' that equates whiteness, nation and citizenship similarly to, for example, the equation of Britishness and whiteness.[37] Hence, although Germany has, at the institutional and administrative level, refrained from racial classification systems, women of colour's lived experiences illustrate how race is evoked at the interpersonal level as a structuring element of everyday encounters.

As this chapter has demonstrated, the embodiment of difference and Otherness excludes the women from Germanness/whiteness, while hairstyling acts as a performative strategy through which the women express, negotiate and challenge their exclusion and entertain alternative modes of identity and belonging. For some women, hairstyling became a means to manage a marginalised identity and to performatively 'become' German through the chemical relaxing of their hair or by wearing weaves and wigs. Other women choose to proudly enact a 'Black' or 'African identity' through the natural texture of their hair. In the women's narratives, hairstyling was then both a site of oppression and a site of recovery from the physical wounds of chemically straightening the hair and the psychological injuries stemming from racism and internalised oppression.[38] The psychology of Black hair has thus much to offer to the project of Black feminist theory in Europe because it enables us to theorise and understand hairstyling as a praxis and epistemology within women of colour's lived experiences in Europe, and Germany in particular.

NOTES

1. R. Chin, 2011. 'From Rasse to race: On the problem of difference in the Federal Republic of Germany'. Unpublished paper, School of Social Science, Institute for Advanced Study, University of Michigan. www.sss.ias.edu/files/papers/Paper42.pdf (accessed 19 February 2019).
2. According to the *Statistische Bundesamt*, a person has a migrant background if they or one of their parents were not born with German citizenship. www.destatis.de/DE/ZahlenFakten/GesellschaftStaat/Bevoelkerung/MigrationIntegration/Glossar/Migrationshintergrund.html (accessed 7 May 2018).
3. Debra Thompson, 2012. 'Making (mixed-)race: Census politics and the emergence of multiracial multiculturalism in the United States, Great Britain and Canada'. *Ethnic and Racial Studies* 35(8), pp. 1409–26 (p. 1420).
4. The term 'women of colour' is not perfect and reflects a compromise vis-à-vis the rejection of 'Black/black', 'mixed-race' and *Afrodeutsch* (read: Afro-German) as identity categories and labels by the majority of women in this project.
5. Uli Linke, 2004. 'Shame on the skin: Post-Holocaust memory and the German aesthetics of whiteness'. In Rodopi Birgit Tautz (ed.), *Colors 1800/1900/2000: Signs of Ethnic Difference*. Rodopi, Amsterdam, pp. 183–211. Damani J. Partridge, 2012. *Hypersexuality and Headscarves. Race, Sex and Citizenship in the New Germany*. Indiana University Press, Bloomington.
6. Tina M. Campt, 2009. 'Family matters: Diaspora, difference, and the visual archive'. *Social Text* 27(1), pp. 83–114. doi:10.1215/01642472-2008-018. Fatima El-Tayeb, 2001. *Schwarze Deutsche. Der Diskurs um 'Rasse' und Nationale Identität 1890–1933*. Campus Verlag, Frankfurt; New York.
7. Campt, 'Family matters'. Johanna Melissa Lukate, 2007. *Colored Families in Deutschland (Beitrag zum Geschichtswettbewerb des Bundespräsidenten und der Körber Stiftung 2006–07)*. Unpublished report submitted to the History

Competition of the President of the Federal Republic of Germany and the Körber Stiftung where it has won two prizes.

8. Campt, 'Family matters', p. 67.
9. In one instance, two women were interviewed jointly.
10. Jennifer C. Nash, 2014. 'Archives of pain: Reading the Black feminist theoretical archive'. In *The Black Body in Ecstasy: Reading Race, Reading Pornography.* Duke University Press, Durham. Sarah Haley, 2016. *No Mercy Here. Gender, Punishment, and the Making of Jim Crow Modernity.* University of North Carolina Press, Chapel Hill. Saidiya Hartman, 2007. *Lose Your Mother. A Journey along the Atlantic Slave Route.* Farrar, Straus and Giroux, New York.
11. Heidi Safia Mirza, 2013. '"A second skin": Embodied intersectionality, transnationalism and narratives of identity and belonging among Muslim women in Britain'. *Women's Studies International Forum* 36, pp. 5–15. doi:10.1016/j.wsif.2012.10.012. Paulette M. Caldwell, 1991. 'A hair piece: Perspectives on the intersection of race and gender'. *Duke Law Journal* 2, 365–96.
12. Bertelsmann Stiftung. *Factsheet Einwanderungsland Deutschland.* 2016. www.bertelsmann-stiftung.de/de/publikationen/publikation/did/factsheet-einwanderungsland-deutschland/ (accessed 7 May 2018).
13. Josephine Beoku-Betts, 1994. 'When Black is not enough: Doing field research among Gullah women'. *NWSA Journal* 6(3), pp. 413–33 (p. 313).
14. Advanced Chemistry is known as one of the first HipHop groups in Germany. The track 'Fremd im eigenen Land' (1995) translates to 'stranger in my own country' and addresses the ambivalence and contradictions of questions of identity and belonging as experienced by people of colour in Germany. The lines quoted here translate to: '"In the future, are you going back home?" / Where to? To Heidelberg? Where I have a home?'
15. Jayne O. Ifekwunigwe, 1997. 'Diaspora's daughters, Africa's orphans? On lineage, authenticity and "mixed race" identity'. In Heidi Safia Mirza (ed.), *Black British Feminism. A Reader.* Routledge, London, pp. 127–52 (p. 128).
16. Hartman, *Lose Your Mother.* Johanna Melissa Lukate and Juliet L.H. Foster. '"Depending on where I am ..." – hair and identity performance in women of colour in Germany and England'. Revised resubmission. *European Journal of Social Psychology.*
17. Helen Haste, 2004. 'Constructing the citizen'. *Political Psychology* 25(3), pp. 413–39.
18. Gerard Duveen, 2001. 'Representations, identities, resistance'. In Kay Deaux and Gina Philogène (eds), *Representations of the Social.* Blackwell, Oxford, pp. 257–70 (p. 259).
19. Linke, 'Shame on the skin', p. 209.
20. Axel Honneth, 1995. *The Struggle for Recognition. The Moral Grammar of Social Conflicts.* MIT Press, Cambridge, MA, p. 131.
21. Linke, 'Shame on the skin', p. 209.
22. However, for a discussion of skin bleaching, see Margaret L. Hunter, 2011. 'Buying racial capital: Skin-bleaching and cosmetic surgery in a globalized world'. *The Journal of Pan African Studies* 4(4), pp. 142–64.

23. Alex Gillespie, 2007. 'The social basis of self-reflection'. In Jaan Valsiner and Alberto Rosa (eds), *The Cambridge Handbook of Sociocultural Psychology*. Cambridge University Press, Cambridge, pp. 678–91.

24. In the German original, Judith uses the feminine denomination *Afrikanerin*.

25. M. Yamada, 1990. 'Masks of a woman'. In Gloria Anzaldúa (ed.), *Making Face, Making Soul = Haciendo Caras: Creative and Critical Perspectives by Women of Color*. Aunt Lute Foundation Books, San Francisco, pp. 114–16 (p. 114).

26. On the Black feminist commitment to recovery work, see Nash, 'Archives of pain', chapter 1.

27. Emma Tarlo, 2016. *Entanglement. The Secret Lives of Hair*. Oneworld Publications, London. Shirley Tate, 2007. 'Black beauty: Shade, hair and anti-racist aesthetics'. *Ethnic and Racial Studies*.30(2), March, pp. 300–19. doi:10.1080/01419870601143992. Cheryl Thompson, 2009. 'Black women, beauty, and hair as a matter of being'. *Women's Studies* 38(8), pp. 831–56. doi:10.1080/00497870903238463. Tracey Owens Patton, 2006. 'Hey girl, am I more than my hair?: African American women and their struggles with beauty, body image, and hair'. *NWSA Journal* 18(2), pp. 24–51.

28. Stuart Hall, 1990. 'Cultural identity and diaspora'. In Jonathan Rutherford (ed.), *Identity: Community, Culture, Difference*. Lawrence & Wishart, London, pp. 222–37 (p. 225).

29. The subtitle is a play on the title of Ifekwunigwe, 'Diaspora's daughters, Africa's orphans?'.

30. Ingrid Banks, 2000. *Hair Matters: Beauty, Power and Black Women's Consciousness*. SUNY Press, Albany, NY.

31. Tate, 'Black beauty', p. 303.

32. Ifekwunigwe, 'Diaspora's daughters, Africa's orphans?', p. 146.

33. Amartya Sen, 2006. *Identity & Violence. The Illusion of Destiny*. Penguin Books, London.

34. Kobena Mercer, 2000. 'Black hair/style politics'. In Kwesi Owusu (ed.), *Black British Cultue & Society. A Text Reader*. Routledge, London, pp. 111–21 (p. 119).

35. Notably, the German term for 'race', *Rasse*, was absent in interviews conducted in German language, which reinforces the notion of race as a taboo.

36. W.E. Burghardt DuBois, 1996. *The Souls of Black Folk. Essays and Sketches*. Penguin Books, New York; London; Victoria; Toronto; Auckland.

37. Paul Gilroy, 2013. *There Ain't No Black in the Union Jack*. 2nd edition. Routledge. Heidi Safia Mirza, 1997. 'Introduction. Mapping a genealogy of Black British feminism'. In Heidi Safia Mirza (ed.), *Black British Feminism. A Reader*. Routledge, London, pp. 1–28.

38. Karen D. Pyke, 2010. 'What is internalized racial oppression and why don't we study it? Acknowledging racism's hidden injuries'. *Sociological Perspectives* 53(4), pp. 551–72. doi:10.1525/sop.2010.53.4.551. Dalia Rodriguez, 2006. 'Un/masking identity. Healing our wounded souls'. *Qualitative Inquiry* 12(6), pp. 1067–90. doi:10.1177/1077800406293238.

10

Love & Affection: The Radical Possibilities of Friendship Between Women of Colour

Ego Ahaiwe Sowinske and Nazmia Jamal

This chapter was shaped by a series of long-distance conversations that took place in the summer of 2017. Our initial motivation for proposing a joint piece of writing came from a feeling of anxiety that others had begun to record our stories in ways that we did not feel comfortable with. The long blur of our labours began to come into focus and we did not want each other's work to simply be an end note in another white academic's history of Western feminism.

The reality of trying to write something together proved more difficult than we expected. Trump, Brexit, austerity – how to concentrate on anything in our personal lives when the political world hasn't stopped spitting out bad news? We are not academics or writers – in times like these you will find us on the streets holding placards, organising a benefit, sharing thoughts on a panel in the hope it will make a change. June Jordan wrote, in the wake of Reagan's election, 'This is not such a hot/ time for you or for me.' For us, in our relative privilege, it remains 'not a good time' to be a Black woman in America or a Muslim woman in London. Rage is a tiring emotion. This summer we became tired.

But, as Jordan also wrote in the same poem, 'From Sea to Shining Sea' (1980):[1]

This is a good time
This is the best time
This is the only time to come together

In the wake of political struggle and personal bereavement we began to finally talk to one another. We don't know what will come tomorrow.

So, we prioritised our friendship over the chapter deadline and began to unpick why we were finding this collaboration so difficult when it was also clear that we very much wanted to do the work. We eventually acknowledged and then examined the breakdown of our friendship several years ago. It is difficult to articulate how a relationship based on such genuine affection and respect ended up in such an awkward stasis but we think this is part of what happened:

1. Archives are a blessing and a curse. We are both deeply interested in feminist organising by women of colour in 1970s and 1980s Britain. At points in our friendship we've ended up playing out age old identity-based rifts. Our arguments have never been personal, they have always been broader. Political Blackness,[2] in particular, is a concept that has caused us such trouble.

2. We started off in different waves. Ego, the last in a long line of custodians at Lambeth Women's Project[3] (LWP), was coming from a second wave tradition when we met. Nazmia sat more in the third wave, having accessed feminism as a teenager in the period immediately post-riot grrrl.[4] Neither of us stayed where we were but, as Ego puts it, Nazmia's arrival at LWP 'was a challenge'.

In the end we have realised that we are not ready to talk about our experiences in a detached way or to historicise them when we are still living with the consequences (both good and bad). We invite you to share this conversation as a documentation of a relationship that radically shaped both of our lives.

* * *

Brixton, September 2017

Dear Ego,

I miss you! These conversations we have been having have reminded me that we make each other laugh, a lot. Perhaps that is why we survived so many meetings together? Even now I can summon up the exact look in your eyes – caught across a table during a string of endless AOBs – that might express frustration, amusement, fury, boredom or hunger. When I think of you you're just nipping off to get food for a meeting, to weed the allotment … you're making that smoothing over/tidying up gesture with both of your hands in anticipation of the next thing you are going to do.

When I was growing up in Wales in the 1980s/90s I would play at being a feminist. I had this outfit that I would wear. I had absorbed some information about Greenham Common from somewhere and spent long hours wishing I was there without really understanding that there were women still camped at Greenham when I was at school. I thought about them in the past tense. I started writing zines, heard about riot grrrl, listened to The Raincoats and I knew I liked girls. In 1997 I came back to London, where I was born but did not grow up, to go to university. I came with high hopes of finding feminist and queer spaces and yet once I was here I did not feel quite at home. Eventually, in 2001 I met my people through organising meetings for London's first Ladyfest.[5] Aside from the chosen family, friends and lovers I met and continue to meet because of that festival, I made connections which dovetailed again in 2007 and led me to the Lambeth Women's Project, and to you.

Sts came to London in 2002 to play at our festival. I had a huge crush on her. In 2006 I was planning to visit her in the Pacific Northwest and ended up volunteering at the Rock'n'Roll Camp for Girls[6] in Portland where she worked. I came home inspired to start one in London. Shanna introduced me to Liz Riches, who lived in London but had worked at the camp in Portland. By February 2007 we were back in Oregon at the first Girls Rock Camp Alliance gathering. We realised very quickly that we'd need to do a trial run that year on some adults so Ladies Rock! UK was born and we came back to London in urgent need of a venue. Tahini Nadim stepped in and suggested I try LWP which felt particularly neat as in 2002 Emma Hedditch who supported the film programme at Ladyfest London had suggested that we use some of the proceeds to buy a drum kit for a women's centre she was volunteering at. That drumkit was for Lambeth Women's Project. Five years later we'd end up using it for Ladies Rock.

The first time I visited LWP was in February 2007. I still experience the memory of meeting the space for the first time as a physical thump, an overwhelming chest spread of arrival and promise. It also felt very much like I'd landed in the 1980s I was pretending to live through when I was a teenager dressing up as a feminist in the 90s. I think we were equally excited to meet one another. We definitely both cried – with happiness or excitement or both. It was clear we had to work together. I felt like I'd come home. At that point in my life I was feeling particularly unmoored. 2007 was the year of my Saturn Return. Many of my friends also turned 28 that year. We talked about race, gender and queerness, read about the recent past, wrote about our lives, put on gigs and strings of workshops while all dating each other. We processed a lot. It was fun but I was struggling to find solid ground – literally ending up on crutches – but LWP, from that first day, was home. I wonder how many other women you must have welcomed into that space over the years? And how many, like me, moved their entire life, cuckoo style, into the space – messy politics, friends and all?

The rest of 2007 is a busy blur. Ladies Rock camp happened and surpassed all our expectations. I spent a lot of time at LWP. I had keys. We hung out a lot. Very soon after rock camp the building started to fall apart. I remember walking in from the rain one day and it was raining just as hard in the hallway … we began to worry about the stability of the stairs … huge orange mould began to bloom on the landing. In 2008 we abandoned planning for a girls' camp in order to focus on salvaging the building we loved. We gathered up our friends and fixed the building as best we could and in the meanwhile we started to battle with the council. We were so bold – marching into Lambeth Town Hall with a highlighted copy of the new Equality Act and all their own policies and demanding an Equality Impact Assessment of their plan to hand our building over to the school next door. We taught ourselves about land rights and property law. I laugh now when I think about that public meeting we went to where Lambeth was trying to encourage BME women to become coun- cillors – at an event in a school hall with caviar on the canapes but no creche – where the organisers were too scared to let you have the mic during the Q&A. It was exciting and exhausting.

Sometimes I worry that I brought a lot of trouble to your door. While it is true that you would not have met your wife if we did not know each other, it is also true that you wouldn't currently be living in Trump's America either! I also don't think anyone who was even peripherally involved in the Race, Privilege & Identity[7] event in Bristol in the spring of 2009 will forget what happened. This was an event organised by people I knew, who I had brought into your life. I remember you left early because things had already started to feel difficult. I hadn't gone at all because I was full of misgivings. On the last day of the gathering we were together, working on a Sunday in the top office on Stockwell Road, when our phones started to ring. It is a strange experience to be asked by a white person you thought was your friend to absolve them from accu- sations of racism made by other people of colour. I'm glad that we didn't have to experience that alone although it was surreal to be caught in that simultaneous, real time, cross country moment with you.

I love this idea that we talked about recently, that when we met you were a twentieth-century wave of feminism smashing together with my twenty-first-century wave. I like to think you were looking forward and I was looking backward. I think our way of being and working is very close to what Allyson Mitchell describes in her Deep Lez statement:

Deep Lez is right this minute and it is rooted in herstories and theories that came before ... Part of the deep of Deep Lez is about commitment, staying power and significance.[8]

Our shared enthusiasm for looking back and looking forward has marked so much of what I brought to LWP over the years. I still can't quite believe Joan Nestle[9] came to present her Lesbian Herstory Archive photos to us in that room where we first met. Projects like The Ladyfest Herstorical Society[10] exhibition and Feminist Activist Forum[11] would not have happened without the space offered by LWP. I learned how to be a curator on Stockwell Road because we had space and you let me fill it.

By 2011, I'd moved to Brixton, partly to be closer to LWP, and then the eviction notice came for Stockwell Road. I'd been following the student protests in Montreal, hearing from friends there about nightly marches through the streets with people banging pots. We started to do the same. Nightly pot banging noise demos in Windrush Square. The last days of the Women's Project were fraught and troubling. There were endless meetings and press releases and strange, terrifying moves from the school and council. I was teaching full time and left class one day to hear women had been locked into the building and were escaping via ladders. I cannot imagine how stressful that time was for you but in amongst the hysteria and exhaustion and deep sadness there were some hilarious moments where we still managed to meet eyes – perhaps over the retelling of how one of the occupying activists had scaled the outside of the building and popped in through the first floor window disrupting a Women's Institute meeting – and fall about laughing.

Eggs, we've done so much together. We've done serious work; remembering Olive Morris[12] and others, learning about ourselves and those that came before in groups like OWAAD,[13] we've made and taken part in Queer Black Spaces.[14] We've also had fun; like that time we saw Joan Armatrading[15] and stood, the only ones dancing on that balcony at the

Albert Hall, because we wanted to and we always dance when we can. I want you to know that as much as I loved LWP, everything that I tried to do in service of LWP was out of love, respect and admiration for you. Ego, sister friend, I am not sure who I would be today if you and LWP hadn't come into my life. I'm so glad to know you.

Love and affection always,

Nazmia

* * *

Minneapolis, September 2017

Dear Nazmia,

I am feeling a sense of gratitude that we have continued to push through with this over the summer. We have both been feeling the impact of the current political climate, which isn't new, mixed with what continues to feel like daily environmental and man-made disasters. Tragedies, loss and grief. This process has been one of patience, understanding, reassurance, confronting the past as well as letting go. I recognise that this only comes from trusting that we know each other well. We had done a good job of completely overlooking the importance of actually having a conversation about this – not just online interactions. I had overlooked how much we really needed to speak and reconnect. Neither of us had ever acknowledged, out loud to each other, that a dis-connect had indeed taken place, after and even during the LWP years and that residue still existed. We had never really talked about the difficult times we had faced being at the Lambeth Women's Project or outside of the project, often by default and being part of the same social networks. I hadn't realised that maybe we had fallen into the feminist trap of keeping up public appearances as a coping mechanism. As a community that can sometimes eat, sleep, organise and intimately love together it can be hard to navigate the moments when things come apart. Our phone conversation revealed we had missed each other and through riding on the same and also different waves of feminism at different points in time over this last decade, we had misplaced and dropped the ball on our actual friendship. We had deprived ourselves, that is how I see it now. I think it's fair to say that on the surface, from the outside looking in it wasn't necessarily noticeable, but we knew. This process had made it clear that organising and feminism had taken a toll on our blossoming friendship.

When we spoke in August you said, 'accessing the archive for us, was a blessing and a curse', and after I had stopped laughing at how accurate a depiction that is of our shared experiences, I realised this statement made our shared experience make more sense. This was exactly it. The past had been silently grating on our present, leaving us, if we were being honest with a bit of an uncomfortable reality. I realise now that when we first met, I was definitely working to keep and maintain the history, policy and politics that the Lambeth Women's Project had been founded on – the guiding principles. Until now, I never really thought of the Lambeth Women's Project as radical feminist space, but its guiding principles were. So describing the project as a women-only building, run by women for women, no boys or men above the age of 11, was language and policy that had become redundant and non-inclusive. LWP took a while to really embrace the landscape of twenty-first-century feminist politics. This often created a clash in reality in regards to its relationship with the council, in meetings including committee, in decision-making, in who could use the building etc.

Nazmia, you dragged LWP kicking and screaming into twenty-first-century feminisms bringing with you a diverse queer DIY community. Previous to this I would be the first to admit LWP was firmly placed in 1986 not sure if it was happy there, it was more legacy and inheritance. The badge/button machine was a testimony to this. I don't even mean this as a criticism, it was definitely those tangible and intangible quirks that kept many of us there for so long. Your curation of the space was a huge contribution to the life and history of the project, from 2007 until the project came to a close in 2012.

READING BETWEEN THE EMAIL EXCHANGES

At the core of our social media exchanges through this year has been the importance of us taking charge of our own history, sharing examples of how we were already being erased from contemporary feminist history and or being asked to literally become footnotes to our own narratives, by feminists we had both once called friends. I wish I had had time to create a timeline based on the decade of email exchanges as we discussed. I needed a starting point, so I went back to our email correspondence over the years. What's maybe most surprising is our consistency. The subject headings alone tell and reveal so much about who we are and what we care about. From queries about Angell Town,[16] 'advice please',

your 'House of Labrys'[17] newsletters, 'Olive Morris Rally[18] minutes/
banners', 'mailing list and meeting' or the amount of emails that begin
URGENT:XXX needs your help. What our emails show is that since we
met, no matter what was going on each year we have carried out some
action that relate to our Black British Feminist sensibilities. I would like
to take some time to actually begin to consciously archive my mail, these
are our modern-day minutes showing where and how the decisions get
made. Sometimes I worry how much we will lose, or what gaps will exist
in regards to twenty-first-century Black British Feminist organising
because so much of it will be hidden away behind our passwords and
locked in servers, lost email accounts and domains.

EVENTS, SOCIALS AND MOVING AWAY

When I think of you I think about all the events that I have been to over
the years that you have put on, a highlight has to be getting to listen to
The Raincoats talk and watching them play a gig in the main room at
LWP the first evening of Ladies Rock Camp. Who would have thought
when you screened Consuelo Ramirez's documentary *Keep it Moving*
about the band Yo! Majesty in 2009 at the BFI London Lesbian Gay Film
Festival[19] (LLGFF) the screening would literally change my life, and
would eventually put me on the path of moving to Minneapolis. When
I saw Anita Castelino in Canada, this summer, we spoke about you at
length (over roti!) and remembered where we had last seen each other, at
'We Have Always Been Here', a benefit to raise legal fees for an LGBTQI
asylum seeker at the Ritzy[20] cinema in 2015 that you had organised with
Sita Balani. This event gave me the opportunity to thank Anita, for the
first time, for being one of 10–12 women who chose to protect LWP
premises and belongings on 14 June 2012, the beginning of the 'sit-in',
not knowing what we would collectively face the next day. I was always
so thankful to those, like Anita and Sita who were prepared to stand up
for the cause and stand strong, no matter the cost. I admired the display
of courage. It was those acts and displays that truly gave me courage
during that dark time. 'We Have Always Been Here' was what I would
consider a typical event of yours; good mixed crowd, an assortment of
zines, badges and second hand books and quality speakers. Many of us
got to hear Antonia Bright from Movement for Justice[21] speak that day
and then many of us booked tickets to protest at Yarl's Wood.[22] I think
the thing we definitely connect on is our love of information dissemina-

tion and mobilising women against injustice (or at the very least telling others what's happening).

I'm so glad that Tahani Nadim forwarded me that email from you, looking for space, back in 2007. Meeting you for the first time and sitting in the front room at LWP, how we laughed, there was a deep sense of excitement that we had finally found each other. Kindred spirits – another proud, queer, brown, black face that enjoyed organising, loved cooking in big pots like our mothers, aunties and grandmas. We saw each other. It felt like neither of us had been seen properly for a while at that point. I feel that somehow, no matter what, we would have met. The 'pink' letter that is now in your archive in Glasgow illustrates that I think. It was for me a treasured item, it was a signifier of what was to come five years later when we ran Ladies Rock! UK from LWP in 2007. That was seriously one of the best things and quite easily the best three days at the Women's Project in my 13-year history. You are also one of the only people I know amongst our peers who has ever deposited their personal papers. I always found this act, even then, so impressive.

What strikes me is how much of you made it over with me to Minneapolis, whether it's mix CDs or beautiful feminist postcards from your travels, event ephemera or my personal favourite – a knitted square you made and gave me of the women's symbol, that had hung in my bathroom in Camberwell for years. I want to thank you for what you brought to the Women's Project and to my life personally. When I moved to Minneapolis, one of the first communities that I was able to tap into was the Girls Rock (She Rock! She Rock!) based here, I am now working with the staff team to develop an intersectional committee. I think of you a lot when I attend these meetings. I am so thankful for the ways we organised and cared not just for LWP but for our communities. It was an empowering time that continues to inform how I navigate and manage my life today. I would say that these moments of critical learning definitely form some of the components in my current survival (invisible) toolkit, that help and support me to navigate current times in a way that just would never be possible without those, shared moments. I treasure the moments we shared during the LWP sit-in, though I also remember these as maybe some of the most challenging times for our friendship, mainly because we were often speaking to each other on behalf of other groups. However, even through the challenges, I remember you as someone I could take solace in and laugh with at how ridiculous or cliched the situation had got so quickly. Do you remember we were going to write a play about the occupation? I have a video recording of me and you. We are making plans and just chatting in your bedroom at Barnes. I think we had been inspired because we had just found out Pratibha Parmar had footage of Audre Lorde visiting London and a discussion that took place in her living room with others like Ingrid Pollard.[23] I must confess I think we really had a thing for the re-enactment of 70s–80s feminism.

I suppose this process in many ways has been some personal archival therapy. At the Raven Row symposium,[24] another moment this year that our lives independently crossed over, I spoke about the politics of running and keeping a women's space. My conclusion was that though exhausting, the provision of space for us to talk, care for one another, build trust, develop relationships, plan and create are rare and actually – priceless. I stated that you can take the women out of the project, but the project remains within our networks, conversations, relationships and our ability to tell the narrative, warts and all. It gives us space to look the uncomfortable truths and realities in the eye and not be afraid to tell the failures alongside the successes.

I'm reminded of the Black Cultural Archive[25] event (organised by Chardine Taylor-Stone) we attended for International Women's Day in 2015. Melba Wilson,[26] when speaking of OWAAD, reminded us to make time for the personal, for the personal is indeed political. I think this has been a step in the right direction to remembering that.

with love, wisdom & solidarity,

Ego

* * *

NOTES

1. Appears in Barbara Smith (ed.), 1983. *Home Girls: A Black Feminist Anthology*. Kitchen Table: Women of Color Press, New York.
2. Political Blackness is an ideology used in parts of Britain, most particularly during the 1980s. For example, the London Black Lesbian and Gay Centre defined those who are 'Black' as being 'descended (through one or both parents) from Africa, Asia (i.e. the Middle East to China, including the Pacific nations) and Latin America, and lesbians and gay men descended from the original inhabitants of Australasia, North America, and the islands of the Atlantic and Indian Ocean.' While some organisations such as trade unions sometimes still use this terminology 'political Blackness' is seen by many as an increasingly problematic identification.

3. Lambeth Women's Project/Lambeth Young Women's Project established in 1979 at 155a Stockwell Road in Brixton, London. Trustees included Susan Mackie of See Red Collective. Lambeth initially allowed the project to pay peppercorn rent and commissioned projects and services out of the building. In 2011 the council evicted the project in order to give the building to the neighbouring school. The history of the project and struggle to resist closure can be found at https://savelambethwomensproject.wordpress.com (accessed 8 February 2019).

4. Riot grrrl was an early 1990s feminist subculture and music genre that started in America.

5. Ladyfest London 2002 was a feminist music and arts festival that took place in August 2002. It was the first Ladyfest in England and the second in the United Kingdom after Glasgow in 2001. The original Ladyfest happened in 2000 and came out of the post-riot grrrl scene in Olympia, Washington. Festivals are independently organised and continue to happen all over the world.

6. Feminist music camp where 8–18-year-old girls spent a week over the summer learning an instrument, forming a band and performing. They also learned things like self-defence, the history of women in music and zine making.

7. Statements detailing the explicit failings of the Race, Privilege & Identity event can be found at https://raceprivilegeidentity.wordpress.com (accessed 8 February 2019). See also Humaira Saeed's journal/zine *Race Revolt* for an understanding of community setting and the breadth of the aftermath.

8. 'Deep Lez//2009/2015' appears in David J. Getsy (ed.), 2016. *Queer*. White-chapel Gallery; London; MIT Press, Cambridge, MA.

9. 'Joan Nestle and Christa Holka: Documenting Lesbian Lives' took place at LWP on 22 May 2011.

10. 'The Ladyfest Herstorical Society' exhibition and event took place at LWP on 13 November 2010. The bulk to the exhibition was then donated to the Lesbian Archive at Glasgow Women's Library.

11. The Feminist Activist Forum was set up at Ladyfest Leeds in 2007. They held several meetings across the United Kingdom including at LWP.

12. Olive Morris (1952–1979) was a community activist who was a member of the British Black Panthers, a founding member of the Brixton Black Women's Group and of OWAAD (see note below).

13. Organisation of Women of African and Asian Descent (1978–82). OWAAD acted as a national umbrella for various groups who came together at four annual conferences; the first of which took place in Brixton in 1979, the same year LWP was established down the road.

14. Queer Black Spaces (2013–15) series of events curated by Caroline Bressey and Gemma Romain at the Equiano Centre, University College London.

15. 'Love & Affection' in the title of this chapter is taken from Joan Armatrading's 1976 song.

16. Angell Town is a housing estate in Brixton.

17. House of Labrys is the unofficial name of Nazmia's home in Brixton – all good punk houses need a name.
18. Rally held on Rush Common 26 June 2015 to celebrate Olive's life and demand that Lambeth council retain a memorial to her when Olive Morris House is demolished.
19. Now known as BFI Flare, the London LGBTQ+ Film Festival.
20. The Ritzy, and other Picturehouse cinemas, have since come into the public eye as part of ongoing industrial action against their owners Cineworld who refuse to pay the London Living Wage.
21. Movement for Justice By Any Means Necessary, established in 1995.
22. Yarl's Wood Immigration Removal Centre, a detention centre in Bedford, has been the focus of regular and increasingly large protests in solidarity with the women detained inside. In February 2017 a group of detainees in Yarl's Wood went on a month-long hunger strike in protest against British immigration policies and the conditions under which they are being kept.
23. Shot by the Late Start Film & Video Collective. Some footage appears in Pratibha Parmar's 1986 film *Emergence*. We believe *A Conversation with Audre*, held at Cinenova, is an edited version of this visit.
24. *Don't break down, break out*, a symposium which took place on 10 May 2017 at Raven Row, London as part of the exhibition *14 Radnor Terrace: A Woman's Place*. Ego presented on LWP in conversation with Susan Mackie from See Red Collective. Nazmia presented on LWP and Sisters Uncut.
25. Black British Feminism: Past, Present & Futures, 14 March 2015.
26. Melba Wilson OBE has written widely on issues of health and social care, with particular reference to Black and minority ethnic communities.

11

Black Pete, Black Motherhood and Womanist Ethics

Lubumbe Van de Velde

Sinterklaas is a Dutch-Flemish tradition that runs from mid-November to the beginning of December. The feast is celebrated on the eve of 5 December, and the morning of Saint Nicholas, on 6 December. In this narrative, the bishop – Saint Nicholas – and his Black servants, who are commonly referred to as *Zwarte Piet* or Black Pete, hail from Spain on a boat and arrive at a harbour in Dutch and Flemish cities. The feast continues in the homes of Dutch-Flemish families through established rituals, such as gift-giving.[1] Black Pete's first appearance in his current aesthetic phenotype, which includes a Black face, thick red lips, an afro curly wig and golden hoop earrings,[2] was in Jan Schenkman's version of the folklore from 1850.[3] While this version is still performed today, some historical gaps such as the nineteenth-century imperial context and the master/slave relations between the bishop and his servant are usually neglected.

The Black Pete debate has created a divide in Dutch/Flemish societies. In 2011, Dutch anti-Black Pete activists, Quincy Gario and Kno'Ledge Cesare, were arrested for wearing a *Zwarte Piet is Racisme* (Black Pete is Racism) t-shirt aimed at promoting a growing protest movement.[4] In 2013, a local court in Amsterdam ruled that the depiction of Black Pete is indeed racist, but a higher court later overturned this ruling.[5] In 2014, a total of 90 people were arrested for both protests and counter-protests in relation to Black Pete. Black Pete opponents argued that the character is derived from colonialism and not befitting of society ostensibly based on equality and respect: 'If we were all equal Black Pete would have changed a long time ago, so that the celebration would be for all Dutch people.'[6] Supporters of Black Pete claim the character is only Black because of soot in chimneys and has no racist connotations or references to the colonial history of the Netherlands.[7]

Although somewhat subdued in Belgium, the character of Black Pete has also been at the centre of discussions between various proponents of the Black Pete character and activists groups such as La Nouvelle Voie Anticoloniale, BAMKO and Belgium Renaissance. In 2016, the Flemish-Dutch house of culture, deBuren, organised a round table discussion about the future of the *Sinterklaas* tradition and how the Black Pete character could be transformed.[8] In typical Belgian pacifying fashion this round table discussion led to the adoption of what has been termed the *Pietenpact* or the 'Pete Pact'. In this pact, a number of children's television broadcasters, schools, toy shops and theatre organisations are committed to introducing new versions of the Black Pete character, such as the soot Pete *roetvegen Piet*, and as such aim at getting rid of the racist aesthetic phenotype of the Black Pete character that promotes anti-Black stereotypes.[9] Not everyone agrees that this is sufficient, for instance, the Belgian minority forum initially refused to sign the pact because according to them, the pact does not do enough in terms of addressing the anti-Black perspectives within Belgian society. By threating to withdraw the minority forum's funding as a reaction to their reservations about the pact, Flemish Minister of Equal Opportunities, Liesbeth Homans, demonstrated just how various platforms in society silence resistance and maintain anti-Black stereotypes and caricatures.

As Townes[10] puts it, Black folk have never controlled the dominant images of ourselves and characters such as Black Pete are the product of the white imagination. This is why, as womanist ethicists, it is our burden to systematically examine and uproot the myths perpetuated about Black people. By omitting certain aspects of the countries' imperial past, both Belgium and the Netherlands manage to contain and control what we understand about the racial hierarchies in both societies. Examples of this collective amnesia,[11] or memory cannibalism,[12] are found in the lack of narratives about Black history and the history and consequences of colonisation in education.[13] This collective cannibalism is also maintained by the state restricting access to primary documents related to the Belgium colonial project.[14] As such, the paradoxes of white privilege within so-called post-racial societies are safeguarded, while consideration for history's subjective nature is left unexamined.

While most recent academic scholarship on Black Pete and *Sinterklaas* focus on the public practices and controversies of the tradition,[15] this work appears to downplay the private dimensions of *Sinterklaas* and Black Pete and therefore neglects to address how culture is also shaped in the home and passed on from one generation to the next. Further, this scholarship seems to ignore the dilemmas in the private spaces of the home that are faced by families with Black children when socialising their children and deciding which practices of the dominant culture their children should participate in, without these families becoming complicit in perpetuating anti-Black stereotypes. Since women are still the primary socialising agents of children, my chapter analyses the lived experiences of Black mothers in both private and public spaces in relation to the *Sinterklaas* tradition.

I argue that previous scholarship fails to address how Black mothers are coerced into being complicit in the continued oppression of Black people in both Belgium and the Netherlands through the *Sinterklaas* and Black Pete traditions. What the seemingly well-intended and innocent Dutch-Flemish tradition might represent in Black homes is the following dilemma:[16]

a) to either silence one's own discomfort and participate in the continued dehumanisation of Black people and therefore reinforcing the notion that to be Dutch-Flemish is to be white

b) or to resist the continued dehumanisation of Black people by not participating in the tradition and therefore making it impossible for the children to fully participate in a foundational part of Dutch-Flemish culture and be once again rendered as outsiders to their own culture.

However, what womanist ethics and the centring of Black women's moral autonomy allow us to see is how Black mothers give preference to an alternative celebration of the *Sinterklaas* tradition which does not include Black Pete. This enables all children to enjoy the festivities while refuting the continued dehumanisation of Black people through the characterisation of Black Pete. I draw on Townes' concept of the 'cultural production of evil'.[17] In this context, the word 'evil' refers to social inequities and forms of social oppressions such as the dehumanisation of Black people through anti-Black stereotypes embedded in culture and traditions. These evils are produced and maintained through what Townes refers to as the 'fantastic hegemonic imagination' that arises from an understanding of history as discipline and memory as subjective. She opposes the notion of historical objectivity and the assumption that history should not be questioned nor criticised. What Townes instead suggests is a reading of history and memory that assumes them both to be subjective. What follows out of this subjectivity of both history and memory is the possibility for one group to create certain narratives and images of another through the use of caricatures and stereotypes that shape a one-sided view of those whom this imagination aims to portray. The one-sided creation and production of a worldview is what Townes terms the 'fantastic hegemonic imagination'.[18] Through the institutionalisation of certain ideas of the 'Other', such hegemony is thus maintained. While her analysis is based on the commodification of Black identity in the United States and how certain images of Black womanhood, such as the 'Mammy', the 'Welfare Queen' and the 'Jezebel' have shaped how we view Black women in the United States, I argue that her concept offers us a tool for an analogue analysis of the Black Pete character as celebrated in Dutch/Flemish culture.

What her womanist ethical framework allows us to address is the ethical dilemma faced by families with Black children when deciding how to approach the Black Pete dilemma within their homes and communities. As a methodology womanist ethics enables us to centre Black women's moral autonomy and gives us insight into the critical and systematic reflection of the moral reasoning that enables them to refuse dehumanisation. This exercise is therefore an epistemological one as it aims at including within the public debate those voices that have historically been marginalised. My chapter is thus organised in two parts. First, I will analyse 'Black Pete' as a structural artefact of contemporary Dutch-Flemish culture. Second, I examine the dilemmas of Black mothers in the context of Black Pete and explore how Black mothers' experiences can be used as a resource for challenging various 'evils' contained in contemporary culture.

'BLACK PETE' AS AN ARTEFACT OF CONTEMPORARY DUTCH-FLEMISH CULTURE

In her book, *Womanist Ethics and the Cultural Production of Evil*, Townes develops the concept of the 'fantastic hegemonic imagination', which draws on Foucault's work on imagination and Gramsci's hegemony. For Townes, the fantastical imagination not only refers to storytelling and mythmaking but also the mundane and the everyday. It 'forms a part of the cultural production of our realities that is in the very fabric of our everyday'.[19]

The 'fantastic' is that thin line between reality and the imagination. It is to be found in ideas and traditions that become commonplace because they are reinforced through different institutions and platforms that are essential to our societies. It is to be found in those moments when we wonder whether what we have experienced actually happened or whether it was an illusion. It is the shock experienced by those who undergo events that do not make sense to themselves and others. Those events that go against the natural order of things, but somehow still manage to take place. Furthermore, what is fantastic is the ability to become comfortable with experiences that might seem extraordinary to others but are your reality for some inexplicable reason. It is everyday life for those who live it because it is weaved in structures of domination and subordination Townes suggests the following understanding of hegemony:

> Hegemony is the set of ideas that dominant groups employ in a society to secure the consent of subordinates to abide by their rule. The notion of *consent is key* because hegemony is created through coercion that is gained by using the church, family, media, political parties, schools, unions, and other voluntary associations – the civil society and all its organizations.[20]

Fantastic hegemony creates images that reinforce its interpretation of the world. Townes specifically addresses the use of imagery as a means to shape a worldview. She gives examples of images that have created certain stereotypes of Black women, such as the 'matriarch' and 'welfare queen'. Townes suggests that these images perform through their ability to make individuals in a given society accept certain ideas of the 'Other'. We consent to these stereotypes and caricatures of the 'Other' because we neglect to examine their origin and therefore accept these images as truth. This power of imagery, and our consent which is obtained from our inability to question these images, whether conscious or subconscious, is how hegemony is maintained.

Using Townes' definition of fantastic hegemonic imagination as a vantage point, I claim that the concept can be applied to the *Sinterklaas* tradition and 'Black Pete' as an artefact of Dutch-Flemish culture. Townes claims the fantastic is woven into our everyday life and reinforced through different institutions. I argue that religious traditions play a significant role in our acceptance of social 'truths', such as equating whiteness with goodness, and investing whiteness with the moral authority to judge what is good and what is evil. In the case of *Sinterklaas*, the representation is explicit. The white bishop, Saint Nicholas, is the moral authority whose judgement determines whether the children have been good or bad. Black Pete, the slave, is given the 'dirty' job of being a tattletale and punishing the bad children. The image of white domination/Black subjugation perpetuated by religious traditions is in turn re-enforced by elite political actors. The current Dutch Prime Minister, Mark Rutte,[21] and Belgian Minister of Foreign Affairs, Didier Reynders,[22] have both publicly endorsed Black face. Rutte stated that 'as opposed to my Black friends in the Dutch Antilles, I have to struggle for days after the festivities to remove my Black face make-up'.

Media coverage of the tradition, everything from the televised arrival of Saint Nicholas and Black Pete to the various images, decorations and Black Pete outfits found throughout both countries from November to December, show how profitable the tradition is and how the fantastic hegemony of a Black stereotype is commodified. Many white Dutch and Flemish people feel entitled to try out being 'Black' for as long as it suits them and then discard this image at the end of the festive period.

No matter how offensive Black Pete is to Black people, for the proponents of Black Pete's aesthetic phenotype, there seems to be no room for discussion because the portrayal of his character is essential to a tradition they view as part of their national identity. As such, it begs the question whether anyone racialised as Black is able to speak out against Black Pete's fantastic hegemony, without them being cast as the 'Other'. In other words, can one be both Dutch-Flemish and Black? Ultimately, any stance against Black Pete quickly evolves into a question of political and national allegiance for the 'new' Dutch or Flemish identity. Thus, hegemony is maintained through coercion because people are forced to buy into the tradition as a demonstration of their loyalty to the national identity.

When a Black person asserts how they 'see' the character as a perpetuation of stereotypes and speak out about how that makes them 'feel', their experiences are dismissed as being 'too sensitive' or 'emotional'. Similar to memory, emotions are considered to be subjective and not a valid argument in 'rational debate' about Dutch/Flemish culture. Deploying a narrow idea of rationality to displace the knowledge gained through lived experiences is one of the many ways in which the fantastic hegemonic imagination operates. But the illusion of rationality evaporates under critical scrutiny as Black Pete is then defended as a harmless joke, not worthy of offence.

In examining the experiences of Black mothers and how they are forced to explain to their children why they, unlike their white friends, cannot fully participate in a tradition aimed at celebrating all 'good children', we are able to get a fuller picture of why the character of Black Pete is at the centre of heated debate. While every parent is responsible for socialising their children, in most societies, the Netherlands and Belgium included, mothers are still assumed to be the primary socialising agents of their children.[23] In our particular dilemma, the question is whether one can participate in a tradition of the dominant culture, such as *Sinterklaas*, while still resisting those practices within that tradition that aim at keeping you in 'your place' such as the character of Black Pete. Take, for example, the approach taken by a Black Belgian mother when asked how they deal with the *Sinterklaas* tradition in her home:[24]

> Saint Nicholas is always welcome in our home. A benevolent saint who brings gifts for well-behaved children? Why would I rob my children of such an experience? Black Pete, on the other hand, isn't welcome. My oldest children know why, the youngest however believes it is due to the fact that we don't have a chimney. When he is old enough, I will tell him the truth.

At first glance, what the *Sinterklaas* tradition seems to do is present Black mothers with one of two options: (a) they are either coerced into silence about the continued dehumanisation of Black people for the benefit of the dominant culture or (b) they resist by doing away with the tradition all together, but risk having their children alienated from other Flemish/Dutch children by the majority because they refuse to be a part of a 'quintessential' Flemish/Dutch tradition. A form of resistance we see happening is the deployment of countermemory to offer alternative pathways to resist and subvert the hegemonic imagination of Black subjugation. According to Townes: 'countermemory has the potential to challenge false generalizations and gross stereotypes often found in what passes for history'.[25] In the case of the Black Pete dilemma, countermemory is to be found in the moral reasoning that enables Black people to refuse dehumanisation. It is found in the ways in which people in the Netherlands and Belgium have used their platform, whether in public or private space to resist stereotypes and caricatures of Blackness in Europe.

It starts with questions such as who is telling our story, who created the images that control our existence as Black people and how do we want future generations of Black people to be portrayed?

CONCLUSION

The aim of this chapter was to demonstrate how an epistemology that centres on the experiences of Black mothers and the moral reasoning that enables them to refute dehumanisation allows us to challenge the continued use of certain traditions that maintain systems of oppression such as the character of Black Pete in the Dutch-Flemish tradition of *Sinterklaas*. By utilising a womanist ethics framework through Townes' conceptualisation of 'cultural production of evil', we are able to examine how the fantastic hegemonic imagination creates and reproduces certain images of the 'Other' that are then institutionalised and redistributed through different platforms such as politics, traditions, education and media. The Dutch-Belgian tradition of *Sinterklaas* is presented as an example of a seemingly well-intended children's festivity that in fact masks racism and heteropatriarchal norms. Even within their own homes, Black mothers' (by extension families with Black children) individual choices about whether or not their children can partici-pate in the tradition will in turn have a bearing on the public sphere and vice versa. At first glance the predicament of Black motherhood seems to coerce Black mothers into either one of two options, (a) either be complicit in the further oppression of people racialised as Black or (b) to 'Other' their own children by refusing their participation in the tradition. Yet, the chapter demonstrates that there is also a third possi-bility, a route of resistance that offers a solution which would enable ALL children to enjoy the festivities equally, namely, to do away with Black Pete completely.

NOTES

1. www.dutchnews.nl/features/2015/11/ten-things-you-need-to-know-to-celebrate-sinterklaas/ (accessed 23 January 2018).
2. www.bbc.co.uk/religion/0/24744499 (accessed 23 January 2018).
3. See Jan Schenkman's version (in Dutch) at www.dbnl.org/tekst/sche039stn io1_01/sche039stni01_01_0011.php (accessed 24 January 2018).
4. See http://zwartepietisracisme.tumblr.com/ (accessed 11 May 2018).

5. See www.thebulletin.be/saint-nicolas-and-Black-pete-belgian-tradition-racist-undertones and www.theguardian.com/commentisfree/2014/aug/19/Black-pete-netherlands-dutch-stereotypes-Black-people-Blacked-up-christmas (accessed 11 May 2018).
6. See www.aljazeera.com/news/europe/2014/11/netherlands-Black-pete-protest-2014111522726689370.html (accessed 11 May 2018).
7. Ibid.
8. www.deburen.eu/magazine/2056/deburen-stelt-pietenpact-voor (accessed 14 May 2018).
9. www.nrc.nl/nieuws/2016/11/11/volgend-jaar-geen-zwarte-pieten-meer-in-vlaanderen-a1531471 (accessed 14 May 2018).
10. E. Townes, 2006. *Womanist Ethics and the Cultural Production of Evil.* Palgrave Macmillan, Basingstoke.
11. See the account 'the great forgetting' given by Mills is his analysis of the management of collective memory through social epistemology. C.W. Mills, 2007. 'White ignorance'. In S. Sullivan and N. Tuana (eds), *Race and the Epistemologies of Ignorance.* SUNY Press, Albany, NY, pp. 11–38. C.W. Mills, 1997. *The Racial Contract.* Cornell University Press, Ithaca, NY, pp. 28–9.
12. Memory cannibalism is used in reference to the management of colonial history and the role played by the churches in devouring that history. Beckford refers to it as 'the process of controlling archives so as to render "dangerous memories" ineffective'. R. Beckford, 2014. *Documentary as Exorcism.* Bloomsbury, London, pp. 94–96 (p. 95).
13. G. Wekker, 2016. *White Innocence.* Duke University Press, Durham.
14. See Parliament resolution brought in front of the Belgian federal Parliament requesting the release of such documents to facilitate research on Belgium's colonial past (in Dutch). www.dekamer.be/doc/flwb/pdf/54/2307/54k2307001.pdf#search="kolonisatie%20%2054%20<in>%20keywords" (accessed 24 January 2018).
15. J. Rodenberg and P. Wagenaar, 2016. 'Essentializing "Black Pete": Competing narratives surrounding the Sinterklaas tradition in the Netherlands'. *International Journal of Heritage Studies* 22(9), pp. 716–28. Y. van der Pijl and K. Goulordava, 2014. 'Black Pete, "smug ignorance", and the value of the Black body in postcolonial Netherlands'. *New West Indian Guide/Nieuwe West-Indische Gids* 88(3–4), pp. 262–91. K. Lemmens, 2017. 'The dark side of "Zwarte Piet": A misunderstood tradition or racism in disguise? A legal analysis'. *The International Journal of Human Rights* 21(2), pp. 120–41.
16. See, for example, an article (in Dutch) in *Mo magazine* at www.mo.be/artikel/welkom-sint-maar-zonder-piet (accessed 14 May 2018).
17. Townes, *Womanist Ethics*, p. 11.
18. Ibid., p. 7.
19. Ibid., p. 19.
20. Ibid., p. 20, emphasis added.
21. www.youtube.com/watch?v=Fk2YkZ2gGDI (accessed 14 May 2018).
22. www.bbc.co.uk/news/world-europe-31962154 (accessed 14 May 2018).

23. See, for example, C. Pateman, 1983. 'Feminist critiques of the public/private dichotomy'. In S. Benn and G. Gaus (eds), *Public and Private in Social Life*. Croom Helm, London. C. MacKinnon, 2006. *Are Women Human?* Harvard University Press, Cambridge, MA. D. Rhode, 1997. *Speaking of Sex: The Denial of Gender Inequality*. Harvard University Press, Cambridge, MA. M. Minow, 1991. *Making All the Difference: Inclusion, Exclusion & American Law*. Harvard University Press, Cambridge, MA.

24. For further reading (in Dutch), see www.mo.be/artikel/welkom-sint-maar-zonder-piet (accessed 14 May 2018).

25. Townes, *Womanist Ethics*, p. 47.

12

Warriors and Survivors:
The Eartha Kitt Files

Alecia McKenzie

My mother sang all the time. She sang while she chopped onions, sorted red beans, cut up chicken. She sang while she drew designs on handbags that would go to an export company based in downtown Kingston, along the waterfront. She sang while she sewed the bags – on one of those old machines with the clunky foot pedal (the same kind of bags that famous fashion designers now produce and sell for hundreds of dollars). She sang when she was angry, sad or worried. Some of the songs were hymns, which we've never heard anywhere else. But most had been recorded by women who became a part of our household and our childhood: Miriam Makeba, Nina Simone and, especially, Eartha Kitt, who was the same age as my mother.

Our home vibrated with these voices, and the volume grew louder after my father died, when I was ten. Grief became melody, and we learned to sing 'Pata Pata' and 'C'est si bon' word for word, even if we didn't understand what we were belting out. (Later, we would move to reggae, but that's another story.) Along with the music, we listened to the accounts of these women's lives, and I can still hear the indignation in my mother's voice. It was as if through the music and narrative, she was determined to inculcate in her daughters and son the strength to overcome – as she had tried to do – whatever life might throw our way.

The Eartha Kitt tale would stay in our heads. The story was that she was born on a cotton plantation in the United States to a teenaged half-Black, half-Cherokee mother and an unknown white father. She suffered so much as a child that even the life of fictional Oliver Twist seemed like paradise. Through talent, she became a star, and things should have gone smoothly then. But in 1968, she stood up at a White House luncheon and let loose a fiery, incensed speech about the Vietnam War, saying that the government sent the 'best of this country to be shot and maimed'. The words upset Lady Bird Johnson and apparently infuriated President Lyndon B. Johnson. Kitt was blacklisted in the United States during the following decade. Scheduled appearances were cancelled, concert organisers couldn't find contracts she had made with them, and her income plummeted.[1]

She left her homeland and journeyed overseas, mostly to Europe where she'd known previous success, and, in 1974, a *New York Times* journalist informed her of the contents of a CIA dossier. Among the things she said she was charged with was being a 'sadistic nymphomaniac whose escapades and loose morals were the talk of Paris in 1956'. She would come to laugh at the memory of these files: 'You know I think I missed a chapter in my life somewhere.'

I would meet Kitt in 1989, after having seen her once before onstage – me a writer and journalist just starting out, and she an icon of 62 making a comeback with a one-woman show, whose signature tune was Stephen Sondheim's 'I'm Still Here'. When I saw the show after our interview, I was struck by one line, delivered with intensity: 'When you've lived through Edgar Hoover, anything after is a laugh ... I'm still here.'

I made a call from London to Kingston to tell my mother about my plans. I didn't know if Kitt would accept my request for an interview, but I knew why I wanted to speak with her. It had to do with all those Kingston Sundays of hearing that voice crooning 'C'est si bon', with my mother singing along in her own singular voice – one forged through hardships.

'I'm sure she'll talk to you,' my mother said.

She did.

We met over lunch at a gleaming Italian restaurant in London that she chose. She walked in wearing leather pants, a sleeveless blouse and an uncompromising expression (unconsciously, I would later use that entrance for a scene with the main character in my novel *Sweetheart*); it was plain that the waiters knew and adored her. The interview got off to an awkward start, but we ended up spending several hours together and by the end, we were promising to stay in touch.

Soon after our meeting, I transcribed the tape but my family and I moved house before I got a chance to publish the interview, and the transcription and tape disappeared amid the dozens of boxes. I found the documents again in January 2017, after having lived in London, Brussels, Singapore and Paris and knowing what it felt like to be far from home. Re-reading the transcript on that chilly day brought home the strength and drive that Kitt needed to survive after the blacklisting, and I thought of my mother trying to do her art with no support. By then, both she and Kitt were gone, but I wish I'd been able to bring them together and tell them how those days of song in Kingston helped to form an individual now able to withstand/stand up being an 'immigrant' artist in Europe. With the raging debate about migration, you feel your status more than ever as an outsider, despite being 'freer' as a woman than in some other regions. I often wonder if Kitt felt the same way in Paris – free, uprooted, different, solitary, hopeful, all at the same time.

In the following interview, I present Kitt's words, alongside insights from other expatriate artists currently living and working in Europe. I've allowed myself some creative liberty with this chapter, and I hope readers will accept it as a kind of song: with solo, back-up voices, improvisation.

THE INTERVIEW

Alecia McKenzie: Is this your first time doing a one-woman show?
Eartha Kitt: I've done concerts, but it's the first time for a one-woman show.

A.M.: I saw you several years ago in 'Timbuktu!', and what really struck me then was that you really seemed to be enjoying what you were doing.
E.K.: Otherwise I wouldn't be doing it.

A.M.: Of course, but is that something that people remark on – that you seem really into what you do?
E.K.: Yeah.

A.M. (*laughing*): I read an interview with you in *The Independent* where they sort of imply that you chew journalists up and spit them out. Is this sort of a regular thing?
E.K.: I have no idea. I do what I do, the best I can. Whatever impression you want to make of it is an interpretation of what you see.

A.M.: Do you get interviewed a lot?
E.K.: Yes.

A.M.: Do you get tired of it? Is it always the same questions?
E.K.: It depends on who is asking the questions. What personalities there are that are asking the questions because sometimes people are out to get me.

A.M.: Well, I'm not out to get you. Are you living here now?
E.K.: I live in Connecticut.

A.M.: You just came here to do the show?
E.K. I came to do 'Follies' in June, and because of the popularity that I had in 'Follies', because of that song that I sing, Mr. Alberry who's the director of the theatre [Shaftesbury] asked me if I would do a one-woman show and stay longer. Here I am, so I've been away from home since June [nine months].

A.M.: You've basically always been a singer, right?
E.K.: I've been everything. I suppose I'm recognized more as a singer because of the recordings.

A.M.: You've done several movies.
E.K.: Yes, but the agents always think of you as ... where the money is, and they think it's in nightclubs more than anything else. Not the theatre. That's why it's very difficult to get things in the theatre. One of the reasons. Plus the fact that if you're a very individual person, agents really don't know how to handle you, particularly if you know how to do more than one thing well. It's confusing, bothers their minds.

Women artists who work in several disciplines often find themselves in this situation. As someone who does creative writing, journalism and visual art, I understood what she meant. Male artists, however, seem free to be 'Renaissance' men.

A.M.: I suppose you don't do the business side yourself?
E.K.: No, I don't like the business side.

A.M.: So do you get a friend, or somebody else? How does that work?
E.K.: People usually call, whatever the number is that they have. Usually through the union or some agent that I have here or in Los Angeles. But I have no contract with agents. Because I'm not very fond of agents. They don't know what to do with me. In general, that is. There's always an exception to the rule. But generally, you do your own work and you tell them what you want. If they want a percentage, they see to it. Like with 'Follies', for instance. Michael Tosh came to me and asked me if I would do 'Follies'. I was in Los Angeles at the Roosevelt hotel. But the producer

of 'Follies' asked me to do 'Follies', and the agent had already said, 'no, she wouldn't do it' six months before I got into it. The agent in London had said 'no, she wouldn't do it because it's only one song'. He didn't discuss it with me at all. And when the producer came and asked me if I would do it, I said 'yes'. Of course I'd do it, why not? It's a good show, and it's a good song. One song or 20 songs. You know what you're capable of doing, and that's what happened. But agents can ruin things for you rather than help you do things.

Friends and colleagues in the music business have had similar experiences. According to DENISE KING, a Paris-based American jazz singer who cites Kitt as a role model (and who performs with me on our JAMERICAZZ project – combining literary readings and jazz improvisation), the most important way to protect oneself is by demanding transparency when you're an expatriate artist. 'I've run into agents who used my inability to speak a language against me,' King says.

Hence the reason I have ALL contracts and correspondence in the original language as well as in English. It's very important to be confident in who you are, your ability and your worth. I ask a lot of questions. In addition, when I'm performing in other countries I ask that I have a translator and guide. I recently had an instance where I asked that people speak in English. Oftentimes it's very uncomfortable when people who can speak English don't. It makes me wonder if everything is above board and question transparency. I, of course, understand that when you're in a foreign country they'll speak their language but as it pertains to business and they do speak English, I ask that they do.[2]

FIGHTING SHARKS AND BEING YOURSELF

A.M.: What are things like in the States for you now? Are you planning to take this one-woman show there?

E.K.: We are deciding now. I think the producers in America are coming in, and they are making the decisions with Mr. Alberry. So it depends on what happens in the next three weeks. I have been extended for one week. It's very scary ... And tomorrow night, I guess they told you that *Sixty Minutes* is coming, so they'll be in the theatre tomorrow night filming.

A.M.: That's great.

E.K.: You never know. Nerve-racking business. Nerve-racking, but I love it. I love what I do, but the crap around the business, it's getting very rough. It's becoming a very sharky business, more so than ever before.

A.M.: How so?

E.K.: Thieves. You never know how much money you've made, you never know how many records you've sold, you never know how honest your accountants are, you never know how honest the producers are, you never know how honest anybody is. Particularly these days. You don't have as many honest people in the background that you used to have. Everybody's got his hands in the pockets. But I think Mr. Alberry is an honest man. He has a reputation for being honest.

A.M.: Are you with a record company?

E.K.: I'm making a record ... they're filming and also making a live recording on the 31st. I just made a single record called 'Cha-Cha Heels' and 'My Discarded Men'.

A.M.: What label is that on?

E.K.: BMG? ... But you never know what label you're gonna be on because they've bought up everybody and it's one big conglomerate. So the record comes out on a different label in Germany or in England. The subsidiaries.

A.M.: In your business, what do you think it takes to be good?

E.K.: I've no idea. I have no recipe except me. The only recipe I know is me.

A.M.: What do you think is important in what you're doing?

E.K.: That you like what you're doing.

A.M.: But every business needs a particular kind of talent, otherwise I'd be in your business and you'd be in mine.

E.K.: Yeah, but if you're exceptionally good at your business, I wouldn't want to compete with that if I was not good at it. But since I am what I am in my business, obviously there's something there that the public says is special. And I like it. I like singing, dancing, fooling around on the stage. You gotta be honest and sincere about it.

*The words reminded me of what my mother instilled in us: rely on yourself;
believe in what you do. These are sentiments echoed by singer LINDA LEE
HOPKINS, an acclaimed African-American gospel vocalist who moved to
France in 1991 and has given concerts around the country as well as in
other European states including Italy and Russia. 'I don't believe in doing
things just for the money, if my heart is not in it,' she has said. 'If you have
faith in what you really want to do in life, it will work for you. You can do
all things through the spirit that strengthens you.'3*

*Her colleague Denise King also speaks of the necessity to be oneself and
to stand firm about one's abilities. 'The greatest difficulties I've had center
around some people deciding what Soul singing is and arguing with me
about it,' King says. 'Soul singing is NOT screaming or screeching, nor is it
endless riff. It almost feels like my Blackness and my life's history and experiences are being challenged. I grew up in the Black musical experience ...
it is my experience. Someone who has not grown up in it can't argue with
me about its origins, root or what it is or isn't. Case in point. I did a festival
where I was asked to perform a Blues program. I pulled from the school
of KoKo Taylor, Etta James, John Lee Hooker and more. It cannot get too
much more Blues than that ... however, the promoter had a preconceived
notion about this music and was highly upset with my program. What he
wanted was Boogie Woogie but had decided that his definition of Blues
was rule of law. I angrily changed my program but, it's about history and
protection of intellectual property. And not allowing others to define who I
am or what African-American music is.'4*

*For Kitt, the road to being herself as an artist began with dance in the
United States.*

BEGINNINGS AND POLITICS

A.M.: How did you start?

E.K.: As a dancer with the Katherine Dunham Ballet Company. In New
York. 1945. All I did was go down to have an audition for the ballet
company, and I got a full scholarship as a joke. I had no intention of
getting into show business because my aunt who brought me to New
York from North Carolina, she didn't think very much of show business
because she was very religious. She wanted me to be a concert pianist.
This was my mother's sister. My mother died when I was almost still a
baby.

A.M.: That's a rough start. (*Long pause*) Did you study ballet, or dance in general?

E.K.: Ballet.

A.M.: Let's go back a bit to politics. I read that you didn't work in the States for 11 years because of the stand you took on the Vietnam War. Did you come to Europe then? What happened?

E.K.: I went everywhere. Thank God for having an international name.

A.M.: That's the hazard of being an artist in the States, that if you really strongly disagree with the politics, you can be blacklisted. It happened to Paul Robeson, lots of others.

E.K.: That's anywhere.

A.M.: It seems to be the unwritten rule that to criticize the government of the States is unpatriotic?

E.K.: Because I think America doesn't have a sense of humor. Not only does she not have a sense of humor, she doesn't want to hear the truth. Not the American people, of course. It's the government. But when Bush says – what did he say? – that we're going to have a more easy attitude with everything in America now ...

A.M.: Do you listen to that and laugh ...?

E.K.: Well, I'm laughing until he actually does what he says. It's gonna be a more loving country, ha ha ha. How many times have we heard that one? Since the beginning of slavery.

A.M.: What happened after leaving the States and going everywhere? When you went back to the States, was it easy working there again?

E.K.: After 'Timbuktu!', it was easy. But some still didn't want to hire me because they considered me a problem.

A.M.: Do you know Nina Simone?

E.K.: Yes.

A.M.: It's similar in her case. A lot of people say: 'We're not going to work with her because she talks too much'. And she talks about record producers, saying they're sharks and things like that.

E.K. They are. (*Laughs*) She's telling the truth.

A.M.: Did it irritate you that nobody would give you a job ...

E.K.: I didn't know anything about it until 1974 ... about why I wasn't working in America.

THE DOSSIER

A.M.: How did you find out the reasons for the blacklisting?

E.K.: Seymour Hersh from the *New York Times* called me and told me that he and Jack Anderson had found this dossier on me. And that's why I wasn't working because it said on one of the dossier pages that President Johnson called the networks and all the media all over the country and said that 'I don't want to see that woman's face anywhere'. Because you're not in accord with his escalation of the Vietnam War, you're out of favor, so out of sight, out of mind. So the American people didn't know what had happened to me, and neither did I. All I knew was that I wasn't working in the same places I had worked in every year. Because if you've been very good at one place, you're always asked to come back, and I was always asked to come back in every place I'd ever worked. And all of a sudden I wasn't asked to come back anymore. The *Ambassador*, three weeks after that luncheon ... I was supposed to open there. And they couldn't find the contract, all of a sudden.

A.M.: Did the *New York Times* do anything about this? Did they publicise the file?

E.K.: That's why he, Seymour Hersh, called, to ask if he could publish it. I think it was January of 1974 that he told me.

A.M.: What I started asking was: is it irritating that nobody would hire you for a certain time, and then you come abroad and you've had great success, and now you go back and people are falling over themselves. *Sixty Minutes* coming in ... is that annoying? People now suddenly starting to call again, after ignoring you. Or is it just one of the hazards of the business?

E.K.: It is one of the hazards of the business because you don't know why you go out of popularity. Your popularity can go cold, of course, but when you cannot find a reason for it going cold ...You can explain it if you're honest enough with yourself that you're not as good today as you were twenty years ago, or ten years ago, or five years ago, or that your style is not in demand now. You can understand all this because it's explainable. You can find words for it. But when there's no reason for it that you can put your finger on, you say: what happened? And you would say: 'Well, I haven't had a hit record,' but I was recording, so why wasn't anybody asking me to work? All of these things that you say, well, my records are still selling. Now they are collector's items. You become a cult, you know. You become a cult for that. Which I think is wonderful to become a cult, as long as the audience is there. It makes me very happy. But if the public doesn't know why you're not there, everybody will say: whatever happened to Eartha Kitt? And even for myself, I was saying, what happened? What did I do wrong? And then suddenly they call you up and tell you what you've done wrong. Then you start being accused of all sorts of crazy things ... well, you know, whatever the case might be. And then you feel so guilty about everything that you wanna do something to have a reason for them to be accusing you. They are accusing you anyway, so why not go ahead and do something that they are accusing you of (*laughs*). You have a great tendency to do that.

A.M.: What was your reaction when you heard? Were you angry?
E.K.: I was shocked. When Seymour Hersh told me, I was laughing and crying at the same time because it was so ridiculous: sadistic sex nymphomaniac. That was on the dossier. That is on the dossier. As if that had anything to do with being against the government. I think I missed a chapter in my book, in my life somewhere (*laughs*). Oh my God. So what's that got to do with anything? Even if I were guilty? You had a great urge to go out and find five men and bring them home. You know I did an interview on radio, and the guy's first question to me was: Miss Kitt, is it true that when you wake up in the morning, you put your feet into mink-lined slippers, you step over seven men, you go into your sable-lined bathroom and brush your teeth with Dom Perignon champagne? And I said: 'Of course, doesn't everybody?' And of course, that's headlines. That's the way she really is. So you gotta laugh. So you should be very careful what you say as a joke. Especially with people who don't have a sense of humor. Because sometimes people think you're putting them down, rather than teasing them.

For women artists, exclusion is often the consequence of speaking up. Ask for your royalties, and a publisher or record producer may stop answering your emails. As Denise King says:

*The other issue that has sometimes come up is the Angry Black Woman
moniker. When I've had a legitimate grievance and raised an issue I have
been accused of being angry, aggressive. I realized that I am not afforded
the luxury of anger or debate without being accused of being aggressive or
angry. My words must be tempered and carefully chosen. Stereotypes are
strong. I'm a mythbuster but also let people know I do have a right to the
same emotions as anyone else.*

SOUTH AFRICA

*At the time of the interview, Nelson Mandela had not yet been released
from prison (after 27 years in captivity), and the South Africa boycott was
in full force. Kitt, as usual, had her own views.*

A.M.: Something else I read about you. You filmed a movie, or part of a
movie in South Africa.
E.K.: I did a whole movie. Two movies.

A.M.: Why? It was against the ban on artists performing in South Africa.
E.K.: I don't believe artists should be banned. We are the ones who keep
the doors open when politicians close them. I don't think that the sports
people or artists should be banned from keeping the doors of the world
open. If anyone can keep them open, it's the artists.

A.M.: But what if South Africans prefer that American artists or international artists don't come to South Africa during this time?
E.K.: That's not true, because I went into Soweto and had a meeting in
the shebeens with the Africans and when the question was asked: do
you believe in sanctions? Only one said yes. But that one is the one that
gets the headlines that say 'yes, we do want sanctions'. And the other
thirty-four say we don't want sanctions. But the thirty-four do not make
the headlines.

A.M.: So the controversy about Paul Simon, for instance, going in to
make an album with Soweto musicians ...
E.K.: I adore him for doing that. He's a very courageous person for
doing that. And he's showing something about South Africa that you
would not see otherwise. It's an exchange of culture. We keep the doors
open while politicians are closing them. Music has no politics and the

artist has no politics. And you go to the sports arena in South Africa – the blacks, the whites, the yellows, the reds, everybody is sitting right next to one another. They don't give a damn. They just want to see the game. And Arthur Ashe was teaching the African kids how to play tennis. And he was harassed to such an extent that the wonderful chance that these kids had of learning what Arthur Ashe could teach them, now it's forbidden. Generally politicians are for business, and these companies that say, oh, we're pulling out of South Africa, they still get their royalties. And the people they say they've sold the business to, the Afrikaner, they put all the people out of work, and they hire their own. So then the families are starving and the children are hungry and those are the ones that go out and throw stones. No, I don't believe in sanctions, honey, because I was there, and what I saw in 1974 ... I did a three-month tour, the first time an integrated show had ever gone into South Africa and the first time, and it's sad to say it, but it was the first time you had integrated audiences. And we went everywhere, except places like Bloem –, the last stand, you know, that says no integration. And on Sundays I went into the black areas and entertained them at movie houses. But it was an integrated audience, an integrated show. We broke the law everywhere. And raised money to build schools for the black kids. I was thrown out of a park because I was 'colored'. And the person who did it was Indian. I could feel the tension in him. But I got back after the headlines because people made up for what had happened by donating to build schools ... The good things that you do don't make headlines.

FINALE

A.M.: So, where are you now?

E.K.: I'm more scared today than I was in the past because now I constantly have to keep proving that I deserve being wherever the hell I am. Nobody wants to believe that you're capable of being broken, and nobody knows what you're going through emotionally. Nobody knows I'm going through my menopause, my baby gets married and I'm doing a one-woman show, all at the same time. It's absolutely crazy. And I cannot go around saying, excuse me, I'm going through my menopause, my baby just left me and here I am standing by myself, naked. (*Laughs, though it could as well be crying.*)

After her one-woman show in London, Kitt became known to a new generation when she voiced roles in Disney films such as The Emperor's New Groove *and starred in a number of films and television shows. She died on 25 December 2008, aged 81. My mother had passed away almost three years earlier; among the things she'd left us was her collection of records, including Kitt's albums, cassettes, which are now with me in Paris. One grey day, as I was wondering how to complete this chapter and questioning my overall writing, I went to a supermarket in the neighbourhood to get ingredients for curry chicken. As I stepped through the doorway, a song was ending, and soon another began. Kitt's voice came through the speakers:* C'est si bon. *The voice sounded like my mother's too. A message not to give up?*

NOTES

1. Seymour Hersh, 1975. 'C.I.A. in '68 gave Secret Service a report containing gossip about Eartha Kitt after White House incident'. *New York Times*, 3 January.
2. Email interview with Denise King, Paris, March 2018.
3. Alecia McKenzie, 2014. 'Spreading the Gospel in France'. *New African Magazine*, April.
4. Email interview with Denise King, Paris, March 2018.

PART IV

Surviving the Academy

13

In the Changing Light;
Daring to Be Powerful

Yeşim Deveci

The quality of light by which we scrutinise our lives has direct bearing upon the product which we live, and upon the changes which we hope to bring about through those lives. It is within this light that we form those ideas by which we pursue our magic and make it realised. (Audre Lorde, *Sister Outsider*)[1]

THE CHANGING LIGHT

More than a decade ago, a good friend introduced me to the work of Audre Lorde by giving me a poster with one of her most famous quotes: 'When I dare to be powerful – to use my strength in the service of my vision, then it becomes less and less important whether I am afraid.'[2] For many years, the poster lived on a shelf in my office at the community centre where I worked. I did not put it on my wall. In part, I did not have the courage to make so bold a statement, Lorde's words are fierce and unapologetic. But also, I did not need it. I worked for a small community organisation with a group of like-minded people who shared a vision for the future and were committed to justice for all. I worked with children and young people – young refugees and migrants separated from their families. My days were spent with young people: going to the Home Office, liaising with social workers, therapists, solicitors, drinking tea, talking, writing funding applications, managing casework, building partnerships, being part of a community. The issues were immediate and urgent, the relationships built over time with trust being paramount. In this context of grassroots solidarity, caring for young people in our community, challenging injustice and creating spaces for safety and belonging, I had the support of friends and colleagues engaged in similar struggles. Community work. The daily work undertaken by women of colour to enable the survival of their children. When I left the centre in 2013, I took my poster with me.

My decision to leave the voluntary sector was largely one of self-preservation; I loved working with young people and the energy of our team but after 13 years the endless struggle of fundraising for survival had worn me down. I had started a professional doctorate in 2010 but the births of my children and flow of life meant the project was one with many stops and starts, speed ups and breaks; a continuing work in progress. Over the years my topic had shifted around but always there were young people, his/herstories, stories of migration, of everyday life, of struggles, hopes and dreams. After a long meander, my research took shape as an exploration of the hopes and dreams, everyday lives and life histories of young people with 'no papers' – with irregular or undocumented immigration status. I hoped that academic research would enable me to have a wider impact on policy-making and practice than was possible from a front-line practitioner position.

In 2014, I took up a part-time post as a lecturer in the social sciences at a 'new' university in London. It had originally been established as a technical institute to serve the local community; the 'people's university'. I knew of the university by reputation; former students talked enthusiastically about their time there, it was home to many 'radical academics' and many of the students were the first generation in their family to attend university. Amongst the student body, people of colour were in the majority, many of them mature students with extensive prior work experience who had entered higher education as a means of moving into graduate employment. Perhaps unsurprisingly, this 'diversity' of the student population was not reflected in the academic staff, much less the management. Where the community centre had become a second home to me, the university was not somewhere I could easily belong; I was a practitioner in a theoretical space, talking about praxis, where lived experience was legitimised by peer review.

In Sara Ahmed's essay 'Being in Question' she describes the experience of being asked, in various contexts 'Where are you from?' as a prerequisite to passing from one space to another, or passing through, or passing as something. 'Passing,' she writes 'is what you have to do because or when your legitimacy is in question.'[3] As the daughter of Turkish-Cypriot immigrants, with neither professional qualifications nor the all important 'Dr' before my name, I am all too familiar with these questions. Despite my 20 years' experience of working with young people with 'no papers', my voice is rarely granted legitimacy. As time passes I realise that regardless of my title, knowledge or experience there will always be questions about my belonging and identity, constant questions about legitimacy, recognition and rights. This is because I am a person who will always, and increasingly intentionally, be inconsistent with the norms of an institution.[4] So after almost a decade of being carried around, always present, never on display, I decided to put the poster up on the wall of my new office at the university. In this new and unfamiliar context, the image of Audre Lorde and her words give me the courage to dare, to resist and to exist in a space where I struggle to belong.

IN THE MOUTH OF THE DRAGON

I began this chapter with the story of the poster as a way of introduction. In my move from 'practitioner in the community' to 'academic at a university' the quality of the light changed. Working with young people, the focus of my practice had always been about making a human connection and working collaboratively together in response to needs. For me, the work of connecting with, caring and advocating on behalf of young people who had arrived in the United Kingdom as refugees or migrants was an intentional practice, a 'conscious decision'[5] to resist the structures and institutions of power which denied them their humanity, justice and right to belong. At the university, the light is more opaque. I am not engaged in daily battles with the Home Office or local authority bureaucracy. However, the 'brick walls' are just as solid if less immediately visible.[6] In this changing light, I have been thinking again about the importance of relational[7] and relationship-based work,[8] this labour of love as a kind of activism; small acts of resistance which sustain the survival and growth of 'space invaders'[9] the black and brown bodies of young people, students and academics whose presence within disrupts and disturbs white space.

Writing about the experience of Black women in the United States, Lorde (1984) reminds us that 'to survive in the mouth of this dragon we call America, we have had to learn this first and most vital lesson – that we were never meant to survive. Not as human beings ... And that visibility which makes us most vulnerable is also our greatest strength.'[10] In this chapter I draw on the work of Audre Lorde (1984) and Sara Ahmed (2017) to discuss my work with Samia, Maryam and Aminatta[11] and explore the ways in which I enact my commitments to justice, solidarity and 'education as the practice of freedom'[12] through these student-teacher relationships. Finally, I consider the consequences of undertaking these small acts of resistance for those of us who do the work and the institutions and structures that are the target.

SAMIA

We are powerful because we have survived, and that is what it is all about – survival and growth.[13]

Samia was amongst the first group of undergraduate students I taught when I joined the university and I became her dissertation supervisor. She was interested in researching the educational experiences of people who came to the United Kingdom as refugees. As we worked together she told me something of her own history of coming to the United Kingdom in her early twenties from Liberia. As we got to know each other, she shared more and more about her life; she talked about her children, the efforts she was making to support them in school and give them every opportunity to grow up with a sense of security. She talked about her determination to complete her degree and to be able to provide for her children. Over time, I learned that she had recently separated from her husband; he had been violent towards her for many years and she had told him to leave. By her final year at university he had moved out but continued to try to maintain some control over her life. Samia felt that he resented her return to education; she was managing on her own and her student status offered the promise of graduate employment and complete independence from him.

As a new lecturer I felt I was barely one step ahead of Samia as I tried to guide her through the process of developing a research project. I was thankful that her topic was one I was familiar with. I could easily direct her to literature and resources and understand something of the experiences she was trying to bring into being. Initially, our work together was fairly straightforward: she'd come for a tutorial, we'd have a quick chat about how she was doing and get on with the work. She told me proudly that her son had passed his 11-plus exam and got into the local grammar school, she worried about overloading her daughter with too many extra-curricular activities and we laughed about my inability to find my way around the labyrinthine university buildings. But by Easter, the weight of all the responsibilities she was shouldering and the constant harassment from her ex-husband were starting to drain her energies. She began to miss tutorials or would attend but be unable to focus. I began to worry about my capacity to support her and sought out organisations I knew who worked with survivors of domestic violence. Samia said thank you but no. She didn't want to speak to anyone else. I struggled with my role; I was her dissertation supervisor not her counsellor, the issues she was grappling with were complex and I didn't feel 'qualified' to help her. Samia was adamant that she didn't need or want input from any other professionals. She was an adult making a decision about her own life and who she wanted to involve in it. So we continued. I tried to offer flexibility within a clear boundary: regular tutorials which provided a time and space in which she could process some of what was going on in her life at present as well as engage with her dissertation project. At times, tutorials consisted of a brief catch-up, then focus on the task in hand. At other times, she simply sat, talked and cried and I would arrange another tutorial for us to discuss her dissertation.

As the deadline drew closer, her home life became increasingly difficult and I became seriously concerned that the pressure to complete the project would push her to breaking point. I sought some advice on her behalf about a possible extension but was advised that she was unlikely to be granted 'extenuating circumstances' and so I should focus on getting Samia to submit her project on time, however incomplete. So we continued with our slow dance; I arranged tutorials for Samia, she came when she felt able and we worked together according to need. Sometimes she talked about how she was feeling, what was going on for her and at other times, sometimes within the same session, we talked and thought about the project. For me, there were two tasks; the first to enable Samia to complete her dissertation and, intimately connected with this, the task of keeping her psychic and emotional needs in mind and making an attempt to meet them with her. Samia for her part worked as hard as was possible in every way she could, she respected the boundaries of the relationship we had established as student and tutor and used the space she was given to help her get through this most challenging time. That summer, Samia submitted her dissertation on time; a testament to her steely determination and capacity to survive and a lesson for me about the value of holding onto a relationship-based practice when navigating unknown waters.

MARYAM

I was thinking that if we all, all of us black, all of us women, all of us deriving from connected varieties of peasant/immigrant/persecuted histories of struggle and significant triumph, if we could find and trust each other enough to travel into a land where none of us belonged, nothing on Earth was impossible any more.[14]

At the end of the summer I picked up a call from Maryam. She reminded me that we'd spoken some weeks before when I'd called to discuss the offer we'd made for her to join our degree programme. She told me then that she was planning to accept an offer to study social work at another university – I wished her the best of luck and did not expect to hear from her again. I was surprised when she called back and asked whether she could be considered for entry to the final year of our degree. She told me that she'd been a student at the university some ten years ago but had been unable to complete her degree when her mother passed away and now was only eligible for one year of student finance. We talked at length and I learned that she had spent the past ten years undertaking short courses and working with young people involved in the criminal justice system. She'd reached a point where she could not progress any further without a degree despite her extensive knowledge and experience.

I've met many 'Maryams' over the years – insightful, intelligent women of colour who do the work, but come up time and again against 'brick walls, institutional walls; those hardening of histories into barriers in the present'.[15] These Maryams are 'space invaders',[16] foreign bodies who don't belong at the experts' table, where the decisions are made that impact the lives of others, those brown and black bodies the system has let down, by accident or design. Without the 'qualifications' which validate their authority, allow them permission to theorise, and recognise their knowledge and expertise – the voices of Maryams, just like the young people with whom they work, are not listened to and rarely heard. As I listen to Maryam I think about privilege and power. About differences and about how, even with papers, she will have to fight to speak and be heard. About Maryam and myself, I see our sameness and differences and the doors we can open and those we have to pass through.[17] As I write, I wonder about my readers and whether I am flattening too many differences between me and my students, making the professional personal, reading too much between the lines of 'overly identified', 'defensive'. So, I turn to those that have been in this space far longer than I have and I read, I read bell hooks, Sara Ahmed, June Jordan, Audre Lorde, Angela Davis. I take a breath and focus. This is the work.

As I listen to Maryam trying to persuade me to accept her directly into the third year of the degree, I am thinking about what she has told me about herself and the bits I have imagined. The familiar known and unknowns, about the demands of the programme, what she will manage and where she might struggle. I think about the final year and try to imagine her in class, the work she will have to do to catch up, how she might juggle work, study and home. I'm trying to get a sense of what it would look like, for her, and for me as the person who accepts her. What extra support she might need to complete the final year. I ask her to email me and include a CV, proof of previous study, anything which can be used to support her case. I tell her that the final decision is not mine but I will do what I can to see what's possible. I'm in advocate mode, working out what I need to know and who I need to persuade to make the case. Over the next few days, I make numerous calls, send emails to colleagues devising solutions, reassuring and persuading colleagues that the concerns they raise are realistic but not insurmountable. A week later, I call Maryam and let her know we are looking forward to seeing her in September. We talk about how she can use the summer to prepare and what to expect. I email a colleague to let her know that I'm happy to be Maryam's final year dissertation supervisor. The final year is demanding and I know that in accepting her onto the programme and persuading colleagues that she will be able to complete I have also taken responsibility for supporting her through this process. I'm apprehensive about the commitment I have made, this leap of faith. But I hear her determination and I am mindful of my own power. I am a gatekeeper. I open the gate.

AMINATTA

It is the storyteller, who makes us what we are, who creates history. The storyteller creates the memory that the survivors must have – otherwise their surviving would have no meaning.[18]

I have a plant on my windowsill given to me by Aminatta. It is a small, spiky succulent, barely visible in the large room but determinedly alive. It is the only plant which has managed to survive in my office at the end of a long dark corridor with no natural light. After the death of my last two plants I started to joke that the toxic air of the neoliberal university was killing them off, but Aminatta's offering has shown me that survival is both possible and necessary.

Aminatta is a survivor and a fighter. In the nine months that I worked with her as a dissertation supervisor she did not miss a single tutorial, deadline or appointment despite suffering with chronic pain and arthritis. She would often arrive out of breath and leaning heavily on her walking stick having trudged around carrying a rucksack full of books. She would spend the morning in the library. She was absolutely determined and nothing, absolutely nothing, would stop her. Aminatta and I chose each other as student and supervisor. It was the start of the final year at the welcome back meeting and Aminatta was greeting all my colleagues; she was on a different programme so I hadn't met her before. She was worried about her dissertation and had been preparing over the summer – a colleague said she should speak to me as I had supervised a dissertation about female genital mutilation/cutting (FGM/C) last year. We spoke briefly and I offered to link Aminatta up with an activist and campaigner I knew who was also from Aminatta's home country.

A week and several email exchanges later, I wrote to my colleague to let her know I would supervise Aminatta's dissertation. It made sense. So we began. Aminatta told me she was a survivor of FGM/C and this project was about giving women like her a chance to speak. In those first few weeks we talked a lot about the importance of survivors being able to speak and write about their experiences and how little of their knowledge was represented in the academic literature. As we talked about telling stories, it became increasingly clear that this project was a way for Aminatta to tell something of her own story. We talked about the ways in which she could include her voice and decided eventually that she would ask a friend to interview her and she would include her interview in the data for analysis. Reflecting on the experience of being interviewed some months later, Aminatta said that she'd told her friend the interviewer 'a lot, but not everything' she'd told me. She said that she wanted to tell her life story and have it written. It had taken her a long time to find the courage to speak and she no longer feared the consequences; she would use her voice.

Aminatta's capacity to theorise and articulate her ideas in relation to her research project was remarkable; but she struggled to get her thoughts onto paper in line with the academic conventions of an undergraduate dissertation project. I understood and felt her frustration as I marked several drafts of each chapter, directing her to additional support around writing and referencing. We spent hours working through the various sections of the project, weaving in the women's voices with the literature she had found, her own story and deep knowledge of her community, the traditions and changing practices across generations; trying to close the gap between language and thought through writing[19] and enabling Aminatta to use her words to speak her truths.

DARING TO BE POWERFUL

… Don't you know
They're talkin' 'bout a revolution
It sounds like a whisper
Poor people gonna rise up
And get their share
Poor people gonna rise up
And take what's theirs.[20]

While writing, I think about Samia, Maryam and Aminatta and the threads that connect our stories: we are all women of colour, engaged in relationships and resistances. We are fighting to survive in spaces which do not welcome our voices. We are connecting across our differences and making solidarities. I write to bridge the gap between experience and ideas; feeling, thinking and theorising, trying to bring together concepts – from therapeutic and social work, education and women of colour feminisms – in ways that can be useful for those of us in search of words. Words which describe our worlds and enable us to speak about that which we know and understand so deeply. And then I stumble, worrying that I am 'just telling stories' and that my argument, the all important single thread which grants legitimacy and defines the text, has got lost within the messy stories of our real lives.

In her brilliant essay 'The Race for Theory', Barbara Christian (1987) reminds us that:

People of colour have always theorised – but in forms quite different from the Western form of abstract logic. And I am inclined to say that our narrative forms, in the stories we create, in riddles and proverbs, in the play with language, since dynamic rather than fixed ideas seem more to our liking. How else have we managed to survive with such spiritedness the assault on our bodies, social institutions, countries, our very humanity?[21]

And then I breathe out again. And walk forwards. Because I have been given permission to speak. To write my truths. And this is what I seek to do when building relationships with my students.

And then, distracted for a moment by the ping on my computer, I check my emails. I breathe in and hold my breath. Not daring to speak as I read with horror the description of the new role I am expected to undertake as an 'Academic Advisor'. This is a new role which replaces the Personal Tutor, in which the psychic and emotional content of the work I do is neatly filed under 'Personal Management' and human relations are reduced to functions. The reconstruction of my pastoral relationship with my students is a travesty of the social relations which are at the heart of engaged pedagogy; relationships which make learning a meaningful exchange and education a liberatory practice.[22] I regret the distraction. The energy drains as I read the details of the policy and guidance, the rush of freedom I felt when reading Barbara Christian's (1987) essay on theory is gone.[23] I am filled with anxiety as I wonder how I will find the time to do the tasks required to meet the demands of this new directive while also doing the work I know to be necessary. The work which sustains our survival and growth.

In a powerful essay in which Lorde (1984) defines the erotic as an assertion of the lifeforce of women, she argues that any system:

> which defines human need to the exclusion of the psychic and emotional components of that need – the principal horror of such a system is that it robs our work of its erotic value, its erotic power and life appeal and fulfilment. Such a system reduces work to a travesty of necessities, a duty by which we earn bread or oblivion for those we love.[24]

The impact of this system of deprivation is, Lorde writes, 'tantamount to blinding a painter and then telling her to improve the work, and to enjoy the act of painting. It is not only next to impossible, it is also profoundly cruel.'[25] The impossibility of the task and its impact on those who dare to try to work while blinded is perhaps what the acclaimed writer Sunny Singh was alluding to recently on Twitter. In a searingly honest thread, which she tags #selfcare #PTSD, she reflects on her experience as a role model for women of colour saying, 'The damn pillar you want to lean on is SO damn brittle because it's stood against all shit for decades before that it will crumble w/a touch.'[26] This thread struck a chord with me as I've been thinking a lot about the consequences of the relational resistance work I have described and particularly how to sustain this as we enter a new academic year.

Unlike Sunny Singh I am not a public figure and so the demands upon us are somewhat different. However, despite our differences we are both, by virtue of our 'nots' – 'not white, not male' – thrown into what Ahmed describes as the political labour of diversity work: 'the work we do when we are trying to transform an institution; or to be more specific the work we do when we are trying to open up institutions to those who have been historically excluded from them.'[27] In a context where work is reduced to a 'travesty of necessities', the time and energy spent working with students in ways which respond to them as whole human beings, with differing needs at different times, is not only invisible but does not count. I use the word 'count' deliberately as the relative value of everything we do at the neoliberal university is now measured in numbers – the number of students who complete their degree, are satisfied with their courses, enter graduate employment within six months and so on. These numbers are the rulers of the university universe and work undertaken is only visible and deemed relevant if it can be explained in terms of these numbers. The complex and complicated stories I have related here do not easily fit the numbers narrative. The consequence of this unquantifiable work is that it does not count as 'workload' and so the time and energy I give comes from my own resources. And so when Sunny Singh tweets: 'Fact is for each person we support, it's a bit out of our lives/hearts that may be keeping us afloat. And no, I don't have a solution' and 'I can tell you that I know how important it is for me to support other WoC. And to live the ethical, moral life. To do the right thing',[28] she speaks for many of us. The struggle to stay afloat, while doing the work we know to be so important, to which we are deeply committed and believe in so fiercely, is constant. It is exhausting. We become brittle and unless we take time to attend to our own needs we cannot survive. Wanting to offer some kind of support, I replied to the thread; 'Take a break – 'self care is a revolutionary act' Audre Lorde. Resist, rest, repeat! So [necessary] to model this 4 other WOC.' She replied: 'Thank you. And very true. Trying to follow her advice.'[29]

These days I take my copy of *Sister Outsider* everywhere, sharing Lorde's wisdom with the sisters in my life. In 'A Killjoy Survival Kit', Sara

Ahmed reminds us of all we need to survive doing this work; books, things, tools, time, life, permission notes, other killjoys, humour, feelings and bodies.[30] I am trying to follow the advice of the women who have walked these paths for many years before me. To learn from their struggles and my own and share this with the women I meet, as a practitioner, an activist, a student and a teacher.

CONCLUSIONS

In writing this chapter I have faltered numerous times as I worry that it is not adequately theorised, that the stories are too simple or too complicated, that it is not 'properly academic'. But what sustains me in writing and in my practice of education is the memory of the joy of recognition when I have read something which resonated with my experience and the knowledge that teaching and learning are indivisible. I learn from my students and they from me, all practice is an attempt to meet the other, a process of connection and collaboration which takes energy and creativity. It is not linear but cyclical. It is relational and the being and doing cannot be separated out.

My intention is to create spaces for connection, to foster creative and critical thought as a means of challenging structures that oppress. The consequences of undertaking this work are that what we bring to the university is rarely what is wanted by the institution – there is a claim to diversify but really, the challenge and the outcome is unwanted. So, I am learning slowly to work quietly. To just get on with the being and the doing without seeking approval. Daring to be powerful and enabling others to do the same. Trusting in my experience and my feelings and respecting those 'hidden sources of our power from where true knowledge, and therefore lasting action comes'.[31]

For those who live without privilege, resistance is part of existence. It is tiring to be continually resisting, with no real sense that the institutions and structures we come up against are in any way diminished by our fight. But we are not merely working in an isolated moment in time, our struggles are long and interconnected. In remembrance let me share the closing words of June Jordan's *Poem for South African Women*:[32]

And who will join this standing up
and the ones who stood without sweet company
will sing and sing
back into the mountains and
if necessary
even under the sea

we are the ones we have been waiting for.

NOTES

1. Audre Lorde, 1984. *Sister Outsider*. Crossing Press, Berkeley, p. 36.
2. The poster references Lorde's statement 'When I dare to be powerful, to use my strength in the service of my vision, then it becomes less important whether or not I am unafraid.' In Audre Lorde, 1997. *The Cancer Journals Special Edition*. Aunt Lute Books, San Francisco. Digital: Location 117 of 1372.
3. Sara Ahmed, 2017. *Living a Feminist Life*. Duke University Press, Durham, p. 120.
4. Ahmed, *Living a Feminist Life*.
5. Lorde, *Sister Outsider*, p. 55.
6. Ahmed, *Living a Feminist Life*.
7. See Kenneth J. Gergen, 2009. *Relational Being*. Oxford University Press, New York. Kenneth J. Gergen, 2015. 'Relational ethics in therapeutic practice'. *Australian and New Zealand Journal of Family Therapy* 36(4), pp. 409–18.
8. See Helen Hingley-Jones and Gillian Ruch, 2016. 'Social work practice in austere times'. *Journal of Social Work Practice* 30(3), pp. 235–48. Patrick O'Leary, Ming-Sum Tsui and Gillian Ruch, 2013. 'The boundaries of the social work relationship revisited: Towards a connected, inclusive and dynamic conceptualisation'. *British Journal of Social Work* 43(1), pp. 135–53. Pamela Trevithick, 2003. 'Effective relationship-based practice: A theoretical exploration'. *Journal of Social Work Practice* 17(2), pp. 163–76. www.tandfonline.com/doi/abs/10.1080/026505302000145699 (accessed 6 September 2017).
9. Nirmal Puwar, 2004. *Space Invaders: Race, Gender and Bodies Out of Place*. Berg, Oxford.
10. Lorde, *Sister Outsider*, p. 42.
11. Samia, Maryam and Aminatta are pseudonyms.
12. bell hooks, 1994. *Teaching to Transgress: Education as the Practice of Freedom*. Routledge, New York.
13. Lorde, *Sister Outsider*, p. 139.
14. June Jordan and Stacey Russo (eds), 2014. *Life as Activism: June Jordan's Writings from the Progressive*. Litwin Books, Sacramento, p. 13.
15. Ahmed, *Living a Feminist Life*, p. 136.

16. Puwar, *Space Invaders*.
17. Ahmed, *Living a Feminist Life*, pp. 119–20.
18. Chinua Achebe cited by Biyi Bandele in Chinua Achebe, 1958. *Things Fall Apart*. Paperback edition, 2001. Penguin Modern Classics, London, p. x.
19. Arundhati Roy, 2017. *An Evening with Arundhati Roy*. Union Chapel, London (5 June).
20. Tracey Chapman, 1988. 'Talkin' 'Bout a Revolution'. Elektra Records.
21. Barbara Christian, 1987. 'The race for theory'. *Cultural Critique*, No. 6. *The Nature and Context of Minority Discourse*, Spring. University of Minnesota Press, Minneapolis, p. 52.
22. See Paulo Friere, 1970. *Pedagogy of the Oppressed*. Reprinted 1996. Penguin Books, London. hooks, *Teaching to Transgress*.
23. Christian, 'The race for theory'.
24. Lorde, *Sister Outsider*, p. 55.
25. Ibid.
26. Sunny Singh, 2017. Twitter, 5 September. https://twitter/sunnysingh_n6 (accessed 8 September 2017).
27. Ahmed, *Living a Feminist Life*, p. 93.
28. Singh, tweet, 5 September 2017.
29. Yesim Deveci, 2017. Twitter, 5 September. http://twitter.com/YesimCDeveci (accessed 8 September 2017).
30. Ahmed, *Living a Feminist Life*, pp. 235–49.
31. Lorde, *Sister Outsider*, p. 37.
32. *Poem for South African Women* commemorates 'the 40,000 women and children who on August 9, 1956, presented themselves in bodily protest against the "dompass" in the capital of apartheid. Presented at the United Nations, August 9, 1978'. www.junejordan.net/poem-for-south-african-women.html (accessed 8 September 2017).

14

Cruel Ironies: The Afterlife of Black Womxn's Intervention

Cruel Ironies Collective

On 15 December 2017, we joined a group of Black feminists in an intervention at the University of Amsterdam's Research Centre for Gender and Sexuality (ARC-GS). This intervention was meant to address the cruel irony that an event designed to address the exclusion of Black womxn[1] from white academic spaces thriving on Black womxn's intellectual labour itself neglected to include Black womxn. The only way in which Black womxn were involved with the staging of this discussion was in the event's promotional image, featuring an unnamed Black woman. The backlash, not only in the moment of the intervention but that has followed us since, has made evident that even the defence of Black womxn's representation in the Dutch academy requires the erasure of Black womxn and that the critique of the absence of Black womxn is valid only when articulated by a non-Black person. Months and a handful of thinkpieces later, the afterlife of this small-scale protest has revealed to us a profound split in the anti-racism scene of the Netherlands. Black womxn's criticism of the instrumentalisation of a non-Black person of colour by the institution, and our declaration that non-Black people of colour cannot represent Black people have brought to the surface a troubling undercurrent of anti-Blackness.

Broadly defined, anti-Blackness is to be 'resistant or antagonistic to black people',[2] and Afro-pessimist theorist Jared Sexton specifies that 'anti-blackness is not simply anti-black racism ... not just distinct and horizontally related to the whole array of mass suffering'.[3] We rely on the analysis of Egbert Alejandro Martina, which shows how anti-Blackness is historically fundamental to the development of the Dutch political language, class system and legal system. In our context, the following insight is particularly important:

Blackness is ... not only the baseline against which non-Black people of colour are measured, it is also the baseline against which risky populations, that is Allochtonen/immigrants, are created. Non-Black people of colour are measured on the blackness scale. Race gathers its libidinal force from anti-blackness; the closer to blackness the riskier you are ... By privileging ethnicity (*ethnic minority* or *Allochtoon*) as an organizing term in Dutch discourse on race, anti-blackness as an organizing principle gets erased, or side-tracked. Even though, the blackened (or in other words *racialized*) Other is a motile concept, as Dutch political discourse suggests, bodies marked as phenotypic Black cannot move out of the political category 'Black' with the same ease as non-Black bodies of colour who are scripted as *Black* politically: phenotypic Black folks are, it seems, permanently fixed in blackness.[4]

This has informed the demonisation of the Black womxn activists who participated in the intervention, the fabricated victimhood of the non-Black academic and the convenient forgetting of her gesture of solidarity by other non-Black academics, and perhaps most importantly the derailment of the intervention's purpose into a sanctimonious panic over Blackness as an identity of its own. We reject the vilification of identity politics by those threatened by its implications for Black womxn's liberation,[5] and embrace this concept as a vocabulary with which to empower ourselves. We have had months to study our (mis) representation in smokescreens and white noise, and are emboldened by the Combahee River Collective's call to 'demonstrate the reality of our politics'.[6] From the place of realisation that 'the only people who care enough about us to work consistently for our liberation are us',[7] we write our version of events.

WHITE SPACES, BLACK THOUGHT

In November 2017, the event page for a lecture titled 'The Trouble with Post-Black Feminist Intersectionality' by the Université de Montréal's Professor Sirma Bilge (Figure 14.1) went live and made the rounds in the Dutch anti-racism activism circuit. The lecture was described as an attempt to think through a so-called 'post-Black feminist turn' in the study of intersectionality, the increasing global popularity of the concept which marked a 'curious move away from Black feminism and actual Black women'.[8] To analyse this exclusion of Black womxn of African descent by academic institutions, Bilge would engage with 'another strand of Black radical thought, namely Afro-pessimism'.[9] The description concluded that in spite of contemporary universities' incorporation of intersectional criticism, 'anti-Blackness remained the changing same'.[10] On the heels of the global 'Decolonise the University' movement's arrival in the Netherlands[11] and the University of Amsterdam's first diversity commission,[12] this declaration rang true but well overdue. Most crucially, the truth of this conclusion was undercut by the irony of its staging: to address the exclusion of Black womxn by institutions that capitalise on Black womxn's thought, ARC-GS invited a non-Black woman. This revealed the move away from actual Black womxn as no longer 'curious', and mostly troublesome. The ARC-GS lecture reproduced the very problem it claimed to address.[13]

The irony was not lost on the Netherlands' Black feminists such as queer activist Jo-Ann With and writer and political scientist Munganyende Hélène Christelle, who took to the online platforms on which the event was being promoted. Christelle argued:

[I]t is necessary for non-black academics working on the subject of blackness to engage with the critique of self. As it is for any academic working on topics that engage with questions of collective and interpersonal trauma. Understanding that a duality is possible: having your non-black women body under siege whilst perpetuating epistemic violence against the black women body too.

The silencing of black bodies within black-centered conversations has never been liberating to the women on the margins Black feminism was designed for *and never will be.*

And that is exactly where it goes wrong: Black feminism is a movement for liberation. Not a *jadijada* [yada-yada] topic just to consume over cups of academic tea.

The intellectualization of collective Black women trauma is hot business.[14]

The heated online debate that followed on whether Bilge might claim political Blackness[15] or if her presumed self-identification as a woman of colour justified her positionality, and the organisation's neglect to respond to these concerns eventually culminated in a call for intervention by radical Black feminist activist J. Tizora.

Following the introduction by ARC-GS director Liza Mügge, Tizora raised her hand and asked the organisers to clarify their silence around the criticism of the event. There had been a lively debate on the ARC-GS Facebook page about this event and at the time, no one from the Centre had responded to any of the criticisms. When the director responded to Tizora's criticism by saying that Tizora and the audience should 'let [Bilge] talk' and demanded an adherence to the academic protocol of 'questions at the end', we did not think the criticism was being taken seriously. In response, we – members of the University of Colour activist collective[16] and our associates – joined Tizora's intervention in solidarity. We asked: How could ARC-GS reconcile their organisation of an event on the absence of Black womxn in academic matters of Black womxn's thought with the emphatic absence of Black womxn in that event? Why, when Black womxn activists had tirelessly organised around the inclusion of Black people in Dutch academic spaces, did the ARC-GS fly a non-Black woman across the Atlantic to tell them what we had been campaigning around for years? And why, when dozens of Black womxn had taken to the promotional platforms of this event to demand expla-nation or accountability for its hypocrisy, were their voices disqualified from a discussion that purported to amplify them? The exchange that followed saw on one side the criticism of ARC-GS's exclusion of Black womxn, on another Mügge's refusal to engage with our critique, and soon, Sirma Bilge's own decision not to give her talk, as 'this discussion [was] much more important'.[17] Bilge explained both her decision and the premise of her talk by quoting Barbara Christian's 1994 essay 'Diminish-ing Returns: Can Black Feminism(s) Survive the Academy?': 'It would be a tremendous loss, a distinct irony, if some version of Black feminist inquiry exists in the academy to which Black womxn are not major con-tributors.'[18] In the ensuing discussion, Bilge declared it would be a 'cruel irony' to carry on this event when the point she had wanted to make – about anti-Blackness and the co-option of intersectionality – was being reproduced at her talk.

It is ultimately the afterlife of this intervention that motivates our writing. Following the ARC-GS's public acknowledgment of the event's shortcomings, we've seen the continuation of extensive conversations and the release of thinkpieces from non-Black womxn and men of colour condemning our intervention as divisive identity politics or contesting the importance of a distinct Black womxn positionality.[19] Misrepresenta-tions proliferate in these pieces, which channel tropes of angry Black womanhood, the intellectual poverty of Black activists and the construc-tion of Black self-representation as aggression and division. We've seen

Amsterdam Research Centre for Gender and Sexuality

Home   About   **Events**   **Publications**   **Education**   People   **Blogs**   **Thesis Prize**   **Links**   **Contact**

15 Dec 2017

15:30 - 17:00

Prof. Bilge

The Trouble with Post-Black Feminist Intersectionality

Lecture by Prof. Sirma Bilge (Université de Montréal)

Lecture

To think through the post-Black feminist turn in intersectionality studies, Prof. Sirma Bilge engages another strand of radical Black thought, namely Afro-pessimism.

Since its initial articulation by Black feminist scholars, the concept 'intersectionality' has travelled across multiple disciplinary and geopolitical boundaries, generating much acclaim and criticism, as well as ornamental deployments to signify theoretical trendiness. Intersectionality's global traction has also been accompanied by a curious move away from Black feminism and actual Black women.

Bilge questions what the evolutionary paths of intersectionality tell us about the specific ways contemporary university incorporates its own critiques, and how despite shifting configurations and rearticulations of racism, anti-Blackness remains the changing same.

Figure 14.1   'The Trouble with Post-Black Feminist Intersectionality' at the Amsterdam Research Centre for Gender and Sexuality

Source: http://arcgs.uva.nl/content/events/lectures/2017/dec/bilge.html

the strawman victimisation of Sirma Bilge and the erasure of her gesture of solidarity to distort this narrative into one in which Black womxn activists are tyrants. For us, our intervention has only ever been about the inclusion of Black womxn in institutions that appropriate Black womxn's thought; an idea that, when coming from Bilge, warranted an academic platform, but when it is articulated by Black womxn in Amsterdam, seems to be unacceptable. And finally, we've seen the premise of our original intervention eclipsed by an identity crisis in Dutch anti-racism that conveniently makes impossible the articulation of our concerns: the problem of political Blackness. Cruelly, ironically, we've found our efforts to represent Blackness as Black people twisted into an alibi for rampant anti-Blackness by non-Black people of colour.

ANTI-BLACKNESS, UN-ACCOUNTABILITY

The intervention at the event organised by ARC-GS allowed for a critical reflection on the academic popularity of Black womxn's thought and the dismissal and erasure of Black womxn in academic spaces – again, the very problem Bilge was flown in to discuss. As such, the collective reflection that took the place of Bilge's lecture was, for everyone in attendance, an opportunity to hear this critique articulated by Black womxn who were familiar with anti-Blackness and misogynoir[20] at Dutch universities. Although the discussion was at first very tense, by the end of the event these tensions had eased significantly and we felt we had been able to show, in different words and tones, and from different Black perspectives, the pressing need for non-Black people to recognise and challenge anti-Blackness, not just in theory, but in practice. After the de-escalation and subsequent ending of the discussion, we spoke more personally with several attendees, including some of the womxn of colour who had been vocal about their opposition to our intervention. We left the building feeling optimistic about having taken an important step towards developing a mutual understanding of our different experiences of racism in the academy, which in our experience is crucial to building solidarity. At this point, we never expected this intervention to attract much attention beyond the University of Amsterdam staff organising under the banner of the ARC-GS. Unbeknownst to us, the misrepresentation of Bilge as a victim of our divisive politics was rapidly going to take on a local and international life of its own, spreading through channels inaccessible to us.

Anti-Blackness itself is not new or at all unique to the Netherlands,[21] but we find it important to share some of the structural similarities in the way people of colour, including Black men, involved in anti-racism in the Netherlands have expressed their anti-Blackness and misogynoir over the past few months in response to our intervention. Specifically, we find that these structural similarities point to an anti-Blackness among activists which colludes with the anti-Black academy. The following descriptions of anti-Blackness were present both during the intervention as well as in a widely shared article written by Miriyam Aouragh[22] which refers to the intervention.

The most obvious examples of anti-Black sentiment in these settings have been the liberal use of stereotypes about Black womxn to delegitimise the intervention we staged. These include, but are unfortunately not limited to: accusations of aggression, assumptions about Dutch Black activists being ignorant, and implications of Dutch Black activists' illiteracy. The use of stereotypes about Black people was directed at Dutch Black activists, which requires both recognition of Black people and an association with negative stereotypes.

Interestingly enough, the same people who managed to identify Blackness in Dutch Black activists so as to apply racial stereotypes to them also claim Black people are divisive for claiming Blackness to empower themselves. This makes it risky for Black people to embrace solidarity through the adoption of the signifiers 'person of colour', and renders unacceptable the identification of non-Black people as 'politically Black'. When Black people and non-Black people are homogenised into a single category based on sameness this can potentially serve to hide and/or deny anti-Blackness. The fantasy in which non-Black people of colour are unable to oppress Black people is upheld by ignoring the lived experience of Black people who have structurally experienced anti-Blackness from non-Black people of colour. It means choosing sameness, at the expense of difference (not a very intersectional approach). Forced sameness is divisive: it forms an impediment to solidarity between different people of colour.

This perspective is a world away from the accusations of divisiveness which non-Black people of colour have used to centre themselves and derail the efforts of the Black womxn who staged the intervention. During the reflection and online discussions we encountered the same difficulties explaining our demand that Black people, and not just Black thought in the form of texts, be valued. It's not that this is a particularly complex position, especially not for academics whose professional activities see them work through much more complex ideas on a regular basis. Rather, the reflection on anti-Blackness in the academy which J. Tizora initiated – specifically as a Black woman without institutional status – was used as an alibi to entertain and a vehicle in which to propose other unrelated criticisms that implied that the intervention was an act of oppression towards non-Black womxn of colour in the space. Following Bilge's act of solidarity, there was an immediate response from several audience members representing our description of Bilge as white-passing as a hostile and insulting act. Before we knew it, we found ourselves in a debate about whether it is possible for non-Black womxn of colour to appropriate and erase Black womxn (to which we would say, yes[23]) and whether a distinction should be made between non-Black womxn of colour and Black womxn in this discussion in the first place (we find these distinctions are necessary in order to address the specific experiences of anti-Black racism).

By far the most effectively derailing question was an extensive discussion on who can claim Blackness. This is certainly not an unimportant or simple question. However, considering Bilge's lecture drew heavily and explicitly on Afro-pessimism, in this particular context the Blackness being discussed self-evidently coincided with being of African descent and historically racialised as 'Black'. That we moved from a discussion about Black womxn being exploited to a discussion as to whether non-Black people of colour might be excluded from a claim to Blackness was deeply problematic. This constitutes a complete refusal to acknowledge the context-specific definition of Blackness which flows from Bilge's lecture topic. Our experience has been that questions about who is and isn't Black are important – but they are simply not what require our focus in this case. Especially not when the non-Black womxn of colour in question are showing they know, to a large extent, who is Black through their use of anti-Black stereotypes. Effectively, accusations of race essentialism, divisiveness and sectarianism have served to move attention away from the anti-Blackness perpetrated against Black womxn.

At this point we find it important to draw attention not just to how anti-Blackness has been perpetrated and simultaneously denied, but that our engagement has been primarily with non-Black womxn of colour in academia. Why is this significant? We believe that the reason we underestimated the amount of anti-Blackness that would emerge in response to the intervention is linked to the investment people who claim to do anti-racist work have in the university. By adopting politics which reject difference, obscure anti-Blackness and require a fantasy level playing field (in the form of implicit or explicit insistence on political Blackness) which refuses to recognise anti-Blackness, they seem to endorse a technocratic and thus a hierarchical vision of who can be an expert in anti-racism. Consider that the Black thought currently being appropriated by many non-Black academics is the foundation of their professional reputation as critical and knowledgeable experts on racism. The lived experiences of anti-Blackness which lead to the formulation of critical Black theory are dismissed as irrelevant. This creates the illusion that anyone who experiences any kind of racism can and should understand and relate to these works in the same way. If we then take into account (1) the exclusion of Black womxn from the academy, and (2) the erasure of their lived experiences in the name of solidarity, it becomes clear that in a context that requires academic technical expertise a Black womxn cannot be recognised as an expert on critical Black theory in the Netherlands where institutions like the university hold a monopoly on expertise. The fact that Black womxn who have experienced anti-Blackness and misogynoir find themselves unsupported by non-Black womxn of colour who claim to represent Black womxn's interests but find the articulation of anti-Blackness acceptable only when coming from Bilge as a non-Black academic (barring Bilge herself) speaks volumes about the anti-Blackness this situation breeds.

This collusion which took place between anti-Black womxn of colour and the university as an anti-Black institution repeats itself outside the walls of the institutions on activist platforms. The privileging of anti-racist activists like Miriyam Aouragh[24] with academic credentials over those with lived experience is in our view a great obstacle to doing justice to the work and sacrifices of Black womxn for anti-racism. In her article she assumes Black activists are ignorant and uneducated, and have not read or heard about the texts, authors or collectives mentioned by Bilge. Never mind that her article is evidence that having read all of these texts does not mean one can make a critical analysis that does right by the Black people whose lived experience of anti-Blackness is affirmed by these texts. Is Black lived experience only valid in activism when expressed through this canon composed by Aouragh, herself a non-Black woman of colour? She wrongly posits that Dutch Black activists are uncritically copying outdated race theory and practice from the United States. Her article wrongly describes Black and decolonial activists as dismissive of class. In general, the piece wrongly claims Black activists are too obsessed with identity and thus do not fight structural racism. Black activists are accused of being so ignorant that we cannot see that we are pushing away our 'allies'. As if to say: if only Black people embraced a class analysis, then they wouldn't be excluding white people and non-Black people of colour. Perhaps surprisingly, this piece uses Black thought to stereotype Black people and critique the Black activism which some white people and non-Black people of colour experience as divisive. Ironically, despite its claim that Dutch Black activists lack a perspective on class it shows many signs of academic elitism. It is made inaccessible with a dose of academic jargon and references. In addition, it is effectively a rejection of intersectional thinking – just because white people are racist to all people of colour doesn't mean that non-Black people of colour don't have some serious work to do on their anti-Blackness. When this anti-Blackness shows, it is usually Black womxn and femmes who take the risk of standing up for themselves and other Black people to demand that we be heard when we speak for ourselves, that we are credited, involved and otherwise respected. This is a structural critique, part of a holistic vision which critically analyses how a broad range of power structures interact and manifest. It is not right to reduce this to 'white privilege theory', or to blame a supposed lack of perspective on class. We must be able to point out anti-Blackness and misogynoir when it manifests without then being blamed for not only being divisive and assuming some kind of supe-riority, but also being made responsible for the weakness of anti-racist politics and policy as a whole in the Netherlands. How can Black people be blamed for being wary of 'allies' when people demand thankfulness without being able to accept critique or accountability?

CONCLUSIONS: #NOTYOURMULE

Honey, de white man is de ruler of everything as fur as Ah been able tuh find out. Maybe it's some place way off in de ocean where de black man is in power, but we don't know nothin' but what we see ... De nigger woman is de mule uh de world so fur as Ah can see.[25]

#NotYourMule first arose on Twitter in 2016 in the aftermath of #Oscars-SoWhite which sought to point out the lack of diversity and representation at the Academy Awards and more broadly in Hollywood. After #Oscars-SoWhite gained attention, its creator April D. Ryan – a Black woman – received criticism from non-Black people of colour for not being 'inclusive' enough and not reflecting the lack of representation of Asian and Latinx Americans. This eventually sparked the creation of another hashtag: #NotYourMule. Ryan explained that the hashtag was an indict-ment of non-Black people of colour who don't act in solidarity with Black people, but still want the rewards of the labour of the Black activist. It seems that many expect Black womxn to do the labour for everyone else.

This idea of Black womxn as the mules of the world comes from Zora Neale Hurston's *Their Eyes Were Watching God*. In this novel, *the mule* symbolises the position of Black womxn in the world. Hurston depicts the Black womxn as carrying the burdens of the world. It would appear that not much has changed since the book was published in 1937 when it comes to our expectations of Black womxn. The Black womxn can never be *a Black womxn*. What was made painfully clear during the intervention and its aftermath was that the actual lives and thought of Black womxn were of no importance, as the experiences from which they derived is all too willingly dismissed when represented by the Black womxn in the room who shared their lived experiences, talked about how they were excluded and expressed their anger. Our specific grief, agony and hardships are not acknowledged as having their specificity. A Black womxn can never be a Black woman, she is not allowed to be a living being, aware of her own condition and position in the world, and create a meaning for herself. Whatever she does is for others, she is always in the service of others. In her struggle, she carries everyone. She is not a Black womxn, she is a mule.

What was significant was not only what happened during the event on 15 December, but also the reactions from certain non-Black womxn in the aftermath. The Black womxn who spoke up were met with criticism and disapproval by both white womxn and non-Black womxn of colour before, during and after the event, with people asking why the Black womxn were so angry. They said to not understand why a non-Black woman of colour would not be qualified to speak on Black feminism. After all, Bilge was a woman of colour, which to them meant that she was a natural ally to Black womxn. All of the sophisticated and critical responses to them by Black womxn both during the event and in online discussions were seemingly dismissed. Black womxn were accused of being divisive, of 'mobbing' a woman of colour and breaking up the solidarity that should exist between 'womxn of colour'.

In our view, the concerns of Black womxn were simply not taken seriously. Black feminist critiques, our anger, is only interesting when it's comfortable, and when it can be co-opted. Instead, non-Black womxn of colour were being centred, which ironically further erases Black womxn. Black womxn were expected to show solidarity to people who were not prepared to return the favour or hear our concerns and needs. Who were not prepared to hear the agony that they did not share and had themselves contributed to, they refused to listen to its rhythms and learn within it.[26] We should let go of our grief, not use our anger, for the sake of unity, they said. At the same time Black womxn were being told about what kind of Black radical politics was and wasn't acceptable. Theirs supposedly wasn't about solidarity, neither was it international or intersectional, as the politics of Malcolm X, Fanon and the Combahee River Collective amongst others had been. They had their own reading of them, a decontextualised one, even though these were all theorists and leaders who spoke explicitly about the lived Black experience, and formulated their ideas from these experiences. Now Black womxn were critiqued for speaking on theirs. It was as if to say that some expressions of the lived experiences of Black people are valid, and others are not.

And they, non-Black people, could be the judge of that. And of course they had the correct reading and interpretation of these acceptable Black lived experiences. Their unwillingness to listen to the critiques of Black womxn, to properly engage with them and the ease with which they dismissed them when they became uncomfortable, show the self-serving nature of their interest in Black radical thought. As Audre Lorde noted, 'Black women are expected to use our anger only in the service of other people's salvation or learning.' And just as Lorde, today's Black womxn proclaim that that time is over, for we are not mules.[27]

NOTES

1. We choose to use the trans-inclusive term womxn to emphasise the autonomy of womxn. We wish to break with the patriarchal and binary dependent relationship of the term 'women' to 'men'. For more information, see Sampaguitagxrl, 2013. 'I don't know what hxstory books you're reading ...'. Sampaguita Gxrl, 5 September. www.sampaguitagxrl.tumblr.com/post/60343 395890/i-dont-know-what-hxstory-books-youre-reading/ (accessed 13 February 2019).

2. 'antiblack'. Dictionary.com Unabridged. Random House, Inc., 6 May 2018. Dictionary.com www.dictionary.com/browse/antiblack (accessed 13 February 2019).

3. Jared Sexton, 2017. Interview by Daniel Colucciello Barber. 'On Black negativity or the affirmation of nothing'. *Society and Space*, 18 September. www.societyandspace.org/2017/09/18/on-black-negativity-or-the-affirma-tion-of-nothing/ (accessed 13 February 2019).

4. Egbert Alejandro Martina, 2014. 'On the containment of Blackness in Dutch anti-racist organizing'. *Processed Life*, 23 May. https://processedlives. wordpress.com/2014/05/23/on-the-containment-of-blackness-in-dutch-anti-racist-organizing/#more-1853/ (accessed 13 February 2019, emphases added).

5. 'This focusing upon our own oppression is embodied in the concept of identity politics. We believe that the most profound and potentially most radical politics come directly out of our own identity, as opposed to working to end somebody else's oppression. In the case of Black women this is a particularly repugnant, dangerous, threatening, and therefore revolutionary concept because it is obvious from looking at all the political movements that have preceded us that anyone is more worthy of liberation than ourselves.' Keeanga-Yamahtta Taylor, 2017. *How We Get Free: Black Feminism and the Combahee River Collective*. Haymarket Books, Chicago, p. 19.

6. Ibid.

7. Ibid.

8. 'The Trouble With Post-Black Feminist Intersectionality'. Amsterdam Research Centre for Gender and Sexuality. www.arcgs.uva.nl/content/events/lectures/2017/dec/bilge.html/ (accessed 13 February 2019).

9. Ibid.

10. Ibid.

11. universityofcolour, 2015. 'The international call for decolonization'. The University of Colour, 28 March. www.universityofcolour.com/post/1148 89477328/the-international-call-for-decolonization (accessed 13 February 2019).

12. Diversity Committee, 2016. 'Diversity Committee presents final report "Let's do diversity"'. University of Amsterdam, 12 October. www.uva.nl/en/content/news/news/2016/10/diversity-committee-presents-final-report.html/ (accessed 13 February 2019).

13. Essed and Nimako show this move away is actually a common practice in the Netherlands and was cemented when the board of the University of Amsterdam, under pressure from white scholars, closed the Centre for Race and Ethnic Studies (CRES) after just five short years. Philomena Essed and Kwame Nimako, 2006. 'Designs and (co)incidents cultures of scholarship and public policy on immigrants/minorities in the Netherlands'. *International Journal of Comparative Sociology* 47(3–4), pp. 281–312 (p. 291). CRES was an institute with a Black director and 'staff, faculty and affiliates consisting of a mix of different racial, ethnic and majority populations, a degree of gender and race-ethnic integration that, to date, has not found its match in another university institute in the Netherlands' (ibid.). Also see Kwame Nimako, 2012. 'About Them, But Without Them: Race and ethnic relations studies in Dutch universities'. *Human Architecture: Journal of the Sociology of Self-Knowledge* 10(1), Article 6, pp. 46–7. Ahead Publishing House. www.scholarworks.umb.edu/humanarchitecture/vol10/iss1/6 (accessed 10 May 2018). Since the closing of CRES and stimulated through much government funding, the – what Nimako termed –'About Them, But Without Them' way of doing research (p. 47), which started in the 1960s according to Prins, is upheld within as well as outside of academia. Baukje Prins, 2000. *Voorbij de Onschuld: Het Debat over de Multiculturele Samenleving* (Beyond the Innocence: The Debate about the Multicultural Society). Van Gennep, Amsterdam, p. 12.

14. Hélène Christelle, 2017. A text post describing the instrumentalisation of academia and exploitation of Black women's labour. Facebook, 15 December. www.facebook.com/events/529983747382196/permalink/538115529 902351/ (accessed 29 March 2018).

15. Political Blackness is understood here as a political signifier which can be claimed by anyone who experiences structural racism. See Uvanney Maylor, 2009. 'What is the meaning of "black"? Researching "black" respondents'. *Ethnic and Racial Studies* 32(2), pp. 369–72.

16. University of Colour (Awethu! et al.), 2018. 'From the hollow of the lion: A testimony of revolt at the University of Amsterdam'. In *Smash the Pillars:*

Decoloniality and the Imaginary of Color in the Dutch Kingdom (Decolonial Options for the Social Sciences). Lexington Books, Maryland, pp. 17–29.

17. Sirma Bilge, 2017. 'The Trouble With Post-Black Feminist Intersectionality'. Amsterdam Research Centre for Gender and Sexuality, 15 December. University of Amsterdam Roeterseilandcampus.

18. Barbara Christian, 1994. 'Diminishing returns: Can Black feminism(s) survive the academy?' In Gloria Bowles, M. Giulia Fabi and Arlene R. Keizer (eds), *New Black Feminist Criticism, 1985–2000*. Reprinted 2007. University of Illinois Press, Champaign, pp. 204–15.

19. Miriyam Aouragh, 2018. 'De Beperkingen Van Wit Privilege: Shortcuts in De Antiracisme Strijd'. *Socialisme.nu*, 4 March. www.socialisme.nu/blog/nieuws/54983/de-beperkingen-van-wit-privilege-shortcuts-in-de-antiracisme-strijd/ (accessed 13 February 2019). Heidi Dorudi, 2018. '"Wit", "bruin", "zwart": huidskleur of politieke identiteit?' *dorudi*, 23 April. www.dorudi.nl/wit-bruin-zwart-huidskleur-politieke-identiteit/. Jazie Veldhuyzen, 2018. 'You can't have capitalism without racism'. *Republiek Allochtonië*, 2 April. www.republiekallochtonie.nl/blog/opinie/you-can-t-have-capitalism-without-racism/ (accessed 13 February 2019).

20. Misogynoir describes 'the anti-Black racist misogyny that Black women experience'. Moya Bailey and Trudy Bailey, 2018. 'On misogynoir: Citation, erasure, and plagiarism'. *Feminist Media Studies*, 18(4), pp. 1–7.

21. Almass Badat, 2016. 'How to tackle anti-Blackness as a non-Black PoC'. *Gal-Dem*, 7 June. www.gal-dem.com/anti-blackness-poc-communities/ (accessed 13 February 2019).

22. Aouragh, 'De Beperkingen Van Wit Privilege'.

23. Ann Phoenix, 1998. '(Re)constructing gendered and ethnicised identities: Are We all Marginal Now?' Ann Phoenix inaugural lecture, University for Humanist Studies Utrecht.

24. Aouragh, 'De Beperkingen Van Wit Privilege'.

25. Zora Neale Hurston, 1991. *Their Eyes Were Watching God*. University of Illinois Press, Champaign, p. 19. Originally published 1937.

26. Audre Lorde, 2007. 'Uses of anger: Women responding to racism'. In *Sister Outsider: Essays and Speeches*. Crossing Press, Trumansburg, NY. Print, p. 132.

27. Ibid.

15

Creating a Space Within the German Academy

Melody Howse

SCENES FROM A GERMAN CLASSROOM

There are spaces both physical and metaphysical in which as you enter, you realise that you do not belong. Frantz Fanon in 'The Fact of Blackness' describes how a child on a train points him out as Black. As the child grows in distress, Fanons' awareness of his body becomes both heightened and dislocated, 'fixed' by the 'atmosphere of certain uncertainty'.[1] There have been many times in my life when I have felt this sensation of being stuck, aware of my every movement and the difference of my being. It is a sensation that always surprises and shocks but somehow fades and becomes forgotten. That is until you and your difference are thrown once again into sharp relief by the environment you find yourself in.

I moved to Berlin in 2010, having previously lived in London for 15 years. London is and was an inspiring city but my work in commercial broadcasting was eating my soul and Berlin with its slow pace offered a place of rehabilitation. I needed a chance to re-collect the parts of myself that the relentless rhythm of London life had scattered to the winds. Having never completed higher education further than a Bachelors, I decided that this was the time to continue my education and found myself drawn to visual anthropology, it seemed like the best fit for my eclectic background in art, journalism and filmmaking. Being back at university was inspiring, I felt myself grow and I was happy. I devoured the readings we were set and sought out other texts. The more I read the more it dawned on me what kind of discipline I had joined. I read works that categorised Black and indigenous populations as biologically incapable of being equal to the 'white race' and writings by great scholars such as Bronislaw Malinowski whose method of participant observation is intrinsic to the foundation of the modern discipline, but whose personal diary revealed his disdain for the people who had allowed him to live on their land and to participate in his research. In his private thoughts they were just 'niggers' that he was dying to get away from.[2]

As my knowledge grew so did my realisation that I was literally 'matter out of place',[3] a body in a space where it did not historically belong. The moment from which I cannot return from seems small in comparison to the painful revelations that I was uncovering through my study, but it was the moment from which something necessary came. I sat in our small dark classroom with our lecturer at the front showing us a selection of ethnographic images that were in some way all problematic. Perhaps it was the compound effect of seeing so many objectified black and brown bodies, but as he started to talk about an image called the 'Boomerang Throwers' (1884) by R.A Cunningham,[4] of three aboriginal people, a man, woman and child (known as *Billy, Jenny and little Toby*) who were taken from Australia and forced to participate in a travelling exhibition – a human zoo, something inside me started to burn ... first my skin, then my ears. I started to tremble, my hands unable to lie still and then my heart started beating faster and faster in my chest. As I became fixed in space, hyper-aware of my body and my presence, the lecturer continued to talk about the man in the image, continually referring to him as a 'performer', inferring that he was a willing participant in this human circus. The fact is that 'Billy' was not a 'performer' with the freedom to choose when and where he performed. He had been enslaved along with countless other men, women and children so that he could be taken across the world and exhibited as the 'lowest order of man' (this wording is taken directly from the 1884 exhibition pamphlet). Much of this was omitted from the lecture and the innocuous word 'performer' was used as a blanket covering up the reality of the situation in which these three people had been forced. I had to question how and why we were being shown images of enslaved peoples from the time of colonial anthropology without much critique and presented in a way that denied their lived reality. As I tried to calm myself, I looked around the room looking instinctively for support. I was one of the few people of colour there. I was also the only one, to my knowledge, descended from enslaved people.

The dishonest narrative used by my lecturer was a betrayal to the people in those images and as I sat there I found the words to challenge him, bringing a halt to his use of the term 'performer' and making everyone aware that what we were looking at were not simply 'neutral' or 'apolitical' images. These were the testaments that remained of a people forcibly taken from their homes and treated like animals. I am proud of my heritage: I am a fourth generation descendant from Nigerian and Cameroonian enslaved people who were brought to the Caribbean. I can never know their story, only the parts that remain as myths within my own family and what lies in my blood, a sanguine history that carries more than just origin. There is a study that shows how trauma can leave a kind of scar on DNA and how this marker can be passed on for generations, influencing our predispositions and sensitivity to stress,[5] illustrating another way that historical and traumatic events not only shape our family tree but also how we develop and respond to the world. It made me think of a healer I once heard from New Orleans who spoke about how our ancestors communicate through our bodies and senses, how an intense reaction or an unfamiliar sensation could also be a way that your past is communicating with your present.

No matter the scientific validity of this notion, in Black literature and most recently in the book *Homegoing* by Ghanaian-American author Yaa Gyasi,[6] this idea of ancestral communication, traces of the past affecting the present are ways in which those of us with forcibly dislocated histories are able to imagine ourselves as whole. I like to think that my reaction in that class was a message from my own past for me to wake up and do something, to not sit by and watch the stories of the lives of countless enslaved and subjugated peoples be taught as if slavery was a choice and colonialism wasn't a brutal force. The effects of the trans-Atlantic slave trade and impact of colonialism isn't something to be relegated to the past, we do not have to look far to see the effect it has all around us in every corner of the globe.

CURRICULUM IN THE GERMAN ACADEMY

My dissent in that German classroom became the spark for other small acts of resistance. First, I consciously included more Black and indigenous scholars in my academic work and educated myself outside of the curriculum. Through this self-directed study, I learned of the work of Sara Ahmed and Linda Tuhiwai Smith, both of whom have become very important to how I position myself in the academy and how I use the platform it provides. I also realised that I could not exist in this space alone, and that I needed support from other like-minded people. I reached out to Black feminist scholars in Europe and the USA and was amazed at the generosity I found in those I sought advice and mentorship from online. This virtual support then led to physical support as I looked for groups in Berlin who were tackling the questions that had become so present and immovable in my mind, and slowly I started to find other academics of colour in the city, many of whom were active in the decolonisation movements of the Berlin universities.

Within this newly discovered community of academics, I found an opportunity to effect a small change. A colleague of mine was developing a course on classic anthropological literature, but her curriculum consisted almost entirely of white men except for Margaret Mead and Ruth Benedict, two of the more famous female anthropologists. I enquired about the lack of women and suggested she include Zora Neale Hurston, who at the time she had never heard of. Hurston was the first Black female anthropologist and arguably the first visual anthropologist, she was not only a peer of Ruth Benedict and Margaret Mead but also a student of Franz Boas, known to many as the 'father of modern anthropology'. Her inclusion in the canon should have been automatic. When Mead and Benedict are included in a curriculum, although I am happy they are there, I often feel it is only as a grudging concession to the fact that women have always been instrumental in the social sciences. But never in Germany have I heard mention of Hurston in anthropology. Zora Neale Hurston was a pioneer whose work has influenced everything from literature, dance, documentary to theatre. Her legacy is endless but yet in Germany she remains largely in the shadows, adding to the narrative that Black scholars don't exist, a narrative that persists today in the proof that so few Black scholars are currently employed in European universities. The inclusion of Hurston is a small victory on the long road of decolonising the curriculum and shifting away from the rigid white patriarchal mode of knowledge production on which anthropology is built.

Germany has one of the largest gender pay gaps in Europe,[7] it is also a country where in 2017 the far-right are the third largest political party in the place I have chosen to be my home. The institutions of learning in this country are steeped in colonial history much of which remains unaddressed. Only recently are necessary public discussions about this history and its impact on the present starting to happen; in 2016 the Deutsche Historiches Museum held an exhibition 'dealing for the first time, with various aspects of German colonialism'.[8] It was a start, but for many did not go far enough in addressing the often downplayed role of Germany in the European colonial project. Although many institutions have been slow to face the past, there is an active base of scholars, artists and activists who have worked for decades to bring this history to light. One example was the installation of a memorial plaque in 1988 at the Otto Suhr Institute for Political Science in Berlin.[9] The building at the Freie Universität formerly known as the Kaiser Wilhelm Institute for Anthropology, Human Heredity, and Eugenics. Now the home of the Department of Political Science, between 1911 and 1945 it was an institute which conducted discredited race science and housed a collection of human remains taken from the German colonies to be studied in an attempt to manufacture and classify 'race' and justify white supremacy. The Otto Suhr memorial was made possible by years of tireless activism to make this deliberatively 'forgotten' history visible and is just one of the many small ways in which the academy is being challenged.

Stories of German activism rarely seem to make it outside of the country so I will take the opportunity to provide a few more examples. In 2015, the University of Bremen came under fire for its attempt to create a Black Studies Unit. The aim was to establish for the first time in the German humanities 'a platform for the interdisciplinary investigation of literary and visual practices and discourses of the Black Diaspora, and to create an international research network'.[10] It sounded promising and essential, but it was a deeply flawed proposal that was ultimately rejected. One of the first points of contestation was that the proposal had listed only white professors, post-doctoral researchers and graduate students as participants and architects of the working group. No scholars of colour from the university were apparently included, which begged the question as to why had they been excluded. The answer demonstrated the politics of knowledge employed by the all-white working group and re-affirmed the marginalisation of Black scholarship. The work of Black German scholars, according to the group, 'enjoy[ed] a very precarious visibility on the fringes of academic scholarship or outside of academic disciplines'.[11] Yet it failed to address why Black scholarship in Germany was marginalised and instead capitalised on the names of a few Black German scholars as prospective 'partners' while excluding their scholarly contributions to the field. Furthermore, it did not seem to occur to the working group that the setting up of a Black Studies Unit might be the opportunity to bring Black scholars from the margins to the centre. The voices of protest came from across Germany, Europe and the United

States and included many Black German scholars who now teach abroad, such as Fatima El-Tayeb and Daniel Kojo Schrade and political activists such as Angela Davis. In an open letter to the university protesting the composition of the Black Studies Unit, they stated that the unit

> reinforces the colonial model of expropriation: Black Germans can serve as the 'raw resource' or 'native informants' for White academics but are not permitted to act as scholars in their own right. White German academics and graduate students, however, stand poised to reap even more monetary and symbolic capital as part of the proposed Creative Unit.[12]

The protest in Bremen informed other similar protests and in 2016 saw echoes at the Freie Universität in Berlin. A lecture series was proposed on 'Climate Change in Africa' at the aforementioned Otto Suhr Institute.[13] Much like in Bremen this lecture series excluded African scholars. This omission, combined with the history of the building in which these lectures were to be held, proved damning. An opposition group was formed that consisted of activist scholars. Their agenda to this day is to decolonise the university. They achieve this not only through protest but by critically engaging in the curriculum and through creating spaces in the city of Berlin where those interested in changing the status quo have a space to speak, share ideas and to combine their efforts. It is in these institutional spaces steeped in colonial history and within a country that doesn't yet legally recognise Black people as an oppressed group that I find myself with a chance to add new voices to the hegemonic perspectives found so frequently within our universities.

CREATING A CONTESTED SPACE

Opportunities come when you least expect them and this one came after a failed PhD proposal. I was invited in for feedback and one of the questions I was asked by my potential PhD supervisor was why are stories of Black people often so negative and why couldn't they be more positive? I didn't quite know what to say. My work looks at the legacy of pain and fear which the state imposes on the Black body, via the visual collective narrative of disseminated videos of police violence against Black people and their effect on the subjectivity of the Black diaspora in Germany. It is an exploration of the historic and lingering perceptions of

Black people which we see played out in these daily and sometimes lethal encounters. Understanding these dynamics, between race, technology, affect and the racial imaginary is of critical importance, particularly in the context of the rise and normalisation of far-right politics and rhetoric. Black people's interactions with the police on both sides of the Atlantic are a collective narrative that shapes everyday interaction with lawmakers and institutions. Ignoring this for a more palatable inquiry into Black experience seems to willfully miss the point.

I felt disillusioned, but to my surprise the conversation proved productive and I was asked to create a course for the visual anthropology programme that would explore race and themes such as 'Critical Whiteness'. I am no expert in critical race theory nor am I a teacher, but I am a researcher and a woman of colour and as I have never had an educator who wasn't white, I knew I needed to take the chance to change that. It turned out to be what I had been looking for, a space to create a place for the difficult and necessary conversations around the discipline and our roles within it. It was also a chance to bring the work of indigenous and Black scholars into the curriculum and to challenge the dominant ethnographic narrative of the 'savage' and the 'primitive', narratives that are still used today. Being a novice I turned to bell hooks to seek advice on how to 'teach critical thinking'[14] and to the other women who had inspired my own work such as Deborah Willis at New York University, who created the first compendium of African American photographers *Reflections in Black*[15] showing work from 1840 to the present day. Her work provides an alternative visual narrative to what anthropologists and ethnologists were producing in the late 1800s, that of the anthropometric image of classic dehumanising anthropology. These alternative realities, representations and histories are what I try and show and debate with my students.

As serendipity would have it, the students who participate in the class have arrived at a perfect moment; they are in the temporally short window before going out to conduct their own fieldwork. It is in this time that they have a final opportunity to thoughtfully position themselves, instead of walking blindly into the field as so many do, unaware of the legacy and impact of our discipline and how research is rightly viewed by many communities as a negative force that should not be engaged. It is within the space that the course provides that I have tried to engender and nurture what I have called a 'vigilant epistemology', a way of knowing which strives not to reproduce knowledge through a colonial lens but a

knowledge system that is conscious of the structures of power and the relationships of power that exist between the researcher and the researched.
A vigilant epistemology considers the implications of research and how
it can be used 'in creating and maintaining a legally-codified system of
discrimination that [has] underpinned structural racism throughout
the 20th century'[16] and continues to do so. As bell hooks argues, 'in
these settings, thinking, and most especially critical thinking, is what
matters.'[17] Therefore, I encourage the students to interrogate their own
ideas and practices. This critical consciousness is not static, rather it is a
constant work in progress which as teachers, researchers and 'producers
of knowledge' we have a responsibility to maintain.

This class is also my contribution to the activism which started long
before me to 'decolonise the university.' It is a space where contested
histories and realities can be brought to light, discussed and explored.
My work in the classroom is an act of resistance, achieved using the tools
and platform that I have to 'interrupt' the way of teaching and learning
that has for so long denied the views of those of us who have been the
subject of research and classified as 'Other'.

EMERGING VOICES

It is from this sensation of being 'out of place', of not belonging, not recognising my own history and the experiences which have defined me and
my entire Black family, that provided the necessary rupture to attempt to
carve out a new space to exist within this academy. In other countries like
the United States, these spaces have existed for a long time within universities but only in 2016 was the first Black Studies course founded in
the United Kingdom at Birmingham City University. Here, in Germany,
there are few. Of note are the 'Black European Studies' programme at the
Johannes Gutenberg University Mainz and the creation of the first Black
Studies journal in Europe in 2014 entitled the *Black Studies Journal* from
the controversial Black Studies Unit at the University of Bremen.

Nevertheless, more conversations are happening and a talk I recently
attended about race, ethnicity and the 'anthropological responses to
contemporary challenges' brought up the familiar topic of the burden
of Black scholarship being a 'double bind', of having to focus on 'Black
issues' as they are not often the focus of White scholarship. I know many
people who feel this bind, even my sister who is an artist tells me in the
words of Reni Eddo-Lodge that she is tired of 'talking to White people

about race'.[18] But yet her artwork reflects and prompts these exact conversations that she may be tired of having, with the audience she is tired of having them with. It can be a complicated position for many of us, but it is not with reluctance or a feeling of burden that I attempt to effect change. It is because I desire to inscribe a history and a way of seeing that resonates and represents the denied and ignored reality of being a woman and a person of colour and yes, I am tired of being told my place in the world through a colonial lens which has only seen me and my ancestors as a commodity and as a source of labour extraction, but never as a human.

Thankfully I know I am not alone. Across Europe there are many new spaces emerging as more of us strive to bring our own and other marginalised perspectives into the disciplines we have chosen, just as I am trying to within Anthropology. We all have a part to play, never more so than now as the work that has been done before us is under threat through the racially divisive politics of the past decade. We find ourselves in a time where once again, racial inequality in many of its invisible forms has gained critical visibility and we need to use the amplification this clarity provides to make more of our voices heard.

NOTES

1. Fanon, F., 2000. 'The fact of Blackness'. In L. Back and J. Solomos (eds), *Theories of Race and Racism, a Reader*. Routlege, London; New York, p. 258.
2. B. Malinowski, 1989. *A Diary in the Strict Sense of the Term*. 2nd edition. Routledge, London.
3. M. Douglas, 1988. *'Purity and Danger': An Analysis of the Concepts of Pollution and Taboo*. Routledge, London; New York, p. 36.
4. R.A. Cunningham, 1992. 'Boomerang throwers'. In E. Edwards (ed.), *Anthropology & Photography 1860–1920*. Yale University Press, New Haven; London, p. 52.
5. R. Yehuda, N.P. Daskalakis, L.M. Bierer, H.N. Bader, T. Klengel, F. Holsboer and E.B. Binder, 2015. 'Holocaust exposure induced intergenerational effects on FKBP5 methylation'. *Biological Psychiatry*, September, p. 373.
6. Y. Gyasi, 2016. *Homegoing*. Penguin Random House, London.
7. 'Gender pay gap in Germany decreasing very slowly'. https://tinyurl.com/y78gwrdx (accessed 22 January 2018).
8. 'German colonialism, fragments past and present'. https://tinyurl.com/yaqso7go (accessed 22 January 2018).
9. Ihnestrasse 22, The Kaiser Wilhelm Institute for Anthropology, Human Heredity, and Eugenics. https://tinyurl.com/ydedwcfx (accessed 22 January 2018).

10. 'Community Statement: 'Black' studies at the University of Bremen'. https://tinyurl.com/y6u5wf96 (accessed 22 January 2018).
11. Ibid.
12. Ibid.
13. 'Decolonize the FU – Ringvorelsung, Klimawandel in Afrika'. https://tinyurl.com/y87dcscj (accessed 22 January 2018).
14. b. hooks, 2010. *Teaching Critical Thinking, Practical Wisdom*. Routledge, London.
15. D. Willis, 2000. *Reflections in Black*. Norton, New York; London.
16. R. Anderson, 'The social role of anthropology's racist uncle'. https://tinyurl.com/y9etf6cz (accessed 22 January 2018).
17. hooks, *Teaching Critical Thinking*.
18. R. Eddo-Lodge, 2017. *Why I'm No Longer Talking to White People about Race*. Bloomsbury, London.

16

A Manifesto for Survival

Sadiah Qureshi

Academia is pale, male and stale. We all ought to know this, but few of us are familiar with the figures that starkly illustrate the profound marginalisation of women, people of colour and Blackness within British academia.[1] Statistics make the whiteness and overall dominance of men in academia immediately obvious: 86.9 per cent of all staff are 'White', including 55.3 per cent women, while only 13.1 per cent are 'Black and Minority Ethnic' (BME).[2] Disaggregating even this small fraction reveals significant variation between ethnicities: the biggest 'BME' group is 'Asian' at 40.3 per cent, only 18.6 per cent of staff are 'Black', 16.6 per cent are 'Chinese', 14.1 per cent are 'Mixed' and 1.3 per cent are defined as 'other'.[3] The age profile of BME staff reveals that there are very few nearing retirement, most are in the middle, but far fewer younger people are entering academia. Only 30 BME academic staff across the country hold positions defined as 'Managers, directors and senior officials'. Such disparities continue to concentrate power and decision-making in the hands of traditionally privileged white men and do little to truly integrate a broader range of identities into academic life and governance.

The United Kingdom has almost 19,000 professors compared to just over 170,000 non-professors. Just over 9 out of 10 UK professors are white, with 67.5 per cent white men, 22.9 per cent white women and 9.6 per cent BME people. Of the 1,820 BME professors in UK academia only 400 are women making up just 2.1 per cent of the overall professoriate. There are only 120 Black professors in the United Kingdom including only 25 women. These abysmal figures are not just an issue of professional prestige, but one of financial security. Among UK academic staff, BME staff earn 2.2 per cent less on average than their white colleagues. Among professional and support staff the gap is even larger, with UK BME staff earning 3 per cent less. The disparities are even more pronounced for non-UK staff. Non-UK BME academic staff earn 12 per cent less while non-UK professional and support staff earn 12.6 per cent less than their

white colleagues. These figures suggest that the overwhelming benefi-
ciaries of white men losing ground have been white women and they are
far from being on an equal footing.

What can we do? In this chapter, I want to focus on learning to
recognise and challenge oppression, being self-reflexive, surviving
and, when possible, thriving within the context of marketised higher
education institutions that are still dominated by patriarchal whiteness.[4]

We can begin with rejecting the assumption that people either are
or aren't prejudiced, whether we mean in relation to race, sex, gender,
sexuality, class, age, religion, nationality, disability or any other kind
of oppression and their intersecting impacts. This makes it too easy
to think of some individuals, possibly ourselves, as immune from all
prejudice and others wholly responsible. More importantly, it overlooks
the fact that prejudice operates along a spectrum, not as a discrete
presence or absence, but as something fluid and shifting. We're all sus-
ceptible to broader social influences, including prejudice. We do not
suddenly become immune to the potentially oppressive nature of these
social and cultural influences when we enter a campus, lecture theatre
or laboratory, even if we are encouraged to think of ourselves as unfal-
tering 'objective' beings in these spaces.[5] This means taking on the task
of self-reflection, recognising our position within structures of power
and acting accordingly.[6] Everyone would benefit from thinking about
how they can foster positive and inclusionary patterns of behaviour in
themselves and others. Once we accept that change requires the labour
of everyone, the burden can be distributed and lightened particularly for
those most likely to carry it.

When reflecting on these issues, I formulated the following advice for
myself (italics below). I never intended these short, sharp cues for publication but would pore over them when I was trying to remind myself
of effective strategies and the reasons why they worked. In the spirit of
lightening burdens, I share my reminders with you.

EXIST. RECOGNIZE. RESIST. ORGANIZE.
INSIST. DECOLONIZE. PERSIST[7]

*Exist and occupy space in the places from which others seek to exclude your
kind. Sometimes the sheer fact of your existence can make a difference to
those in your wake or at your side.*

Statistics illuminate the stark inequalities embedded within academia, but they can only hint at the everyday lives of the marginalised within academia. Making such experiences visible is an important way of challenging marginalisation, both for ourselves and those around us.

I am often asked for advice on how to enter academia by students and people considering a change of career. Many of them are unsure of how to secure funding, what qualifications they will need or the processes involved in applying to courses.[8] Everyone is nervous about different aspects when making these choices, from personal confidence to the resources they have available. In my experience, Black and South Asian people, especially women, are particularly interested in knowing what it is like to be *myself* in academia. By this they usually mean my *brown* self, and occasionally my *hijabi* self, in overwhelmingly white spaces. Such questions are often directly prompted by the task of navigating institutions where they cannot recognise their own identities well represented among staff. Such conversations are some of the most important experiences I've had in academia.

Several years ago, I met a young South Asian woman studying in Cambridge where I studied some years earlier. She found the institution a difficult place to inhabit and knew of my work because it was assigned reading on her course. She said that she had once held my book in her hands and told herself that if I could be successful in that environment, then she could also make it. I could so easily never have known of this act. It would be easy to characterise this an example of someone senior making a difference to a student, but it also made an indelible impression on me. Moments like these are too rare, but they are sustaining through difficult times. I was astonished; and yet, I have done the same with my own admiration of many Black and South Asian professors, especially women and those in my discipline, because their existence highlights what is possible, no matter how unlikely. Role models are especially important given their scarcity and recent professional recognition. After all, the first women of colour to become professors within British universities were Heidi S. Mirza and Lola Young. When I learned that they had been appointed to chairs only in 1998, I realised that there had never been a female professor of colour within British academia when I became an undergraduate.[9]

When we are the first to achieve particular kinds of success, whether in our families, institutions or communities, it may be obvious that we will make a difference to those following. Recognising how our existence affects others is powerful. However, we must not forget that being the first or even knowing someone personally isn't necessary to secure lasting change. Meaningful transformation often comes when the second, tenth and even the hundredth person sharing our identity achieve the same success and with fewer obstacles, whether that's among our juniors, peers or seniors. In this climate, it is especially important to create and maintain a sense of solidarity between Black women and other women of colour in a collective effort that unites us across Europe.

Recognise structural violence, pay attention to power relations and reflect upon the assumptions that such inequality is predicated upon. People in power will always protect their position as they reproduce the structures that benefited them.

Structural violence was originally defined as indirect violence 'built into the structure' that 'shows up an unequal power and consequently as unequal life chances'; thus, from its inception, recognising structural violence was rooted in making 'social injustice' visible.[10] More recently, Kimberlé W. Crenshaw's theory of intersectionality is helpful both in learning to discern structures and as a means of ensuring that new policies remain alert enough to difference to create truly equitable effects. Although the term has become common, it is worth revisiting Crenshaw's original work and reflecting on her insistence that she is not seeking to provide a 'totalising theory of identity'. Instead, she seeks to transcend identity politics that ignore 'intragroup differences'. For instance, she argues that the

> failure of feminism to interrogate race means that the resistance strategies of feminism will often replicate and reinforce the subordination of people of colour, and the failure of antiracism to interrogate patriarchy means the antiracism will frequently reproduce the subordination of women. These mutual elisions present a particularly difficult political dilemma for women of colour.[11]

Crenshaw's original work focused on race and gender, but she pointed out the broader possibilities of intersectionality for addressing class and her work has laid the foundation for even broader discussions of identity such as sexuality and disability.

Advantages in academia can be accrued in numerous ways. Some of the most obvious privileges include knowing people who have been to university unlike those who might be the first in their family, attending and working at elite institutions with large endowments versus less prestigious and financially secure institutions, having sufficient personal funds to survive on a temporary contract until one can secure a permanent job, not taking career breaks due to maternity leave or sick leave and caring duties, forgetting that early career researchers are often saddled with enormous student loan repayments while international colleagues are forced to pay extortionate visa fees to the Home Office as it appeases the worst elements of an electorate obsessed with immigration.[12] I have focused on race, class and gender specifically within academia here, but there are many ways in which systemic inequalities can affect our prospects. By paying attention to the different ways in which multiple factors can make us vulnerable to structural violence, we are better placed to both acknowledge differences and constructively address their needs. Refusing to engage with the structural violence embedded within the academy allows it to be reproduced. By learning to recognise and challenge such systemic disparities we keep ourselves focused on achieving broader social justice.

Resist the gas-lighting of your experience. Meet micro-aggressions with micro-resistance and remember even the humblest of beginnings can bring unexpected effects.

In 2015, the University and College Union (UCU) surveyed its 'Black and Minority Ethnic staff' to understand their experiences of working in further and higher education. The subsequent report is shocking: 52 per cent of respondents within further and higher education 'did not see a positive future for their career with their current employer' and 7/10 respondents reported that 'they were "often" or "sometimes" subject to bullying and harassment by managers' while 68 per cent reported the same from their colleagues; 86 per cent of those working in higher education reported that 'they were "often" or "sometimes"' subject to cultural insensitivity, with 73 per cent reporting the same in further education; 90 per cent of respondents within further and higher education felt that they had 'faced barriers to promotion'.[13]

In this environment, it is especially important that the racially marginalised feel able to express their experiences. Yet, as Sara Ahmed observes,

'Race equality as a positive duty can translate into an institutional duty for BME staff not to dwell on "negative experiences" of racism.'[14] It's understandable why people want to focus entirely on the positive: dwelling on problems can take its toll and be overwhelming. Advances have been made: nonetheless, rather than expecting people to be satisfied or grateful for *some* improvements, we ought to measure ourselves against the truly equitable future we dream about, not the known and profound inequalities of the past. If we only ever use the often exceptionally low standards of the past to calibrate our progress, then we risk becoming complacent and failing to acknowledge the work that remains. Insisting that the marginalised always remain positive makes discrimination significantly harder to talk about and less perceptible.

Likewise, insisting that colleagues who raise concerns about discrimination only do so in particular tones is an attempt to control how the oppressed express and protest their oppression. It is rooted in the false promise that studying harder, speaking politely, working in a respectable profession and not complaining will outrun racism.[15] Asking the oppressed for solutions unfairly transfers the burden of securing change onto people who are already bearing too much. For those suffering, even small acts of resistance can bring benefits because they are conscious refusals to allow someone else to determine one's response. It's very easy to think of resistance solely in terms of grand gestures, but smaller refusals have their place especially for someone trying to build confidence. From saying 'I prefer not to' or 'no' to yet another request for unpaid labour, only answering emails during regular working hours and when you've had time to digest the contents rather than immediately, to connecting with broader communities sharing your identity and politics through hashtags such as #readmorewomen and #blackgirlmagic, every step matters.

Organise, individually and collectively, to build communities that support each other.

Systemic problems require collective effort. In a recent *Guardian* investigation, it was found that only 36 people from BME groups were amongst the 1,000 most powerful people in Britain and only 23 per cent were women. This 'snowy peak' is obvious in the government, the military, the press, the legal profession and universities.[16] On the social implications Kalwant Bhopal argued: 'White privilege often operates as a form of self-legitimising power in higher education. It reinforces, protects and perpetuates its own sense of eliteness. The same sorts of people from the same elite universities set the ground rules for who will and won't succeed.'[17] This self-perpetuation maintains an unjust status quo and requires collective resistance. After all, solidarity can never be taken for granted, rather it must be created and maintained.[18]

There are many ways to build communities around ourselves and to contribute to broader efforts. Reading the work of our forerunners and peers can help us learn from a vast range of experience.[19] Social media can help forge links with other academics, activists and writers. At its best, it allows me to transcend the limitations of working within my institution, discipline and country to connect with an immense range of Black feminists that I would probably not otherwise encounter.[20] Likewise, there are impressive shared endeavours to which we can contribute. Publishing ventures such as Media Diversified and *gal-dem* magazine are creating new spaces for us to be published and it is important that academics contribute to such ventures. The IF project university-level arts and humanities summer courses are taught by academics who volunteer their time and expertise to students who would otherwise be unable to attend university. By contributing and supporting such ventures with social justice at their core, we can use our expertise and skills for personal and collective benefit.

Of course, many of us face challenges in contributing. The marketisation of British higher education brings greater demands on time and barriers. Some activists are calling for a return to 'slow scholarship' as a form of feminist resistance and thoughtful alternative to the idealised neoliberal academic.[21]

Insist on the recognition of your dignity. Self-care is a refusal to accept the burden of being worthless or worth less. Do not aid violence through silencing yourself of your kind.

Reading Claudia Rankine's *Citizen*, there were so many moments that I found my heart pounding and a knot in my stomach from uncanny recognition:

You take in things you don't want all the time. The second you hear or see some ordinary moment, all its intended targets, all the meanings behind the retreating seconds, as far as you are able to see, come into focus. Hold up, did you just hear, did you just say, did you just see, did you just do that? Then the voice in your head silently tells you to take your foot off your throat because just getting along shouldn't be an ambition.

Rankine's evocative words capture those moments when you have mere seconds to process an 'ordinary moment'. As Rankine notes, the physiological cost of trying to outrun 'the buildup of erasure' through achievement can be deadly.[22]

Given the impact of oppression, it is particularly important that we learn to draw boundaries, allow others a platform and care for ourselves. As Audre Lorde battled cancer, she wrote that 'Caring for myself is not self-indulgence, it is self-preservation, and that is an act of political warfare.' Forced to acknowledge her mortality, she finally accepted that she could not 'do anything' in favour of 'an open-eyed assessment and appreciation of what I can and do accomplish, using who I am and who I most wish myself to be'.[23] We are often taught that giving is good, but we are not necessarily taught how to set boundaries. Critics argue that too often self-indulgence is said to be self-care; however, for too many the struggle comes in valuing self-care to begin with. Finding internal validation is essential within many walks of life but especially so for a career in academia. There are so many opportunities to be turned down and ostensibly 'fail', whether it's an article rejected by a journal or unfunded grant application. One of the most important ways to deal with this is to always give things a go but learn resilience in the face of 'no' or 'not this time'. I often advise colleagues to find value in their work independent of metrics and performance targets. Doing so means that, even when external recognition does not come, they can remain motivated by their personal values. I think this is particularly important for Black women and women of colour who can often feel as if they're swimming against the tide.[24]

Decolonise, reconfigure and rebuild rather than diversify and endorse the status quo. Consider who truly benefits from the changes you seek. Effective action requires changing the balance of power and building space for alternative ways of being. Remember inclusion is worthless if you are not valued, respected and safe as you are.

In *Living a Feminist Life*, Sara Ahmed beautifully observes some of the difficulties encountered by those doing 'diversity work'. She writes, 'If you are not white, not male, not straight, not cis, not able-bodied, you're more likely to end up on diversity and equality committees. The more nots you are, the more committees you might end up on.' The diversity workers she interviewed often described encountering, even hitting, 'brick walls' as institutions created new policies as proxies for meaningful structural change.[25] It is a feeling that is likely familiar to anyone doing diversity work.

With increased numbers of Black women and women of colour, there are more of us than ever, but mere numbers have not secured equality or equity. Audre Lorde's warning that 'The Master's Tools Will Never Dismantle the Master's House' remains pertinent.[26] Allowing institutions and individuals that are already powerful to determine how changes should be made will bring some diversity as some marginalised peoples are included. However, this cannot eliminate systemic obstacles because that requires changing the balance of power. Within academia, these debates have been become particularly pressing with the 'Rhodes Must Fall!'(RMF) and 'Why is my curriculum white?' protest movements.[27]

Departments may be diversifying the curriculum through adding a few alternative writers and scholars here and there. Yet, even such minor interventions can prompt intense backlash. In 2017, the *Telegraph* ran a front-page story headlined 'Student Forces Cambridge to Drop White Authors', illustrated with a photograph of Lola Olufemi, then Women's Officer for the Cambridge University Student Union. The paper falsely claimed that students, and Olufemi in particular, were demanding the removal of white authors from the syllabus, when students had simply *requested* the *addition* of Black authors and those of colour to English Faculty reading lists. The paper later issued a correction, but the targeting of Olufemi and gross misrepresentation of decolonisation was telling.[28] Meanwhile, one of the most remarkable responses has been Birmingham City University's decision to offer a degree in Black Studies from September 2017. Black Studies courses are common in the United States but this is the first time that the positive connotations of that phrase have been embraced by a European university.[29] Crucially, the course exemplifies meaningful attempts to decolonise, not just diversify, a curriculum. Ultimately, to demand decolonisation over diversification is to commit to dismantling the Master's House.

Persist for you will face disappointments. Do not grant another person's 'no', or 'not yet', the power to quell your desire for justice. Withdraw if you must, but return and remember it is a privilege not afforded to many. Grieve, rally and confute.

Change can come in fits and starts and there is never a guarantee that progress is permanent. Recent domestic and global political developments, whether the 'hideous whiteness of Brexit' or the installation of the forty-fifth President of the United States, have shown us that we cannot afford to assume we have successfully defeated even obvious forms of bigotry let alone tackled subtler shades.[30]

I often read the news and feel utterly aghast at the rhetoric used to vilify Blackness, women, people of colour, immigrants, Muslims, the LGBTQ+ community, disabled people and welfare claimants, amongst others. When teaching on racism and discussing how marginalised communities are targeted for dehumanising rhetoric, I often go to a major news website, search for articles on immigration, choose the first one shown in the search results and scroll down to the comment section. Whether I'm searching the broadsheets or tabloids, the students are often shocked at the vilification and abuse masquerading as commentary. It would be easy to feel defeated or in despair in this climate.

As a historian of race and empire, I often feel as if I'm witnessing the worst prejudices of the long dead being regurgitated for a new audience. Yet, taking a historical perspective also reminds me of all the people who've come before, who fought for better and from whose efforts I, and others, benefit from every day. Whether those oppressed were my ancestors or from communities whose identities I do not share, I know that the dead about whom I read and write would have rights today denied to them in their lifetimes but secured through cumulative and infinite refusals to accept injustice. It is just as naive to expect constant progress as it is to expect nothing to ever change. Knowing this can help us ask of ourselves 'what kind of change would I like to ensure and how can I contribute?' In that spirit, our best response is to take the time we need to grieve, rally ourselves, rise again and confute.

NOTES

1. All statistics from Advance HE, 2018. *Equality in Higher Education: Staff Statistical Report 2018.* Advance HE, London. Also Advance HE, 2018.

Equality in Higher Education: Students Statistical Report 2018. Advance HE, London. Both reports available via www.ecu.ac.uk/publications/equality-higher-education-statistical-report-2018/ (accessed 15 March 2018). For staff, I explicitly discuss 3.1, 3.2, 3.3, 3.11, 3.20, 3.26, 3.30, 3.31, 5.2, 5.6 and 5.9a. The data was collected between 2003/04 to 2016/17. Staff counts represent full person equivalents, rounded to the nearest five and, unless otherwise stated, include UK and non-UK staff. Percentages are calculated on unrounded data. Consult the report for further details of methodology. Also Claire Alexander and Jason Arday (eds), 2016. *Aiming Higher: Race, Inequality and Diversity in the Academy*. Runnymede Trust, London.

2. Advance HE break down the data into UK and non-UK nationals. For the sake of brevity, I have combined the data in places. I use the term 'BME' to describe the data as it is the term used by Advance HE. Otherwise, I use alternatives. Aggregating people on the basis of ethnicity and reducing complex identities to acronyms for administrative surveillance is not welcome; however, I believe the data is an important way to showcase the inequalities I'm discussing and so I include it here.

3. These ethnic categories are used in the report. Even this small number is an improvement of the last 15 years: since 2003/04 BME staff have increased from 4.8 per cent to 7.6 per cent among UK nationals and 3.8 per cent to 5.5 per cent for non-UK nationals. White staff fell from 83.1 per cent to 73 per cent for UK nationals, but rose from 8.3 per cent to 13.9 per cent for non-UK nationals.

4. Deborah Gabriel and Shirley Anne Tate (eds), 2017. *Inside the Ivory Tower: Narratives of Women of Colour Surviving and Thriving in British Academia*. Trentham Books, London.

5. For a thoughtful rejection of 'objectivity', consult Donna Haraway, 1988. 'Situated knowledges: The science question in feminism and the privilege of partial perspective'. *Feminist Studies* 14, pp. 575–99.

6. One widely used example for identifying biases is Harvard's Implicit Association Test. The tests are designed to help an individual identify possible unconscious bias. Project Implicit at https://implicit.harvard.edu/implicit/takeatest.html (accessed 15 March 2018). Many have raised concerns about the test's predictive reliability such as Frederick L. Oswald, Gregory Mitchell, Hart Blanton, James Jaccard and Philip E. Tetlock, 2013. 'Predicting ethnic and racial discrimination: A meta-analysis of IAT criterion studies'. *Journal of Personality and Social Psychology* 105, pp. 171–92.

7. These reminders were inspired by a meme of the motto 'exist & resist & indigenize & decolonize', the earliest use of which I have found is by @ dignidadrebelde, www.flickr.com/photos/dignidadrebelde/11724557353/, posted 2 January 2014 (accessed 15 March 2018).

8. Kalwant Bhopal, 2018. *White Privilege: The Myth of a Post-Racial Society*. Policy Press, Bristol. Heidi S. Mirza, 2008. *Race, Gender and Educational Desire: Why Black Women Succeed and Fail*. Routledge, London.

9. Sadiah Qureshi, 2018. 'Why are Women of Colour still so underrepresented in academia?' *Media Diversified*, 17 January. https://mediadiversified. org/2018/01/17/why-are-women-of-colour-still-so-underrepresented-in-academia/ (accessed 15 March 2018). Gabriel and Tate, *Inside the Ivory Tower*.

10. Johan Galtung, 1969. 'Violence, peace, and peace research'. *Journal of Peace Research* 6, pp. 167–91 (p. 171).

11. Kimberlé Crenshaw, 1991. 'Mapping the margins: Intersectionality, identity politics, and violence against Women of Colour'. *Stanford Law Review* 43, pp. 1241–99 (pp. 1242, 1244 and 1252).

12. Bhopal, *White Privilege*. Amelia Hill, 2017. 'Home Office makes thousands in profit on some visa applications'. *Guardian*, 1 September. www.theguardian. com/uk-news/2017/sep/01/home-office-makes-800-profit-on-some-visa-applications (accessed 15 March 2018).

13. UCU, 2016. *The Experiences of Black and Minority Ethnic Staff in Further and Higher Education*. www.ucu.org.uk/media/7861/The-experiences-of-black-and-minority-ethnic-staff-in-further-and-higher-education-Feb-16/ pdf/BME_survey_report_Feb161.pdf (accessed 15 March 2018).

14. Sara Ahmed (@SaraNAhmed), 7 September 2017, 9:22, tweet. https://twitter. com/saranahmed/status/905707842673532928 (accessed 15 March 2018).

15. Shekinah Mondoua, 2017. 'Systemic racism couldn't care less about your respectability politics'. *The Nation*, 16 June. www.thenation.com/article/systemic-racism-could-care-less-about-your-respectability-politics/ (accessed 15 March 2018). Compare with the treatment of 'uplift suasion' in Ibram X. Kendi, 2016. *Stamped from the Beginning: The Definitive History of Racist Ideas in America*. Nation Books, New York.

16. Pamela Duncan, 2017. 'Revealed: Britain's most powerful elite is 97 per cent white'. *Guardian*, 24 September. www.theguardian.com/inequality/2017/sep/24/revealed-britains-most-powerful-elite-is-97-white. The research was conducted in conjunction with Operation Black Vote. www.thecolourof power.com/ (accessed 15 March 2018).

17. Kalwant Bhopal, 2017. 'A nearly all-white diversity panel? When will universities start taking race seriously', 31 May. www.theguardian.com/higher-education-network/2017/may/31/a-clash-of-personalities-why-universities-mustnt-ignore-race (accessed 15 March 2018). Kalwant Bhopal, 2016. *The Experiences of Black and Minority Ethnic Academics: A Comparative Study of the Unequal Academy*. Routledge, London.

18. Akwugo Emejulu, 2018. 'On the problems and possibilities of feminist solidarity: The women's march one year on'. *Institute for Public Policy Research Review* 24. https://onlinelibrary/wiley.com/doi/full/10.1111/newe.12064 (accessed 15 March 2018).

19. The literature is vast. Most recently, I have found the following especially inspiring in articulating my personal experiences: Claudia Rankine, 2015. *Citizen: An American Lyric*. Penguin Random House, London. Nikesh Shukla (ed.), 2016. *The Good Immigrant*. Unbound, London. Mona Eltahawy, 2015.

Headscarves and Hymens: Why the Middle East Needs a Sexual Revolution. Weidenfeld & Nicolson, London. Reni Eddo-Lodge, 2017. *Why I'm no Longer Talking to White People about Race*. Bloomsbury, London. Audre Lorde, 1984. *Sister Outsider: Essays and Speeches*. Reprinted 2004. Crossing Press, Berkeley. Sara Ahmed, 2017. *Living a Feminist Life*. Duke University Press, Durham.

20. Twitter has significant problems with trolling and abuse, but I still find it useful as so many amazing feminists still use the platform. Some of my favourite tweeters include Akwugo Emejulu (@AkwugoEmejulu), Ash Sarkar (@AyoCaeser), Adrienne Keene (@NativeApprops), Sunny Singh (@sunnysingh_n6), Mona Eltahawy (@monaeltahawy), Guilaine Kinouani (@KGuilaine) and Priyamvada Gopal (@PriyamvadaGopal).

21. Alison Mountz, Anne Bonds, Becky Mansfield, Jenna Loyd, Jennifer Hyndman, Margaret Walton-Roberts, Ranu Basu, Risa Whitson, Roberta Hawkins, Trina Hamilton and Winifred Curran, 2015. 'For slow scholarship: A feminist politics of resistance through collective action in the neoliberal university'. *ACME: An International Journal for Critical Geographies* 14, pp. 1235–59.

22. Rankine, *Citizen*, pp. 55, 11. Professor Sherman James coined the term John Henryism to account for the higher rates of hypertension and death among African-Americans caused by living in a racist society. Consult Fariha Roisin, 2015. 'John Henryism and the life-threatening stress affecting Black people in America'. *Vice Magazine*, 24 August. https://broadly.vice.com/en_us/article/qkg537/john-henryism-and-the-life-threatening-stress-affecting-black-people-in-america (accessed 15 March 2018).

23. Audre Lorde, 1996. 'Epilogue' for *A Burst of Light and Other Essays*. Reprinted in *The Audre Lorde Compendium: Essays, Speeches and Journals*. Pandora, London, pp. 332–35 (p. 335). Consult also Sara Ahmed, 'Selfcare as warfare'. https://feministkilljoys.com/2014/08/25/selfcare-as-warfare/ (accessed 15 March 2018).

24. Further practical advice can be found in Otegha Uwagba, 2016. *Little Black Book: A Toolkit for Working Women*. 4th Estate, London.

25. Ahmed, *Living A Feminist Life*, pp. 115–60 (p. 135).

26. Audre Lorde, 1984. 'The Master's tools will never dismantle the Master's house'. In *Sister Outsider: Essays and Speeches*. Reprinted 2004. Crossing Press. Berkeley, pp. 110–13.

27. 'Why is curriculum white?', dismantling the Master's house. www.dtmh.ucl.ac.uk/videos/curriculum-white/ (accessed 15 March 2018). Much of the campaigning was spearheaded by Nathaniel Adam Tobias Coleman, @natcphd.

28. Anna Menin and Caitlin Smith, 2017. '*Telegraph* issues correction following criticism of article on curriculum decolonisation'. *Varsity*, 26 October. www.varsity.co.uk/news/13874 (accessed 15 March 2018).

29. Kehinde Andrews, 2016. 'At last, the UK has a black studies university course. It's long overdue'. *Guardian*, 20 May. www.theguardian.com/

commentisfree/2016/may/20/black-studies-university-course-long-overdue (accessed 15 March 2015).

30. Akwugo Emejulu, 2016. 'On the hideous whiteness of Brexit: "Let us be honest about our past and our present if we truly seek to dismantle white supremacy"', 28 June. www.versobooks.com/blogs/2733-on-the-hideous-whiteness-of-brexit-let-us-be-honest-about-our-past-and-our-present-if-we-truly-seek-to-dismantle-white-supremacy (accessed 15 March 2018).

17

At the Margins of Institutional Whiteness: Black Women in Danish Academia

Oda-Kange Midtvåge Diallo

This study builds on four months of ethnographic fieldwork among a culturally, ethnically, linguistically and nationally diverse group of Black women in Copenhagen, in which the majority were born or grew up in Denmark, and a few moved there later in life. What they share are their 'African' looks and roots, as well as being cis-women, with either Danish citizenship or residence permit. During the time of the fieldwork they were all part of an academic institution (as students or faculty). The women were recruited via a Facebook post encouraging women of African descent who were interested in discussing issues of race, gender and identity in Denmark to contact me. Through the four months of data collection I have had extensive conversations with the women over coffee, while hanging out at hair salons, during semi-structured interviews and focus groups, and during breaks between lectures and lab work in their respective university environments.

What I learned first and foremost is that because race and especially Blackness is an issue which is rarely discussed in Denmark, within and outside academia, the participants were relieved that they were finally able to voice their experiences in the company of other Black women. With a methodological starting point in Black Feminist Thought,[1] and an analytical foundation in critical race theory, I will explore how these women's experiences are shaped by hidden colonial processes which influence the fabric of their Blackness.

As a mixed-race Black woman and academic, myself, I am part of the studied group, and continuously work to understand the intersections of race and gender within myself and among other Black women in Denmark.

BEING THE ONLY BLACK WOMAN IN A WHITE, MALE-DOMINATED SPACE

At a university party in the 1990s when Aisha, a mixed-race, Afrodanish sociologist in her forties, first started her Bachelor programme in Copenhagen, she was sitting opposite someone she described as a 'very white guy'. He wore a nicely ironed shirt and was eagerly pressing his fingertips against each other, while licking his lips as if he was about to say something. All of her classmates were sitting at one long table, and there was loud conversation and laughter. And then, not unlike Fanon's[2] encounter with a white boy on a train, the guy saw his chance and blurted out directly at her:

Hvordan er det så at være *neger*!? (what is it like to be a *n-word*!?)

The whole party went quiet, and everyone was staring at her. 'I just said quietly "I don't know", and sunk deep into my chair. I think it was the most humiliating moment of my life', she recalls. From that point onwards she was denied the possibility of defining herself.

Being a Black woman in Denmark means being confronted with exclusion on many different levels. Despite the participants' educational and prospective class privilege, they deal with continuous experiences of sexism, racism and in some cases Islamophobia as the only Black women in their respective university milieux. Shirley Ann Tate describes how being a Black person in a predominantly white university creates the position of a 'body out of place' which can engender a role as either 'the exception' or 'the representative of the race'.[3] Universities in Western countries like Denmark are historically white, male and upper class institutions that centre a certain worldview, and thus also reproduce specific criteria for access and acceptance. This makes the mere presence of a Black female body almost *impossible*.[4] Accepting only a few 'Others' into that space can thus be a way of exercising 'diversity', while maintaining privilege, power and the ability to define valid knowledge production.[5] The few that manage to enter these spaces might be ignored – or rendered hyper-visible – which can lead to stress from the constant alertness that is required.[6] Tate's work on racism in British academia is useful here as she looks at the implications of 'negative affects'[7] towards the few Black academics in predominantly white universities.[8]

Tate argues that a Black person will never reach the same level of inclusion as their white peers, and as Black *women* it becomes even more difficult to be included and taken seriously.[9] Aminata, who came to Denmark from Gambia at age 13, described her experience as a feeling of always being *watched*. She had been surprised by the hostility of her working environment, and was missing more social interaction and conversation amongst her colleagues. Despite her neutrality, she often found herself in the middle of conflicts, where she was blamed for all sorts of indiscretions, such as having lost important lab samples. Tate has also observed this tendency in academic environments, and explains the white gaze on the Black body as an act of *touching*. It is not meant as touching in the material sense, but a symbolic touching in the shape of the values, expectations and stigma that is placed on the Black body.[10] Tate explains that within touching there is a simultaneous 'seeing without being seen'. It is in this encounter between the only Black body in a white space that Blackness becomes uncomfortable not only for the one who inhabits it, but for the white gaze as well. Similarly, Heidi Mirza explains the particularity of hyper-visibility that Black women experience, as being 'an exotic token, an institutional symbol, a mentor and confidant, and a natural expert on all things to do with "race"'.[11] Universities, though they portray themselves as sophisticated and post-racial, embody a sort of 'racial melancholia' in which it is not possible to speak of race, and racism will be silenced yet nevertheless become the fabric of the university.[12]

Sibongile and Jill from Zimbabwe, who studied public health, were also talking about experiences of stigmatisation in the classroom. Jill helped Sibongile remember one time she had been at a lecture, where she was the only Black African. The lecturer had a large map showing where different diseases were measured at the highest rates. Jill recalled that in discussing a tuberculosis epidemic in Zimbabwe, a classmate raised their hand and asked 'Is it OK to sit with someone ... from *those* countries', and Sibongile, sighing, continued: 'I just put two and two together, and thought OK, so this person thinks, because I am from Zimbabwe, if they sit close to me, then they will get TB?!' She was shocked by the question, but she decided not to do anything about it. 'I just let it pass, you know.' Before coming to Denmark, Sibongile and Jill did not expect to be judged on the basis of their skin colour. It was not until moving to Denmark that Jill experienced her peers looking at her, while not seeing her. When she spoke in class, they would all turn their heads towards her. 'They did not think I could speak English', she laughed, 'they think we are stupid.' Laughing about the stupidity of people's prejudice can be a way of dealing with it, and moving on. Similarly, choosing not to act or react when experiencing the feeling of being singled out and misjudged is a way of self-protection.

It is important to note that many of the women had difficulties describing their experiences of everyday and institutionalised racism. 'It is like this little thing in the back of my head', Aisha once said when talking about her experiences with being the only Black woman at her workplace. That little thing in the back of her head would make her think about how she talks, walks and acts in front of her colleagues and her students. 'I always have to consider my way of presenting myself,' she explains. 'I can't just walk into a room and not think about it.' Aisha is always aware. This hyper-awareness is a direct result of the specifically gendered racism that Black women experience, also called misogynoir.[13] In her early twenties, she went to New York to study a semester. One of the first things she did was go to the top of the Empire State Building and take a deep breath. 'I was not being noticed', she said. She could just blend in. 'I was simply not being noticed', she repeated, '... for the first time in my life.' She talks about this experience with much joy and glowing eyes. Being noticed all the time is a burden and this hyper-visibility requires a specific kind of self-consciousness. One of the other participants, Mona, a Somali-Danish woman, in her twenties, studying to become a teacher, also said:

> I am, or we [Black women] are forced to think about our identifica-
> tion. We cannot just be, because people will ask questions. They will
> want to know where we are from, and how we identify, so we have to
> think about it. We have to have an answer.

As a Black Muslim woman, wearing a headscarf, Mona has been forced to reflect upon her identity and bodily representation, possibly much earlier in life than her white classmates. Mona encounters these types of heightened expectations everywhere she goes, as there is almost always friction in her everyday interactions with people. Occupying the marginal position of Black woman is about always acting against the norm. Regardless of their background, and whether they were born in Denmark or not, my participants feel that their visible difference will 'give them away' as non-Danish, as Other. The way in which the women all use the category 'Danish' about someone who is white, and words such as 'Brown', 'Black' or 'African' about themselves shows this distinction quite clearly. 'I mostly have Danish friends' means 'I mostly have white friends', and 'I wish I had more African friends' might not necessarily mean that they are African by birthplace. When Amirah, who grew up in a predominantly white neighbourhood, said she had 'learned to be friends with Danes', she also meant Danes with white skin, and not Danes with 'different ethnic backgrounds', as she then would refer to people of colour. When Mona, who grew up in Denmark, talked about how she 'still had to learn to be Danish sometimes', in terms of her way of communicating, being modest and speaking differently, she also did not include herself in the category 'Danish'. What is crucial here is how the hyper-visiblity of Black women in white spaces creates instant discomfort, they are always seen without being seen. Being confronted with bodies whose presence is unexpected can create discomfort among the white majority, who are also reminded of their privileges.[14] Aisha put it this way:

As a Black person in Denmark, it is not very difficult to stand out.

While higher education, especially at undergraduate level, is a time where many young people 'find themselves', Black women are somehow, in their quest to get a degree, forced to leave parts of themselves outside academia.[15] Or as Patricia Hill Collins puts it, they become outsiders-within.[16] In the first focus group discussion, this issue came up. One participant said, 'I feel like I have to be *even* more normal, *even* more bright', and another added, 'it is like having your guards up all the time', and a third person said, 'when you walk into the canteen, it's like – oh, there is a Black or Brown girl over there ... interesting'. They continued talking about how being a Black woman in Denmark means being hyper-visible and as being tied to two distinct stereotypes. 'You are either Sheneneh[17] or Istedgade',[18] one said, and someone else asked 'what is Sheneneh?'. 'Ghetto', one said, and another continued 'it means they think you are from America or something, and you have a lot of attitude ... so when you walk into a room and you speak Danish they are like "oh, are you adopted?"'.

The issue of respectability politics is relevant here as it highlights the strategies the women employ to avoid as much friction as possible, by trying to be 'even more normal'.[19] To be seen as 'Sheneneh or Istedgade' is an example of the Black female body as preconditioned in its mere existence.[20] It became clear that many of the women do not walk down Istedgade at night in fear of being mistaken as sex workers. Regardless of these women's socio-economic status as academics, they experience being stereotyped as hyper-sexual beings with a certain attitude. The stereotypes of 'Sheneneh or Istedgade' – which could be analytically translated to a representation of US-American Black popular culture or undocumented migrant sex worker – are both embodied positions that are not part of the everyday image of mainstream Denmark, let alone Danish academia. And finally, the assumption that a Black woman who speaks Danish fluently is adopted is another way of erasing Black citizens as an independent part of the Danish narrative.

DIASPORIC RESISTANCE

How can we look at the women's everyday strategies of dealing with institutionalised racism, misogyny and nationalism through a lens of resistance? I suggest we employ the very theme of this book 'To Exist is to Resist'. Now that we've examined the different structures of oppression that Black women in Denmark face, it is important to remember the physical and mental strain it puts on us daily. I suggest we look at resistance slightly differently than as directly impactful actions and words. Rather, I see the strength to show up to work and school every day, writing papers, reading literature by white men, being graded by white men and women, being the only Black woman among one's peers is resistance in itself. I see the women's refusal to engage in the silently enforced stereotypes at play as well as not wanting to react when reactions are expected from their white peers and faculty as resistance. There are different spaces at play, inside and outside academia; and a lot of the identity-work and community-building that these women also engage in happens outside academia. Many find solace through social media networks, by engaging in voluntary community work as role models for younger Black women and people of colour. In her exploration of Nordic 'race-thinking' Gullestad,[21] drawing from Stuart Hall, looks at modern identity-making and the focus on autonomy as a way of picking and choosing aspects of one's identity from the cultural resources available in a given society. Thus, self-fashioning is a play between different roles, identities and experiences that the bodies we inhabit make possible. However, in order to fully embody a self-styled identity, we are dependent on the acceptance and acknowledgement of others, of the society in which we live. In this regard, the people who are the most vulnerable are people of colour, living in predominantly white societies like Denmark.[22] It is a struggle against the hegemony of whiteness and patriarchy that exists in most European nation-states. Claiming one's own identity while living in a racialised body is radical, or more specifically, 'claiming blackness is paradoxically challenging race',[23] which can be understood as an adaptive strategy.

Zaynab, a student in her late twenties, who came to Denmark from Somalia as a young child, told me a few months after the fieldwork that she felt like she had developed a lot since I last saw her. When we first spoke, she was very conscious about the intersections of race, gender and religion, as well as the diasporic struggle of being home and away from home simultaneously. However, all these thoughts were somehow detached from her everyday life as a student. She expressed that her being *the only one* was not a big issue for her, and that she is a 'huge loner' anyway. When we spoke again she had realised that she was missing more representation in her study environment.

> I am sort of in an identity crisis right now. You know, thinking about what it would be like if I was in a class *'full of Black people'*.[24] Maybe my general satisfaction with student life would be better. You know, the bar would be decorated differently, people would dance differently. Now, if there's a really nice R'n'B song coming on, I can't just walk into the middle of the dance floor and do my thing. They would just stare at me.

Zaynab was intrigued by the idea of going to a university with 'a bunch of Black people', so much that she had applied for a semester abroad. Her experience of the pressure of being 'the exception'[25] and the feeling of isolation has made her seek other spaces of support, for example, by listening to Hip-Hop. In her imagined classroom 'full of black people' she wouldn't have to be hyper-aware of her position all the time. This example calls for an acknowledgement of community-building and the practice of safer spaces as tools of resistance.[26] For example, de Witte[27] explores self-styling and 'Afro-cool' among Black youth in Amsterdam as a way to resist. The group in de Witte's study is similar to the women in my study in terms of the diversity of their roots and identification, but they are all of African descent. Their identification with Africanness and Blackness is closely connected to their backgrounds and how they have been exposed to and lived with their ethnicities and cultures growing up.[28] The Afro-coolness is created in communities and as a way of making separate standards of success, in which the cultural conception of 'African' music and fashion creates new ways of collective identification. Further, the 'Blackness' and 'African heritage' can be contested and seen as a way of self-creation that requires insider knowledge of what it means to be 'Afro' or 'African', while the idea of 'Afro-cool' is based on consumable culture and thus a more negotiable way of identity-styling.[29] Similarly, the women in Denmark have ways of speaking inclusively of an 'us' that only means Black women of African heritage. They practise a form of Black diasporic solidarity by talking about 'us' and 'them'. They would often say things like '*we* are like this', '*we* laugh and joke a lot', 'hair is very important to *us*'. And they would be keen on asking me if I experience the same things, sometimes when we were in a room where the majority were white, to establish something only 'we' were a part of. One situation that illustrates this quite well is from an afternoon at Aminata's lab, where she was doing an experiment with two white colleagues and started talking about vitamin D deficiency among Black women. She directed her words at me, and spent no time explaining herself, which resulted in her colleagues being left out of the conversation, clueless. Creating these (momentary) feelings of community in the shape of redefining the 'we' can be a way of maintaining self-confidence, and ultimately resisting the narrow standards of white collegiality, or whiteness altogether.

CONCLUDING REFLECTIONS

What this project tells us about racialisation in Denmark is that it works in many different ways and on different levels. It can be the directly racialising gaze 'what is it like to be a *neger*?', or the experience of other people's devaluation or doubt towards one's ability to participate on equal terms, 'they think we are stupid, you know?', or the invisible, discreet feeling of being seen in a different light, 'it is the little voice in the back of my head'. Black women in the predominantly white and male world of Danish academia thus produce friction, discomfort and become impossible presences merely because of the conceptualised political value of their skin, gender and bodies. By being there, and doing their work they are in constant conflict with the narrative of the academic sphere as white, male and 'Danish'. They move through their studies mostly on their own, quietly, but surely in the most professional manner they can perform. Being a Black woman at a Danish university requires a performance, as well a constant neglect of one's self. You cannot be too loud, but you also cannot be silent when a reaction is expected of you, but you are expected to be Black in a specific sense of the word, regardless of your own interpretation of Black embodiment. With Denmark avoiding its colonial past, and race being left out of the discourse, those who experience racism are left without words to express themselves. Instead, they find other spaces of Black expression and belonging, which mostly happens in safe environments and outside of the professional world. Essentially, being a Black woman in Danish academia requires the ability to walk an incredibly thin line, balancing institutional, yet well-hidden racism, sexism and Islamophobia, while also fulfilling one's own ambitions. It is a multi-layered marginality, which does not leave much room for personal movement. Yet Black women show up every day, and keep distorting these white, male spaces with their presence, and their work. It seems as though standing at the margins makes you able to see the absurdities of white, male-dominated academia very clearly. Finally, this study calls for more critical analyses of academic institutions as spaces where oppressive norms are constantly reproduced. We need to make space for knowledge production by Black women as well as others who every day break down barriers just by existing in the academic space.

NOTES

1. Patricia Hill Collins, 2000. 'Black feminist epistemology'. In *Black Feminist Thought*. Routledge, New York, pp. 251–71.
2. Frantz Fanon, 1967. *Black Skin, White Masks* (C.L. Markmann trans.). Pluto Press, London.
3. Shirley Anne Tate, 2014. 'Racial affective economies, disalienation and "race made ordinary"'. *Ethnic and Racial Studies* 37(13), pp. 2475–90.
4. Laurie McIntosh, 2015. 'Impossible presence: Race, nation and the cultural politics of "being Norwegian"'. *Ethnic and Racial Studies* 38(2), pp. 309–25.
5. Collins, 'Black feminist epistemology'.
6. Philomena Essed, 2005. 'Gendered preferences in racialized spaces. Cloning the physician'. In K. Murji and J. Solomos (eds), *Racialization, Studies in Theory and Practice*. Oxford University Press, Oxford, pp. 227–48 (p. 229).
7. Inspired by Sara Ahmed's affect theory on how feelings of 'hate', 'fear' and 'disgust' are perpetrated onto racialised Others, and have a way of 'sticking' to the body. Sara Ahmed, 2004. *The Cultural Politics of Emotion*. Edinburgh University Press, Edinburgh.

8. Tate, 'Racial affective economies'.
9. Ibid., pp. 2480–1. Essed, 'Gendered preferences in racialized spaces'. Heidi Mirza, 2015. 'Decolonizing higher education: Black feminism and the intersectionality of race and gender'. *Journal of Feminist Scholarship* 7(8), 1–12.
10. Shirley Anne Tate, 2016. '"I can't quite put my finger on it": Racism's touch'. *Ethnicities* 16(1), pp. 68–85 (p. 79).
11. Mirza, 'Decolonizing higher education'.
12. Ibid., pp. 75–7.
13. Moya Bailey, 2013. 'New terms of resistance. A response to Zenzele Isoke'. *Souls* 15(4), pp. 341–3.
14. Linda Martín Alcoff, 2006. *Visible Identities: Race, Gender and the Self.* Oxford University Press, New York, p. 103.
15. Cerise L. Glenn, 2012. 'Stepping in and stepping out. Examining the way anticipatory career socialization impacts identity negotiation of African American women in academia'. In G. Gutiérrez y Muhs, Yolande Flores Niemann, Carmen G. Gonzalez and Angela P. Harris (eds), *Presumed Incompetent: The Intersections of Race and Class for Women in Academia.* Utah State University Press, Utah, pp. 133–41.
16. Collins, 'Black feminist epistemology', p. 268.
17. 'Sheneneh' is an African-American pop cultural figure of a loud-spoken and stereotypical Black woman from the series *Martin* from 1992.
18. Istedgade is a street name, and the historical home of Copenhagen's red light district. An increasing number of Black women, mostly from West Africa and without documents, do sex work in the area.
19. Hedwig Lee and Margaret Takako Hicken, 2016. 'Death by a thousand cuts: The health implications of Black respectability politics'. *Souls* 18(2–4), 421–45.
20. Kimberlé Williams Crenshaw, 1989. 'Demarginalizing the intersection of race and sex: A Black feminist critique of antidiscrimination doctrine, feminist theory and antiracist politics'. *University of Chicago Legal Forum* 1(8), pp. 139–67 (p. 149).
21. Marianne Gullestad, 2006. *Plausible Prejudice, Everyday Experiences and Social Images of Nation, Culture and Race.* Universitetsforlaget, Oslo.
22. Ibid., pp. 251–3.
23. Didier Fassin, 2011. 'Racialization: How to do races with bodies'. In F.E. Mascia-Lees (ed.), *A Comparison to the Anthropology of the Body and Embodiment.* Blackwell, West Sussex, pp. 419–34 (p. 424).
24. Said in English with an American accent, despite the rest of the conversation being in Danish.
25. See Tate, 'Racial affective economies'.
26. Glenn, 'Stepping in and stepping out'.
27. Marleen de Witte, 2014. 'Heritage, Blackness and Afro-cool'. *African Diaspora* 7(2), pp. 260–89.
28. Ibid., pp. 262–3.
29. Ibid., p. 266.

18

Africanist Sista-hood in Britain: Creating Our Own Pathways

Chijioke Obasi

Attempts have been made to provide an analytical framework for Black women that centralises our experiences and perspectives both as individuals and collectives. Much of this work has focused on Black feminism emanating from America, but this does not provide adequate reflection on the specific situation in Britain. Developments in Black British feminism have gone some way to address this,[1] however, it is the British context that brings with it issues of contestation around who is considered Black that are also translated into this discourse. Difficulties around the use of existing feminist frameworks with their roots embedded in racism and the marginalisation of Black women has caused many to declare their difficulty with the theory and more resolutely the terminology of feminism. Womanism has provided a useful alternative but in Britain has had much less appeal or recognition.

The chapter seeks to build on existing works in Black womanhood and to contribute to emancipatory frameworks that foreground the cognitive authority of subjugated knowers.[2] A theoretical framework termed 'Africanist Sista-hood in Britain' is offered as a Black female-centred framework for analysis.[3] Within it is recognition of the importance and value of collectivity, connectivity, commonality and difference amongst Black women, where lived experience and self-definition are held in high regard.

Given the position put forward by Hudson-Weems in her discussions of Black feminism that 'for many in the academy who reject it and who go beyond by creating alternative paradigms, they experience blatant unsuccessful attempts to silence them via ostracism and exclusion from the academic circle of either publication ... and/or dialogue,[4] it could be concluded that any attempt to truly move outside of a feminist frame will be met with contempt and result in a fruitless endeavour. However, for those of us Black women who participate in the courageous act of rejecting Black feminism,[5] we owe it to ourselves to at least try!

FRAMING AFRICANIST SISTA-HOOD IN BRITAIN

Guest et al.[6] discuss the work of Bruce Lee in developing his own fighting style due to his dissatisfaction with existing styles. The end product is not a new fighting style but a synthesis of the most useful techniques from numerous existing ones. In reflecting on this fighting style Lee describes it as something that is fluid and flexible, inviting practitioners to take from it what they choose rather than trying to follow a prescribed process. In Africanist Sista-hood in Britain a similar fluidity is built in, a fluidity that allows for incorporation of the work of our Sistas without being constrained by the frames of feminism.

The framework evolved as part of a PhD study[7] by a Black woman with Black women at the centre of the research. It looked at perspectives of equality and diversity from women working in a range of public sector organisations mainly in the north of England. The centrality of Black womanhood did not, however, negate the inclusion of others, as the research also included culturally Deaf women in the workplace. Although the majority of the participants were Black (hearing) women (25), there were also five culturally Deaf (white) women participants. Like Patricia Hill Collins' Black feminist thought and Alice Walker's womanism, Africanist Sista-hood in Britain also seeks alliances with other social groups in an attempt to address social inequality in all its forms.[8,9] In this case, the alliance is sought with culturally Deaf women and with the incorporation of Deaf cultural discourse as a contribution to the study.[10]

The central tenets of Africanist Sista-hood in Britain are set out below.

Self-naming

As Black women when we connect to the many historical journeys of our African (an)Sistas – enslavement, colonial rule and the different ways many of our African countries have been raped and pillaged and re-named by our oppressors – the issue of self-naming becomes ever more important. The legacy of the Anglicised names many of us still carry should not be overlooked.

Asante[11] in his discussion of Afrocentric principles points out the attempts of Black people, whether from the Caribbean or elsewhere, seeking to reconnect to our histories and original connections to Africa by adopting African names as part of that connection. It is an empowering process we can undertake on an individual level, but as a collective of Black women, claiming a name created by white women for white women (feminism) does seem to help maintain the structures of the oppressors. A valid point made by Jain and Turner is: 'when we look at the term feminist through the lens of the politics of naming we see that it is not an impartial label and that there are multiple reasons why women are reluctant to identify with it'.[12] The dissent that has been voiced for many decades both in Western and African women's discourses still remains active and unsatisfied.

'Africanist Sista-hood in Britain' takes from womanism and Africana womanism the importance of self-naming and as such makes no attempt to seek a variant within a feminist label. It acknowledges and responds to the voices of a significant number of women who have rejected both the terminology and framework of feminism as steeped in a history of racism, exploitation and white supremacy. In addition to women of colour, Jain and Turner also highlight similar rejections of feminism from Lesbian and disabled women. They state: 'it is still not something we feel comfortable identifying with and we are not alone.'[13]

Self-naming outside of existing models leads to greater freedom and creativity in self-definition. Sofola[14] points out the limitations of the English language in which women are seen as an appendage to men: wo*man* or fe*male* or the universalising use of *man* or hu*man* to refer to both sexes. She further contrasts this with African languages that use neutral terminology: *Nwa-oke* (male) and *Nwa-nyi* (female) as examples from the Igbo language of Nigeria with both deriving from the neutral word *Nwa* (child). A framework that embraces Sista-hood removes the appendages implicit in feminism and womanism and the words from which they derive, because in doing so there is no reliance on the masculine and thus womanhood and indeed Black womanhood emerges as the central focus.

The centrality of Black womanhood

Like any work on Black womanhood, Africanist Sista-hood in Britain seeks to centralise the experiences and perspectives of Black women. It is this positioning of Black womanhood though that causes some tension in the field. Hudson-Weems[15] in 'Africana Womanism' provides a clear message about the pervasive state of race as the major factor in the sub-jugation of Black women. She promotes the importance of prioritising race for Black women as a prerequisite for dealing with questions of gender. Black feminists in their criticism of Hudson-Weems' Africana womanism point to the work of the Combahee River collective in America, who stated: 'We believe that sexual politics under patriarchy is *as pervasive* in Black women's lives as are the politics of class and race'[16] (emphasis added). In this statement it is clear that for the Black feminism they speak of, neither race nor class can be seen as more pervasive than patriarchy. Gender is always to be seen as at least equally significant to all other aspects of identity. However, as Black women our lived reality often challenges this position.

When we consider these academic debates in the context of the everyday lived experiences of Black women in the United Kingdom it brings these complexities to life. For the Black female research partic-ipants in my study it was clear that, for some, race was interpreted as the primary source of oppression. The public sector, which houses many female-dominated professions, can also often test those gender bonds where Black women report the main perpetrators of racism as white women.

In considering these issues the framework of Africanist Sista-hood in Britian adopts a similar approach to Africana Womanism, in the recognition that race can and does often become *more pervasive* than gender even at the intersections. While recognising that there is no single universal position of womanhood, or indeed Black womanhood, our frameworks need also be reflective of the fluidity of our everyday interactions that in many cases highlight race and/or other aspects of our identity as more influential than gender. This is not to negate the importance of intersectionality, which is significant to the Africanist Sista-hood framework.

Intersectionality

For Crenshaw[17] there is a need to acknowledge the validity of creating a space for recognition of Black women that reflects the diversity of their experiences in order to protect them from legal, theoretical and political erasure. She introduces the notion of intersectionality as a useful way of understanding the multi-dimensional aspects of human identity by applying this specifically to Black women. 'Intersectionality entails thinking about social reality as multi-dimensional, lived identities as intertwined, as systems of oppression as meshed and mutually constitutive.'[18]

Intersectionality is central to Africanist Sista-hood in recognising the different ways multiple oppressions can impact simultaneously on Black women from all backgrounds. However, within the findings of my research there is a recognition that our intersectional identities are not static and impact on us differentially in different environments. Any discussions about the pervasiveness of race, class and gender should also include the fluidity that accompanies it. The pervasiveness of the different aspects of our identities can be place and time specific. My own position as a researcher working with two different participant groups provides a good example of this. As a Black female hearing researcher, my identity has many facets. When researching with Black female participants my hearing status pervaded little if any of the space we occupied, but my status as a hearing person became materially important in the research with culturally Deaf women. Issues of power surfaced in terms of existing histories of oppression in Deaf/hearing research relationships but these were further complicated by existing histories of race and power as all the Deaf participants were also white women.

An Africanist approach

The term 'Africanist' similar to Afrocentric principles adopts a Pan African perspective in seeking to make diasporic ties. In this way, it makes connections to our (an)Sista-ral or direct heritage in Africa. Like Toni Morrison,[19] however, there is also recognition of both a geographical and ideological notion of Africa. In her writing in *Playing in the Dark: Whiteness and the Literary Imagination* one of the key themes is the way in which Africa's or Africanist historical influences continue to shape the current position of African-American people in America.

For many in Britain, 'Black' has become a political identity as an all-inclusive term for all who experience racism.[20] In taking an Africanist approach within the framework, there is recognition of the way that there has been an overcrowding of the Black space where all who are not white British have legitimised claim within the political term Black. However, in practice, the separation does not always end with the white demarcation, as illustrated by Henry's[21] writing about participating in a Black History Month event in London, where Irish dancing was being presented as one of the celebrations of Black history. There is of course a need to recognise Irish oppression at the hands of the English, however, locating this within notions of political Blackness can and does result in decentring, dilution and lack of recognition of Black people's specific experiences of structural racism. It also draws false equivalences between different people's experiences of nuanced forms of systematic oppression.

One impact of how the notion of political Blackness is mobilised is the potential invisibilising of Black people's lives and struggles, especially where they are a minority within a larger minority ethnic population. This was a finding in many of the northern towns and cities where I did my research. This invisibilising is a position demographically evident in localities of many Black people, but curiously absent from policy debates which more often than not focus on a wider discussion of Black and Minority Ethnic (BME) or 'Black' (in the political sense), which have become more homogenising than they should be. In taking an Africanist approach there is more opportunity to make links with the importance of our histories, and connections to our (an)Sistas be that via our links with Africa, the Caribbean or any other diasporic lines.

Pooling resources with Black men

The complicated histories between Black men and women makes our relationship with our Black brothas[22] historically and necessarily a boundaried one, but one that is more complex than first appears in any feminist analysis.

In Britain capitalism has thrived on the exploitation of Black people, not just in terms of the trade in enslaved Africans but also in relation to postwar migrations and employment patterns in the United Kingdom. This creates white privilege which white men and women work in unity to preserve.

Carby points out that 'Racism ensures that Black men do not have the same relations to patriarchal/capitalist hierarchies as white men.'[23] UK data shows poorer outcomes for Black people in education, housing, employment, wealth and hereditary entitlements. These are positions we share with Black men, who in some cases fare worse than their Sistas in these areas. As Black women we are for the most part born into Black families where we will have shared our formative years with our Black brothers, fathers, uncles, grandfathers – many of whom will have provided a positive contribution to our very being. This is not the experience of all Black women, due to reasons such as the UK care system, absent parents, interracial parenting, fostering, adoption and differing individual circumstances. However, Black women and men often need to pool resources in order to fight the race struggle and to nurture our children (male and female) to equip them for the same fight.

Womanism has been recognised as making stronger links with Black men than with white women when compared to Black feminism.[24] At the same time, it has been criticised for overlooking the problems of sexist oppression from Black men towards Black women.[25] In Africana womanism this issue is linked to African traditions of male and female working partnerships. For others, however, Africana womanism 'effectively thwarts critique of sexism in Black communities'.[26]

Black feminism by definition with its identification within the feminist frame has been criticised for stronger associations with white women and issues of gender oppression being prioritised over that of racial oppression.[27,28]

An Africanist Sista-hood perspective takes elements from all these discourses to reflect on and recognise the shifting position we share with our men. It recognises the way 'racism divides certain categories of women and unites them with men'.[29] The aim is not to ignore the significance of the sexist oppression that is present within Black communities in Britain. It is more about recognising the value in relationships between Black men and women, while also trying to eradicate oppression. Africanist Sista-hood adopts from Africana womanism the partnership approach in which there is recognition of the different, but equal, roles for men and women set out in many traditional African communities.[30] At the same time, it adopts both womanists' and Black feminists' thinking of seeking to fight racial oppression while working to fight gender oppression.

The British context

Black British feminist discourse incorporates a politically Black identity that is specific to the UK context. Discourses and terminology around political Blackness have been criticised because of the unrealistic expectations encompassed in terms of the differences which are overlooked, simplified and stereotyped,[31] as well as the differences in gendered racisms which can have differing impacts on Black and Asian women.[32] A Black British feminist discourse that operates within this political Blackness should also be open to criticism. 'Scholars and activists who continue to utilise "Black" to describe groups other than Africans and Caribbeans risk the accusation of being outdated and out of touch with the realities of multiracial Europe.'[33] Taking an Africanist approach such as that built into Africanist Sista-hood removes this contestation and provides further validation of diasporic connections.

In adopting the terminology of Black *British* feminism, further limitations arise not just for those who object to a feminist frame. Its link to Britishness may also work to exclude those who are Black in Britain but do not identify as British, and for others, such as refugees and asylum seekers, who, despite living in Britain, may not be considered British. Reference to Africanist Sista-hood 'in Britain' addresses this issue and widens the scope of Africanist inclusivity within that shared location, including through its lack of emphasis on Britishness.

The importance of experience

Calling on the work of Collins,[34] Reynolds[35] discusses the concept of 'knowing without knowing'. Within the framework of 'Africanist Sista-hood in Britain', the concept of 'knowing without knowing' is linked back to earlier positions described in Black feminist theorising, where white professionals strip experiences presented by Black women and re-present partial or distorted accounts more palatable to white frames of analysis. hooks demonstrates this point well: 'Frequently college educated Black women ... were dismissed as mere imitators. Our presence in movement activities did not count as white women were convinced that "real" blackness meant speaking the patois of poor Black people, being uneducated, streetwise, and a variety of other stereotypes.'[36]

Lived experience is a central tenet where validation and authenticity from within the Sista-hood is gained. Authenticity, autonomy and agency are therefore key elements. The centrality of lived experience does not mean only Black women can contribute to the discourse but within any contribution the limitations of knowledge and experience should also be acknowledged.

'AFRICANIST SISTA-HOOD IN BRITAIN':
FINDING OUR OWN WAY BACK

In Africanist Sista-hood there is (re)Sista-nce to attempts to define individuals and groups in relation to socially constructed norms. The framework in its epistemology takes account of the situated ontology of individual Black women, in which there is an automatic recognition of diversity that exists simultaneously with collectivity, commonality and difference. It is also important to recognise that all the women in a Sista-hood collective will have a shared experience of being a Black woman in Britain, no matter how diverse those experiences are.

Like many emancipatory frameworks, for Africanist Sista-hood, the interpretivist paradigm is particularly appropriate as it recognises that different and often contested constructions exist, but further seeks to highlight the way particular majority group constructions are dominant and influential, often at the expense of alternative subaltern construc-tions from the minority. Issues of power, control of power and agency are central to this understanding. Those furthest from the control of power and resources that shape society are least likely to have their con-structions validated or acknowledged. Africanist Sista-hood challenges other dominant power relations which support hegemonic assumptions of what it is to be Black and female in contemporary British society, by foregrounding Black female experiences as a source of validation.

Like Africana womanism, though Africanist Sista-hood in Britain moves away from existing feminist frameworks and works from a self-determined and self-structured position, it is not defined by oppositional status. Instead, it can be understood as recognising the potential that can be born from Black women's collectives. The idea of collectiveness associated with Africanist Sista-hood is not intended to imply essentialist homogeneity. Rather, it is a perspective that is organic and developing out of diverse Black female contributions to knowledge, and 'intellectualising',[37] which comes from many different arenas, most of which are situated outside of academia. It therefore brings together epistemology and ontology as validated by Black females within the collectives.

The terminology of Africanist Sista-hood in Britain can be broken down into its component parts as outlined in the following.

An 'Africanist' perspective keeps the focus on diaspora and those within it. The Africanist perspective within the framework allows a clear diasporic link to Africa whether via the Caribbean or elsewhere. Recognition of Africanist identities also often work to replace geographical separations with ideational connections or reclamations;[38] in this sense, an Africanist identity is not just restricted to African people along a traditional geographical line, it is more inclusive and includes everyone within the wider diaspora.

The term 'Sista', and therefore 'Sista-hood', has a vernacular home within many Black female narratives in the United Kingdom, as well as many of the paths along the routes of the African diaspora. There are traces of this in many forms of popular culture, for example, fashion, music, art and entertainment. Unlike the term feminism, it does not carry the negative history of Eurocentrism and white middle class privilege. Unlike the debates about womanism, it is not one that could be confined to privileged Black women as asserted by Collins.[39] It is a term that has originated from within Black communities and is recognised or used by Black women and men across the class structure, so should not imply any implicit disunity between Black men and women.

To be a Sista is different from being a 'sister'. It is to embrace more than the blood ties in a familial relationship. Familial terms like sister, brother, aunty and uncle are used simultaneously in the same way and differently to indigenous populations. As in keeping with the womanist metaphor, the familial relationship extends to the community too; 'family is community and community is family'.[40] Unlike womanist origins, Sista-hood is not age specific, a Sista can be across the age spectrum, and also recognises the relational aspect of the term. With this in mind, though, the importance of generational variations is also considered, Springer's paper on third wave Black feminism involves recognition of older Black feminists' 'mix of disappointment and understanding at young Black women's seeming lack of interest in feminism'.[41] She concludes her paper by calling on Black feminists to find creative ways to engage young Black women, including ideas about fusing intellectualising with music as an untapped source of education. Africanist Sista-hood in Britain, with its recognition of many different forms of intellectualising, seeks to encourage diversity in the many ways contributions can be made to this organic framework both in and outside academia; be that music, poetry, fashion, technology, literature, art, media and so on. When also considering collaborations and fusions across different fields, our creative potential extends even further.

The hyphenated '-hood' component of the term is about the collectivity and connectivity which is a driving force behind the concept. Written into the terminology then is a visual representation of the points at which we both connect and diverge. A *Sista-hood* rather than *Sistahood* has built in recognition of the points of our departure as well as the bond to our historical connections; it has recognition of the hyphenated space[42] and those who inhabit it.

The 'in Britain' (as discussed) focuses on the locational context of Britain, rather than restricting it to women with British citizenship. It offers space for recognition of diversity in epistemological and ontological geographies. In sustaining an 'in Britain' focus rather than British, it aims to capture more of the diasporic diversity this offers to Black women within the same location.

CONCLUSION

In moving away from feminism, it is not in an attempt to deny the numerous achievements of Black feminists and womanists, rather it is an attempt to continue and build on that work but in a way that recognises and encourages the beauty and freedoms offered within our own originality. The importance of connecting with history is a key issue running through all the tenets of the framework. In connecting with our foremothers along the feminist terrain we uncover a shared history of marginality, invisibility, (re)Sista-nce and creativity which highlight the inadequacies of the original feminist structures.

Ann duCille in her work around the depiction of beauty and the introduction of a Black Barbie doll made by pouring brown plastic into the existing mould makes the point about how white beauty is held as the ideal against which Black women are often measured. 'Today, Barbie dolls come in a virtual rainbow coalition of colors (sic), races, ethnicities, and nationalities – most of which look remarkably like the prototypical white Barbie, modified only by a dash of color (sic) and a change of costume.'[43] They are as she describes them 'dye-dipped versions of the archetypal white American beauty'.[44]

Black feminist perspectives have been developed that challenge many of the assumptions and omissions made by mainstream feminist theorists. 'The struggle of Black women to claim a space within the modernist feminist discourse, and at the same time to engender critical racial reflexivity among white feminists, consumed the Black feminist project for more than a decade.'[45] In remaining within the existing framework, this leaves us as Black women vying for a place at the table we have previously been excluded from. It cannot be denied that the space eventually afforded us was as a result of Black feminists' combined efforts but my point is that rather than channelling those resources in that direction a more fruitful endeavour would be for Black women to create their own table within their own space and according to their own needs. A table at which we determine whose or what interests are served.

Africanist Sista-hood does take from Black feminist writers many of the criticisms of mainstream feminism and its marginalisation of Black women, but it is the feminist framework itself that provides a valid point of departure. Going back to the Barbie doll example given earlier, a similar analogy can be made with the dash of colour of Black feminism and the original feminist frameworks. Has the hegemonic structure really changed?

Hudson-Weems in relation to our creative potential states: 'I cannot stress enough the critical need today for Africana scholars throughout the world to create our own paradigms and theoretical frameworks for assessing our works.'[46] As a Black woman living out my experience in Britain, I can only write of an Africanist Sista-hood in Britain. To our other Sistas throughout the world there are many spaces for many more contributions.

We are beautiful, we are talented, let's come together and create!

NOTES

1. Heidi Safia Mirza, 1997. In H.S. Mirza (ed.), *Black British Feminism: A Reader*. Routledge, London.
2. Vivian M. May, 2014. 'Speaking into the void?' Intersectionality critiques and epistemic backlash. *Hypatia* 1(Winter), pp. 94–111.
3. The focus of this chapter is the theoretical framework but for more detail on the research study, see Chijioke Obasi, 2016. '"The visible invisibles": Exploring the perspectives and experiences of Black women and Deaf women of equality and diversity in the public sector through the prism of Africanist Sista-hood in Britain'. PhD Thesis. University of Central Lancashire.
4. C. Clenora Hudson-Weems, 2003. 'Africana womanism: An overview'. In Delores P. Aldridge and Carlene Young (eds), *Out of the Revolution: The Development of Africana Studies*. Lexington Books, Oxford, p. 205.
5. Ibid.
6. Greg Guest, Kathleen M. Macqueen and Emily E. Namey, 2012. *Applied Thematic Analysis*. Sage, London.

7. Obasi, "'The visible invisibles'".

8. Patricia Hill Collins, 2000. *Black Feminist Thought: Knowledge, Consciousness, and the Politics of Empowerment*. Routledge, London.

9. Alice Walker, 1983. *In Search Of Our Mother's Gardens*. Harcourt, Bruce Jovanovich, New York.

10. Obasi, "'The visible invisibles'".

11. Molefi K. Asante, 2006. 'A discourse on Black Studies: Liberating the study of African people in the Western academy'. *Journal of Black Studies* 36(5), pp. 646–62.

12. Dimpal Jain and Caroline Turner, 2012. 'Purple is to lavender: Womanism, resistance, and the politic of naming'. *The Negro Education Review* 62–63 (1–4), pp. 67–88 (p. 76).

13. Ibid., p. 76.

14. Zulu Sofola, 1998. 'Feminism and African womanhood'. In Obioma Nnaemeka (ed.), *Sisterhood, Feminisms & Power – From Africa to the Diaspora*. Africa World Press, Trenton, pp. 51–64.

15. Hudson-Weems, 'Africana womanism: An overview'.

16. Nikol G. Alexander-Floyd and Evelyn M. Simien, 2006. 'Revisiting "What's in a name?": Exploring the contours of Africana womanist thought'. *Frontiers* 27(1), pp. 67–89 (p. 77).

17. Kimberlé Crenshaw, 1989. 'Demarginalizing the intersection of race and sex: A Black feminist critique of anti-discrimination doctrine, feminist theory and antracist politics'. *University of Chicago Legal Forum*, pp. 139–67.

18. May, 'Speaking into the void?', p. 96.

19. Toni Morrison, 1993. *Playing in the Dark: Whiteness and the Literary Imagination*. Pan Macmillan, London.

20. Stuart Hall, 1992. 'New ethnicities'. In James Donald and Ali Rattansi (eds), *'Race' Culture and Difference*. Sage, London, pp. 252–9.

21. William L. Henry, 2007. *Whiteness Made Simple: Stepping into the Grey Zone*. Nu-Beyond Publishing, London.

22. Kimberly Springer, 2002. 'Third wave Black feminism?' *Signs: Journal of Women in Culture and Society* 27(41), pp. 1059–82.

23. Hazel Carby, 1997. 'White women listen! Black feminism and the boundaries of sisterhood'. In H.S. Mirza (ed.), *Black British Feminism: A Reader*. Routledge, London, p. 46.

24. Patricia Hill Collins, 1996. 'What's in a name? Womanism, Black feminism and beyond'. *Black Scholar* 26(1), pp. 9–17.

25. Ibid.

26. Alexander-Floyd and Simien, 'Revisiting "What's in a name?"', p. 83.

27. C. Hudson-Weems, 1998. 'Africana womanism'. In O. Nnaemeka (ed.), *Sisterhood, Feminisms & Power – From Africa to the Diaspora*. Africa World Press, Trenten, pp. 149–62.

28. A. Mazama, 2001. 'The Afrocentric paradigm: Contours and definitions'. *Journal of Black Studies* 31(4), pp. 387–405.

29. Floya Anthias and Nira Yuval-Davis, 1992. *Racialized Boundaries: Race, Nation, Gender, Colour and Class and the Anti-Racist Struggle.* Routledge, London, p. 106.

30. Sofola, 'Feminism and African womanhood'.

31. Tariq Modood, 1994. 'Political Blackness and British Asians'. *Sociology* 28(4), pp. 859–76.

32. Julia Sudbury, 2001. '(Re)constructing multi-racial blackness: Women's activism, difference and collective identity in Britain'. *Ethnic and Racial Studies* 24(1), pp. 29–49.

33. Modood, 'Political Blackness and British Asians'.

34. Patricia Hill Collins, 1998. *Fighting Words: Black Women and the Search for Social Justice.* University of Minnesota Press, Minneapolis.

35. Tracey Reynolds, 2002. 'Re-thinking a Black feminist standpoint'. *Ethnic and Racial Studies* 25(4), pp. 591–606.

36. bell hooks, 1984. *Feminist Theory: From Margin to Center.* South End Press, Cambridge, MA, p. 11.

37. Intellectualising is not about academic expertise but about those who have a valuable contribution to make (Collins, *Black Feminist Thought*).

38. Floya Anthias, 2010. 'Nation and post-nation: Nationalism, transnationalism and intersections of belonging'. In Patricia Hill Collins and John Solomos (eds), *The Sage Handbook of Race and Ethnic Studies.* Sage, London, pp. 221–48.

39. Collins, 'What's in a name?'

40. Elsa B. Brown, 2004. 'Womanist consciousness: Maggie Lena Walker and the Independent Order of Saint Luke'. In Jacqueline Bobo, Cynthia Hudley and Claudine Michel (eds), *The Black Studies Reader.* Routledge, New York, p. 55.

41. Springer, 'Third wave Black feminism?', p. 1064.

42. Brenda J. Brueggemann, 2009. *Deaf Subjects: Between Identities.* SUNY Press, Albany, NY.

43. Ann duCille, 2004. 'Dyes and Dolls: Multicultural Barbie and the Merchandising of Difference'. In Jacqueline Bobo, Cynthia Hudley and Claudine Michel (eds), *The Black Studies Reader.* Routledge, New York, p. 269.

44. Ibid., p. 267.

45. Heidi Safia Mirza, 1997. 'Introduction: Mapping a genealogy of Black British feminism'. In H.S. Mirza (ed.), *Black British Feminism: A Reader.* Routledge, London, p. 10.

46. Clenora Hudson-Seemed, 1997. 'Africans womanism and the critical need for Africana theory and thought'. *The Western Journal of Black Studies* 21(2), pp. 79–84 (p. 79)

PART V

Digital and Creative Labour

19

But Some of Us Are Tired: Black Women's 'Personal Feminist Essays' in the Digital Sphere

Kesiena Boom

'Personal feminist essays' draw on lived experience of racism, sexism and other 'isms' in order to explain how systems of oppression operate in an everyday context. Such essays are an embodiment of 'the personal is political'[1] and are increasingly published on websites such as Slate and Buzzfeed. Many of these essays are written by Black women, yet our experiences of producing this emotionally taxing work have been thoroughly overlooked by the academy. In order to address this oversight, this chapter explores why Black women are motivated to begin writing and publishing personal feminist essays and the emotional demands that are placed upon them by doing such work in the digital, monetised context. By employing autoethnography within a Black feminist framework, this chapter explores why I, as a Black woman, began writing personal feminist essays. Namely, to effect social change; to validate myself as a source of valuable knowledge about how intersecting oppressions operate; and reassure other Black women that their dehumanising experiences of misogynoir were not unique to them. The chapter also explores the fixation by white editors on Black, female suffering which characterises some sects of online personal feminist essay publishing. Ultimately, the chapter concludes that online personal feminist essay writing is a site of contradiction. That is, it is arguably exploitative and traumatic for its writers, yet also brings a myriad of educational and self-affirming benefits for both writers and readers.

* * *

Within Black feminism, the use of personal/political writing has been particularly important. For instance, in *Home Girls*[2] Barbara Smith weaves tales from her life seamlessly into her creation of, defence of and advocation for Black feminist theory. As Hill Collins states, 'lived experience as a criterion of meaning'[3] is one of the central tenets of Black feminism. For Black women, knowledge and wisdom (the latter being of more weight) are discerned from each other by the presence of lived experience. 'Knowledge without wisdom is adequate for the powerful, but wisdom is essential to the survival of the subordinate.'[4] This wisdom gained from lived experience, and the retelling of it to others 'has been key to Black women's survival'.[5] Barbara Christian notes that in the eyes of dominant (white, male) society only the 'abstract logic'[6] of the academy has been qualified as a valid source of knowledge. Black feminism inverts this by acknowledging the political power contained within personal narratives.

The deep entrenchment of positivist values in sociology[7] means that attempts at knowledge creation which do not conform to the quantifiably measurable are often looked upon as second-rate.[8] To use one's own life as a basis for writing about structures has been dismissed as unprofessional or inappropriate, particularly when one's life is that of a Black woman.[9] Because feminism has been invested in advocating for women's self-expression in order to challenge the fact that 'knowledge, truth and reality have been constructed as if men's experiences were normative',[10] it has for the most part advocated for women's personal writing, which is regarded as a site of catharsis and liberation. Robin Boylorn, a Black feminist, intertwines personal narrative with interview data in order to invite the reader 'to embrace the positionality of Blackness'.[11] Narratives pertaining to women's everyday lives have the power to make explicit the way in which structures shape our stories – and when harnessed correctly can have revolutionary potential.[12]

This chapter is intended to tread new ground by critiquing this mode of writing from a feminist perspective, by taking into account the modern, online, monetised setting of personal feminist essay writing and how it affects Black women. To the best of my knowledge, this chapter represents the first attempt to marry questions about personal feminist essays, digital publishing in the 'clickbait' age[13] and Black women's emotive experiences of personal/political writing. This seems a travesty, as the digital has become an 'embedded, embodied and everyday'[14] experience and personal feminist essays are enjoying a resurgence.

It's not just Salon and Buzzfeed running deeply personal essays ... it's *The New York Times*, the *LA Times* – almost every respected news source. The personal essay has taken over our way of writing and communicating.[15]

The chapter begins with a portion of autoethnography which explores the question: Why do Black women write and publish personal feminist essays? I use an adapted version of the 'structured vignette analysis' developed by Pitard[16] to present my autoethnography.

IF NOT ME, WHO? BLACK WOMEN'S WRITING AS RESISTANCE

In May 2014, I had been living in Brighton for nearly two years, after moving there to attend the University of Sussex. In 2013, after approximately one month of my second academic year, I dropped out due to a period of debilitating depression, exacerbated by a series of negative racist experiences. I floated through a variety of insecure jobs and found myself miserable as I questioned whether I would ever return to university.

I had chosen to study at the University of Sussex for one central reason: to live in Brighton. Brighton was hailed as a queer, progressive utopia. For a lesbian, mixed-race, Black woman who had endured her teenage years in white conservative suburbia, it represented an escape from taunts, abuses and feelings of isolation. I was desperate to feel accepted somewhere. I threw myself into queer and feminist communities. I chaired a women's group, joined a feminist collective, sang in an LGBTQ choir, dated like my life depended on it and generally lived a very gay and feminist life. Though I expected to be happy, the truth was that Brighton was not what I had hoped it would be.

*   *   *

My gay white male housemate tells me he is going to rape me as I sleep because he is 'threatened' by my outspoken Black lesbian self. He has exposed himself to me before and I really believe in my bones that he would take sick pleasure in raping me. I don't believe it is an empty threat. Later that night I ask my other housemates, a mix of straight and bisexual white women, if we can ask him to move out. I explain what has happened and how I don't feel safe under my own roof. They laugh and tell me to just ignore him. 'Just try and get over it, he's our friend and we want him here', says one of them. So I go upstairs and I lie in bed too afraid to shut my eyes. I think of how me and my male housemate are meant to be one under the LGBTQ umbrella. I think of how my female housemates are meant to be my sisters as feminists and women. I see solidarity as a sham and a facade.

* * *

I go to a gay club and am sexually assaulted by a white man. He repeatedly grabs and fondles my breasts and ass and when I eventually hit back he begins to kick and punch me. My two white friends come to my aid and start attacking the man. They are pulled off and are brusquely told to leave. The man who has hurt me is allowed to saunter off without so much as a word. A white bouncer yanks my arms behind my back, so sharply I think my shoulders will dislocate. As he roughly bundles me out of the club he deliberately bangs my head three times into the wall as we descend downstairs. He calls me a 'jumped up bitch' and a 'cunt'. When I cry out he says 'I can do anything I like to you'. The next day is my twentieth birthday and my face and arms are covered in dark bruises. I walk slowly to the house of the white woman I have been dating for the last couple of months. She is a self-proclaimed feminist but when I recount the story of last night to her she is horrified, not because of the violence inflicted upon me, but because I dared to hit back at the man who violated my body. 'You're always so angry' she says. 'You're no better than any of them'. I go home and cry in the bath.

* * *

The above events, alongside others, are clawing for space in my head as I begin to write one evening. Since dropping out of university I have been increasingly reliant on my community to structure and shelter me, and repeatedly they have let me down. I am sick of suffering in resentful silence. I lie on my tummy on my slight single bed, the plastic mattress pooling sweat into my belly button as I shift uncomfortably. I decide that it will be cathartic to pour my rage and sadnesses and frustrations into an essay which derides the many failings and apathy of my supposed queer, feminist community. I spin my experiences into a wider structural critique and I let my white hot anger suture sentences into shape. To construct something out of the gaping devastation I feel is soothing, to know that my words might *just get someone out of their sleepy ignorance is satisfying, to know that I can locate my pains within something bigger than myself lets me begin to come to terms with them. If I tell the truth about what lies beneath the progressive facade of Brighton, perhaps I can make people interrogate their assumptions about what progress means and for whom it marches onwards. If I tell the truth, maybe I can let other queer women of colour know that they are not alone and they are not to blame. I write in one long scrawl, not noticing as it gets dark around me. When I am finished the sense of satisfaction I feel is momentous.*

* * *

MY SILENCE WOULD NOT PROTECT ME[17]

I came to personal feminist essay writing from a place of distress and found that articulating some of my experiences provided a way for me not only to experience catharsis but also to feel as though I could make a difference to other women's situations. I thought that perhaps my essay would push the white queers and feminists around me, and beyond, to step up and do better, to practise meaningful solidarity. I had read 'White Woman Listen!'[18] I knew that Black feminists had been 'demanding that the existence of racism must be acknowledged as a structuring feature of our relationships with white women'[19] for many years. I seethed in my realisation that nearly 20 years had passed since Hazel Carby had written about the racially delineated 'boundaries of sisterhood'[20] and yet very little appeared to have changed. White women were still dismissing women of colour's particular raced and gendered oppression, they were still leaving us in the dust. When I remember the 'white hot' anger that flowed through me as I wrote, I cannot help but understand this in the context of 'The Uses of Anger' by Audre Lorde. Here Lorde deconstructs the assumption that anger is an emotion devoid of political utility.

> Focused with precision [anger] can become a powerful source of energy serving progress and change.[21]

The simple reason of 'why' I began to write was because it was the only way I knew to focus my fury 'with precision'. As a Black lesbian my body had, as expressed in the vignettes, been a site in which the raced/ gendered power relations I was caught up in manifested. My body made me vulnerable, my body was not my own. But words gave me a sense of power, words gave me space to define my life on my own terms and to push back against the violence, both symbolic and literal, that sought to keep me down. My anger was intensified because of my isolation – I was deeply aware of my Blackness because I had been thrown against a 'sharp white background',[22] that is, Brighton's queer/feminist scenes. So this anger, focused and furious, gave me a way to begin the process of righting the wrongs around me. My words could let other Black women know that they were not crazy, that their experiences of frustration were not their burden alone, and that they were connected to something outside of themselves. In the Combahee River Collective Statement,[23] the authors discuss how once they came together they realised that their individual experiences of girlhood had all been similar in terms of the dismissals that they faced. By linking these incidences to systems of patriarchy and racism, they were soothed and empowered. By 'joining the dots' through my personal feminist essays, I accessed the same sense of reassurance. The essay ended up being published on Autostraddle, the world's largest website for lesbian, bisexual, queer and transgender women. The response was overwhelming and the piece became one of the top read articles on the site in 2014. I was flooded with messages from Black women who were relieved to hear that they were not alone, that the thoughts they had were my thoughts too. From then, I was hooked. I had found my voice and I knew I could use it to help.

VIOLENCES AND VIOLATIONS:
WHITE FASCINATION, BLACK PAIN

In the summer of 2015 I have been a freelance writer and copy editor for approximately a year, I have a contributing writer position at one website, a copy-editing position with a small business and am in the process of being interviewed for another position. I earn steady, if under-whelming money and am beginning to feel confident enough to say 'I'm a writer' when people ask me what I do. However, this modicum of confidence has been hard earned, because I do not write straightforward journalism, nor do I have a book bearing my name on the spine upon my shelf. The writing I do, centred as it is on Black women's lived experience and largely published online, isn't the 'serious' writing people imagine as necessary to claim the title of writer. It is not the writing of white men. It is not the writing of power. Despite this, personal feminist essay writing has been good to me in many ways (and draining in others), yet up until this point the positives have always outweighed the negatives. This is about to change. As a present to myself, in honour of my much awaited return to university, I have gone to California alone to couch-surf.

* * *

I am sat in an Oakland coffee shop, surreptitiously siphoning the free wi-fi, hoping I'm not thrown out. The woman whose floor I'm sleeping on does not believe in that which makes life easier, pleasurable or more bearable. Hence the lack of wi-fi in her apartment and why I endured a meal last night at her small round kitchen table which consisted entirely of unseasoned kale and sweetcorn (!?). So it is here in the coffee shop in which I am typing out an essay for my latest publication, the ubiquitous BuzzFeed.[24] My editor is a white queer woman. She reached out to me instead of me having to approach her, a rarity in the freelance world. She told me that she enjoyed a previous piece of mine, one which details how a combination of internalised misogyny and racism lead to me spending most of a decade struggling with bulimia. The essay I am writing for her centres around how my internalised racial hatred lead to a previous pathological need for white women's sexual validation. The idea for it was suggested amongst three other stories I wished to write, yet it was this one that she is keen on. I re-read our previous correspondence in which she implores me to make it as personal and specific as I can, to dig deep into experiences which still leave me cold when I recall them. I had only included the original pitch amongst the others because I knew it would get her attention, but I didn't really want to write it. I just wanted her to keep me in her memory, to not lose me in her sea of emails. I tried to demur, explained my discomfort with getting specific when she pressed me. But she was insistent and was offering me $300, which would cover the majority of my rent for a month. The world of freelancing is tough and frequently demoralising. I have lost count of the number of pitches I have emailed out into the void. I know it is part of the job, but every email met with resounding silence tears at my confidence. The fact that this editor had come to me, had sought me out, specifically wanted me ... it was intoxicating. The validation and opportunity to reach the masses was too sweet to turn down. If I said no I would be shooting myself in the foot, shutting myself off from an unthinkably large audience and alienating an editor with a significant amount of power. I would be shrugging off the mantle that was being handed to me and that *was unthinkable. So I am writing about desire and desperation and I am writing about aspects of my life of which I am deeply ashamed. And I'm doing it because I want that $300 and a byline on one of the biggest websites in the world and I want to effect change, even though I'm deeply uncomfortable with what I have to write in order to obtain these things. I feel sick as I write about the cruel, callous things I let other women say and do to me. The shame rises in my stomach and I tilt the screen of my laptop further down, so that no one sat around me can read what I'm writing. I feel pathetic, as if it is happening all over again, and I have no sense of self-worth. Or rather I know precisely how much I'm worth ... the grand sum of $300.*

* * *

CAN THE PRICE EVER BE RIGHT? EXPLOITATION AND GUILT

I am aware of a marked turning point at which the emotional demands of producing personal feminist essays began to take a toll on me. I felt trapped in something uncomfortable, not just on a personal level but on a political one. I was caught between two truths. I wanted to represent the stories of Black lesbians, I wanted to reach out to other women like me who would otherwise struggle to find representation of their lives. Yet, simultaneously, I felt creeping guilt because if I listened to my discomfort and sat on this story, refused to hand it over to whiteness, then who would tell such stories? If not me, who? If not now, when?

I bristled at the editor's brazenness. Who was this white woman to push me and cajole me into exploring traumatic racial experiences which I was clearly reticent to discuss? While our interactions were pleasant and light, what did it mean that she must have known the leverage she held over me in terms of the money and exposure she could offer me? What did it mean that she chose to use it to push into soft parts of me that were not done healing? It seemed to me that her white fascination with Black suffering was not merely a personal interest, but indicative of the wider impulse by whiteness to reify the position of Blackness as a site of lament as a 'possessive investment in whiteness'.[25] As bell hooks notes, 'voices and beings of non-white women [are turned] into commodity, spectacle'[26] for the benefit of whiteness. A month after my piece was published on BuzzFeed, a former BuzzFeed content creator, Kat Blaque (a Black transgender woman) created a video on her YouTube channel about how BuzzFeed maintains a reputation as a site of racial, sexual and gender diversity, yet is ultimately exploiting marginalised voices for its own profit.[27] My pain, my suffering would gain my editor clicks, which in turn would gain her company money, perhaps she would even be praised for benevolently deigning to 'give' me a voice, to have fought past her socialised impulse to 'not see' me as a racialised woman.[28] Our Black, female traumas marketised and monetised are white people's guilt assuaged and pockets lined.

Tens of thousands of people read my essay in its first month of being published, arguably far more than would have read it had it been published in print. The digital sphere gifted me an audience from all over the world. But how many of those people took something of use forward after reading it? And how many of those merely forced it down and spat it back out and pitied me/mocked me/thought me just another stupid Black girl desperate for acceptance from a white world too good for her?

Intersectionality is the buzzword of the day, both within and outside academic feminism.[29] Yet the fact that this interest in the experience of the multiply marginalised has been incubated in a racist, sexist society means that it is often marred by sexist/racist intentions. I was forced to confront the notion that my white editor's primary dedication was to the service of white supremacist capitalism, rather than to me and my liberation goals. I felt sick realising the essential tension in what I was doing. I understood that 'a lack of universal acceptance of Black women's experiences that are not confined to a victim/problem arena ... reflects the desire by dominant groups in society to exploit these experiences in order to serve their own interests'.[30] Yet despite my editor's structural advantage over me, it was not a clear-cut case of oppressor/oppressed. As Lyon puts it, I was colluding and co-operating with my own means of control.[31] I was raised by a middle class mother, I would not have been out on the streets if I hadn't taken that $300. I made a choice. An uncomfortable choice, but a choice. 'As Black women we see from the sidelines, from our space of unlocation, the unfolding project of domination.'[32] I saw quite clearly what was happening, the 'project of domination' in which I was enmeshed and yet I still continued, I did not say no.

To suggest ... that Black female writers are completely powerless in this process would be an oversimplification of their relationship to publishing. Black women are not simply passive victims, they are active

254 · TO EXIST IS TO RESIST: BLACK FEMINISM IN EUROPE

agents in this relationship because they are themselves implicated in this process of commodification.[33]

I knew I was perpetuating the insidious idea that Black women's pain exists as entertainment. I pitched the story because I *knew* it would catch her attention:

in the current market specific stories about Black womanhood are going to sell; namely, the stories that centre on dysfunctionality, anxiety and marginalization. [I] therefore recreate[d] such stories.[34]

In a much shared piece on the 'First-Person Industrial Complex', Jia Tolentino, an editor at online women's magazine *Jezebel* was quoted as saying that women writers online are in 'a situation in which [they] feel like the best thing they have to offer is the worst thing that ever happened to them'.[35] Women's pain in particular has long been fetishised. In the Western imagination, influenced by Christianity, women are 'deserving of pain and suffering'.[36] While Black people's pain has literally facilitated white people's pleasure for time immemorial. When these two social positions collide, woman and Black, our misery practically begs to be packaged up and sold. This is particularly dangerous in the world of online writing, whereby editors are fighting low attention spans and the oversaturated online space in order to gain clicks to their websites.[37] A simultaneous feeling of exploitation and guilt flourished in me as I wrote the essay. What was the price I was willing to put on myself? While the original goal of my writing was to help dissolve webs of oppression, as I thrashed around in them seeking to destroy them, the tighter I was gripped. I grappled with the contradictions embodied by my work. It was born from a desire to soothe myself and others, yet in order to produce such work and have it be seen widely, I felt I had to inflict the trauma of white gaze back upon myself and submit to its pressures.

At this point, a few years on from the events described above, I still feel torn about what is 'right'. The messy knot of liberation work and money and guilt and shame leave no easy answers. I often read the phrase 'There is no ethical consumption under capitalism.' Perhaps I can add 'There is no ethical online personal feminist essay writing under capitalism.' Less catchy, but just as true. If I could reverse time I would have stood my ground and kept the experiences closer to my chest for a while longer. Eventually I would have written the essay and sold it to a publication aimed specifically at, and edited by, other Black people. I would have given it over to a space in which I could trust that, despite the commercial setting, my sickly shameful words would be met with innate understanding born from shared experience. I would not let whiteness hurt me twice over.

CONCLUSION

This chapter utilised autoethnography in order to explore the reasons why Black women might be motivated to write personal feminist essays and questioned the difficulties associated with the commercial online publishing of personal feminist essays. The reasons for producing such work were shown to be centred around creating social change for the better, reassuring other Black women, and asserting the importance of Black women's narratives, as well as to reap financial compensation. Primarily and most urgently, the personal feminist essay process was something that I felt compelled to do because of my frustrations at the realities of living a Black lesbian life. It was a political as well as personal decision. As Mittlefehldt notes, Black women's essays are a way to counter the white, male hegemony and to push back against the mistruths that are perpetuated about our existences.[38] However, the contradiction between wishing to help dismantle structures of racism and sexism through my personal feminist essays but feeling as if I were inadvertently reifying said systems by playing into problematic discourses[39] about the tragedy and trauma of Blackness and womanhood was particularly striking. I conclude that online personal feminist essay writing in a marketised context is inherently a site of contradiction and tension. It is certainly true that I gained valuable benefits from personal feminist essays, namely, an avenue for catharsis and an opportunity to validate myself and earn money. Furthermore, it is true that personal feminist essays undoubtedly helped readers and are an important source of education, reassurance and information. However, the multitude of emotional demands, the feelings of exploitation, guilt and exhaustion that were commonplace and debilitating represent the negative consequences. Ultimately, unsurprisingly, there is no way to locate online personal feminist essays as either exclusively liberatory or exploitative, there are no such easy answers in the realm of power. The price that Black women must pay in our quest to see a better world is currently characterised by struggle, as it has always been. The marketised digital context merely changes the ways in which it is so.

In highlighting my negative experiences in contrast to my liberatory goals, I believe I have contributed a valuable addition to the literature by complicating the discourse around the liberatory character of personal feminist essays by considering their modern creation and dissemination in the monetised digital context. It is my hope that going forwards, not only does academia do better by listening to the personal experiences of Black feminists, but that the online personal feminist essay industry alters its fixation on Black, female suffering. I propose that this would be best achieved by the hiring of more Black women to editing positions, so that nuanced portrayals of Black women have a better chance of gaining a platform.

NOTES

1. Carol Hanisch, 2006. 'The personal is political' (original feminist theory paper at the author's website). www.carolhanisch.org/CHwritings/PIP.html (accessed 2 May 2017).
2. Barbara Smith (ed.), 2000. *Home Girls: A Black Feminist Anthology*. Rutgers University Press, New Brunswick.
3. Patricia Hill Collins, 2000. *Black Feminist Thought: Knowledge, Consciousness and the Politics of Empowerment*. Routledge, New York, p. 257.
4. Ibid.
5. Ibid.
6. Barbara Christian, 1987. 'The race for theory'. *Cultural Critique* 6, pp. 51–63.
7. Martin Slattery, 2003. *Key Ideas in Sociology*. Nelson Thornes, London.
8. Arthur Bochner and Carolyn Ellis, 2000. 'Autoethnography, personal narrative, reflexivity: researcher as subject'. In Norman Denzin and Yvonna Lincoln (eds), *The SAGE Handbook of Qualitative Research*. Sage, London, pp. 733–68.
9. Kathryn Church, 1995. *Forbidden Narratives: Critical Autobiography as Social Science*. Routledge, New York.
10. Personal Narratives Group (eds), 1989. *Interpreting Women's Lives: Feminist Theory and Personal Narratives*. Indiana: Indiana University Press, p. 3.
11. Robin Boylorn, 2006, 'E Pluribus Unum: (Out of Many, One)'. *Qualitative Inquiry* 12, pp. 651–80 (p. 657).
12. Patricia Ewick and Susan Silbey, 1995. 'Subversive stories and hegemonic tales: Toward a sociology of narrative'. *Law & Society Review* 29, pp. 197–226.
13. Ben Frampton, 2015. 'Clickbait: The changing face of online journalism'. BBC News, 14 September. www.bbc.co.uk/news/uk-wales-34213693 (accessed 2 May 2017).

14. Christine Hine, 2015. *Ethnography for the Internet: Embedded, Embodied and Everyday.* Bloomsbury, London, p. 13.

15. Eli Rubel, 2016. 'What the rise of the personal essay can teach you about customer service', 10 March. www.forbes.com/sites/theyec/2016/03/10/what-the-rise-of-the-personal-essay-can-teach-you-about-customer-service/#32781f2432a7 (accessed 3 May 2017).

16. Jayne Pitard, 2016. 'Using vignettes within autoethnography to explore layers of cross-cultural awareness as a teacher'. *Forum: Qualitative Social Research* 17, p. 1.

17. Audre Lorde, 1980. *The Cancer Journals.* Aunt Lute Books, San Francisco.

18. Hazel Carby, 1997. 'White woman listen!: Black feminism and the boundaries of sisterhood'. In Heidi Safia Mirza (ed.), *Black British Feminism: A Reader.* Routledge, London, pp. 45–53.

19. Ibid., p. 46.

20. Ibid., p. 45.

21. Audre Lorde, 1997. 'The uses of anger: Women responding to racism'. *Women's Studies Quarterly* 25, pp. 278–85 (p. 280).

22. Zora Neale Hurston, 1999. 'How it feels to be colored me'. In Eleanor Stoller and Rose Campbell Gibson (eds), *Worlds of Difference: Inequality in the Aging Experience.* Sage, Thousand Oaks, pp. 95–7.

23. The Combahee River Collective, 1982. 'A Black feminist statement'. In Patricia Bell-Scott, Akasha Hull and Barbara Smith (eds), *All the Women Are White, All the Blacks Are Men, But Some of Us Are Brave.* The Feminist Press at CUNY +, New York, pp. 13–22.

24. buzzfeed.com, 2017. '*BuzzFeed receives 200+ million unique visitors per month'.

25. George Lipsitz, 2006. *The Possessive Investment in Whiteness: How White People Profit from Identity Politics, Revised and Expanded Edition.* Temple University Press, Philadelphia.

26. bell hooks, 1989. *Talking Back: Thinking Feminist, Thinking Black.* South End Press, Boston, MA, p. 14.

27. Kat Blaque, 2016. 'The dark side of BuzzFeed', 2 July. www.youtube.com/watch?v=oQYqDDPQfo8 (accessed 20 February 2018).

28. bell hooks, 1992. 'Representing whiteness in the Black imagination'. In Lawrence Grossberg, Cary Nelson and Paula Treichler (eds), *Cultural Studies.* Routledge, London, pp. 338–42.

29. Anna Carastathis, 2014. 'The concept of intersectionality in feminist theory'. *Philosophy Compass* 9, pp. 304–14.

30. Tracey Reynolds, 2002. 'Re-thinking a Black feminist standpoint'. *Ethnic and Racial Studies* 25, pp. 591–606 (p. 595).

31. David Lyon, 2013. *The Electronic Eye.* John Wiley & Sons, Hoboken.

32. Heidi Mirza (ed.), 1998. *Black British Feminism: A Reader.* Routledge, London, p. 5. Originally published 1997.

33. Reynolds, 'Re-thinking a Black feminist standpoint', p. 595.

34. Ibid.

35. Laura Bennett, 2015. 'Why did the harrowing personal essay take over the internet?', 14 September. www.slate.com/articles/life/technology/2015/09/the_first_person_industrial_complex_how_the_harrowing_personal_essay_took.html (accessed 20 February 2018).

36. Angela Padilla and Jennifer Winrich, 1991. 'Christianity, feminism and the law'. *Columbia Journal of Gender and Law* 1, pp. 67–116.

37. Aneya Fernando, 2013. 'Are personal essays the future of digital journalism?', 2 October 2. www.adweek.com/digital/are-personal-essays-the-future-of-digital-journalism/ (accessed 20 February 2018).

38. Pamela Klass Mittlefehldt, 1993. 'A weaponry of choice'. In Ruth-Ellen Boetcher-Joeres and Elizabeth Mittman (eds), *Politics of the Essay: Feminist Perspectives*. Indiana University Press, Bloomington, pp. 196–209.

39. Wendy Brown, 1993. 'Wounded attachments'. *Political Theory* 21, pp. 390–410.

20

Coming to Movement: African Diasporic Women in British Dance*

Tia-Monique Uzor

I have always felt the most connected to those around me when we dance together. Inhibitions gone, eyes shut and only pulsing rhythms between us. As a British Caribbean diasporic woman, there have always been frequent occasions to dance together in community. These collective experiences of movement shaped my understanding of myself and heritage as I grew up in south eastern England. I would eventually formally train in Western contemporary, classical, African and African diasporic dance forms and become a scholar. As Stuart Hall notes, 'we all write and speak from a place and time, from a history and a culture which is specific.'[1] I write from my experiences as a British Caribbean diasporic woman navigating the field of dance in Britain.

In this chapter, I will present hooks' theory of 'coming to voice' from an alternative perspective that focuses on the use of choreographed movement as a medium by which female choreographers of African and African diasporic heritage subvert systematic racial oppression and prejudices by creating spaces of radical creativity. Using Alesandra Seutin's *Ceci n'est pas Noire* (2013), Vicki Igbokwe's *The Head Wrap Diaries* (2016) and the collaborative duo Project O's (Alexandrina Hemsley and Jamila Johnson-Small) piece *O* (2013), I will discuss how these case studies expand hooks' discourse on coming to voice, by coming to *movement* through hooks'[2] ideas of resistance, empowerment and self-transformation. I demonstrate how embodied artistic expression acts as a necessary site of resistance against the hostility of the European environment to African and African diasporic women.

As I began to critically study the field of dance I realised there was a lack of value placed on narratives of African and African diasporic choreographers and dancers. Many Black and brown artists face more complex challenges in comparison to their white counterparts when navigating the politics of funders and programmers within the British Dance industry. These artists, particularly Black women, are often segregated from 'mainstream' dance and ghettoised in a space known as the 'Black Dance Box'. Operating within this space often leaves artists restricted to specific types of funding and programming that are often concerned with ticking diversity boxes. These restrictions directly affect the type of work that these artists create, where these artists perform and which audiences are able to see their work. This struggle to be seen beyond the confines of the Black Dance Box has been extensively discussed within dance scholarship[3] and elsewhere I have also presented a series of conversations with artists talking about their experiences within British Dance.[4]

I use the framework of 'coming to movement' to examine how African diasporic women might embody the multitude of emotions that they experience as part of their daily lives. Feelings such as despair, anguish and rage help to shape the multiplicity of a woman of colour's identity. Understanding how African diasporic women in British Dance negotiate their emotions and identity offers new insights into their artistic expressions in movement vocabulary, genre and production. Re-focusing hooks' coming to voice to movement allows for a shift of analysis that transcends the restrictions of written languages. In 2015 hooks identified language as being a place of struggle for those that are oppressed when attempting to articulate resistant speech,

> Dare I speak to you in a language that will not bind you, fence you in, or hold you? Language is also a place of struggle. The oppressed struggle in language to recover ourselves, to reconcile, to reunite, to renew. Our words are not without meaning they are an action, a resistance. Language is also a place of struggle.[5]

Movement is often able to transcend the restrictions of written language as within any one body a multitude of movement languages/vocabulary can exist. Within African diasporic choreographers we see varied embodiments of African, African diasporic and Western movement vocabularies. Movement in this sense becomes a solution and a way of negotiating the multifaceted nature of an African diasporic identity.

For hooks, recognising that for all women, but in particular women of colour, the act of coming to voice is multifaceted and not unilateral is key.[6] This is replicated in the way that women of colour come to movement and choose to employ the use of their own individual movement languages within their own body and through their choreography. The nuanced nature of this means that within the British context alone there is a myriad of unique movement languages being produced that act as a tool to transform and transcend the hostility of the environment in which artists move. Analysing the artistic expressions of movement by these choreographers will, as C.L.R James identifies, allows for a unique insight into how diasporic women experience British society. James notes,

> They will be intimately related to the British people, but they cannot be fully part of the English environment because they are black. Now that is not a negative statement ... those people who are in western civilisation, who have grown up in it, but made to feel and themselves feeling that they are outside, have a unique insight into their society.[7]

There are three key ideas that constitute hooks' coming to voice that I will use for understanding dancers and choreographers coming to movement: coming to resistance, coming to empowerment and coming to self-transformation. The case studies within this chapter all respond to these ideas differently and demonstrate how notions of resistance, empowerment and self-transformation operate through their varied artistic productions. I will document three choreographers/dancers:

- Vicki Igbokwe is the Artistic Director and Choreographer of Uchenna Dance. Igbokwe's movement language is one that she describes as 'free-up',[8] it encompasses House dance, Waacking, Voguing, African traditional dances, Hip-Hop styles and contemporary dance techniques. This creates a unique creolisation of movement that is 'empowering' for Igbokwe.
- Alesandra Seutin is a widely trained dance artist based in the United Kingdom and Belgium and is the Artistic Director of Vocab Dance. Alesandra defines herself as an 'art-activist' and her choreographic work reflects this, often taking on a theme with a strong female presence and concern. During her choreographic process, Seutin often works from the inside out to produce work that has integrity and is raw.
- Project O is a collaboration between Jamilla Johnson-Small and Alexandrina Hemsley. Both conservatoire trained, the duo also

make work outside Project O. Johnson-Small also makes solo choreographies as 'Last Yearz Interesting Negro' and has other long-term collaborations with other artists. Her practice disrupts the many gazes directed body. Hemsley also works in a collaborative and often interdisciplinary way. Her work celebrates her mixed-race identities and reclaims the space of her body.

These artists' different approaches to movement and artistic production are key in recognising that not all African and African diasporic feminist voices move in the same way or respond to the same ideas. The case studies of this chapter work together to create a dialogue that demonstrates how movement within artistic production can communicate resistance in a variety of ways.

COMING TO RESISTANCE

Resistance, at root must mean more than resistance against war. It is a resistance against all kinds of things that are like war ... so perhaps, resistance means the opposite to being invaded, occupied, assaulted and destroyed by the system. The purpose of resistance, here, is to seek the healing of yourself in order to be able to see clearly ... I think that communities of resistance should be places where people can return to themselves more easily, where the conditions are such that they can themselves and recover their wholeness.[9]

The above conception of resistance by Thich Nhaht Hahn highlights its necessity to humanity as a process of sustainability. This, in particular, is necessary for oppressed groups living within Euro-American societies who are systematically 'invaded' on a daily basis. When articulating this in her theory on coming to voice, hooks differentiates speaking as an act of resistance from 'ordinary talk'.[10] There is intentionality within the speech of resistance that causes one to listen to it. An intentionality using the 'liberatory voice' that does not conform to the status of the oppressed or object, but it is characterised by opposition, by resistance'.[11] When analysing Igbokwe's *The Head Wrap Diaries* the question of resistance is really a question of visibility. The statement that this piece makes through its presence, intentionality in movement vocabulary and artistic production is one that not only resists dominant narratives of beauty within Britain but, as Hahn suggests, creates a place of recovery for themselves and the community.

Igbokwe uses hair as the central theme of her piece *The Head Wrap Diaries* (Figure 20.1). Set in a salon, the piece presents the hidden narratives of the hair experience within the African and African diasporic communities in Britain. She explores the ways in which the nuanced cultural practices place different values and meanings on hair. For those whose experience *The Head Wrap Diaries* reflects, it is an empowering acknowledgement of our narratives. It becomes a space of visibility and a place in which the community can return to themselves, embracing themselves as a process of recovery from colonial efforts to dehumanise African and African diasporic people through hegemonic white beauty standards. To those outside of this community, it is an invitation into a world to which they would not normally have access. Through installations and a head wrap bar in the foyer, the audience is invited to learn about Afro hair before they enter the theatre. This educational experience conveys cultural and historical knowledge allowing the audience to enter these narratives.

The hair of African diasporic people has always been politicised in Europe and the West. It has been a signifier of racial ideologies to those who categorise African and African diasporic people as other, it is a site of difference. For African diasporic people hair has been a site of agency, a place where the energy poured into creating a multitude of ways of wearing it has acted as a way of countering racial oppression experienced in the West, whether relaxed, braided, locs, natural, extended or short, it has been key in the self-expression of African diasporic people. These creative responses to oppression have become part of the diasporic history and culture and there have been many 'movements' of hairstyles across the African diaspora.

Igbokwe's piece claims a positive space for hair stories from African diasporic women in Britain and carves out a space in which our stories are presented. The piece takes us on a journey and the audience encounters three dancers who transform, by embodying different movement vocabularies, to represent different stories. Igbokwe utilises a range of movement languages within her choreographies; during *The Head Wrap Diaries* we see Afro-house, House, Contemporary, Hip-Hop Waacking, Voguing, as well as traditional African Dance aesthetics such as undulations. When considering hooks' conceptualisation of resistance within coming to voice, we can see this melange of movement styles that Igbokwe uses as her liberatory voice. It is the voice that is reflective of her own diasporic experience, one that is intracultural, informed by both

European and Africanist aesthetics. The vernacular of movement choice and language Igbokwe chooses is one that is owned by the community. The intentionality in choice causes a shift that demands those outside of the community to take note and listen to a narrative that has been hidden from them. Igbokwe resists the othering of African diasporic beauty and also attempts to shift the us/them binary of beauty standards. Igbokwe uses her movement to resist narratives assigned to her African diasporic womanhood and instead claims a space for it and other narratives to flourish.

Figure 20.1   Shanelle Clemson and Habibat Ajayi in *The Head Wrap Diaries* (2016)

Photo credit: Tia-Monique Uzor.

COMING TO EMPOWERMENT

Alesandra Seutin challenges the conventions of the theatre space by creating an immersive experience within which the audience can connect with the multiple characters she plays in *Ceci n'est pas Noire*. At the beginning of the piece, Seutin encourages the audience to participate in a call and response rhythm. This creates a vibe within the auditorium that allows the audience to shed any inhibitions and become present in the moment. Trinh encourages this type of non-conventional disruption in which conventional spectator/performer roles are subverted. In doing so, those watching are no longer passive in their discovery of the piece, but instead 'complete and co-produce'.[12] Once Seutin has drawn you in, she asks the audience to answer a series of questions, 'Am I a sex symbol? Am I Black? Am I a Rasta?' Answering these questions out loud forces the audience to confront their perceptions within a public setting. Seutin, a tall, dark-skinned woman of mixed white Belgian and Black South African heritage, asks the audience if she is Black. When I attended the answer from the audience was a resounding 'yes'. In asking these questions Seutin reveals the very problematic nature of the signifiers that are employed to represent 'Blackness' and their arbitrary nature.

Seutin as object has her identity assigned to her by those in society, and by using a movement vocabulary anchored in Western, African and African diasporic forms to resist reductive ideas about her assumed identities instead tells you who she is. Stuart Hall affirms that our identities are created out of difference by external judgements. He explains, 'identities actually come from outside, they are the way in which we are recognised and then come to step into the place of the recognition which others give us. Without the others there is no self, there is no self-recognition.'[13] Seutin refuses to 'step into' the identity assigned for her. During an interview with me, Seutin explained that she defines herself as Afropean, intentionally rooting herself within both dominant aspects of her identity through her use of language. Embodying this through her art, we see Seutin rooting/routing herself through her African heritage with the traditional grounding African Dance aesthetics, we see the multiplicity of African diasporic movement languages manifest through her body in voguing and complex footwork. Seutin dances on demi-pointe with a makeshift skirt which alludes to both ballet and the iconic Josephine Baker simultaneously. This is all underpinned by a contemporary dance aesthetic that brings these forms together.

Seutin reconstructs the unique positioning of her mixed European and African heritage. She embraces and acknowledges the competing facets of this identity and articulates her notion of self through her movement vocabulary. When Seutin directly addresses the audience, she creates an intrigue that challenges those watching to actively participate and to meet her in the place in which she exists. The audience is empowered to hear and Seutin can be heard. With Seutin, she creates spaces of movement that harbour possibility.[14] The performer is empowered to be heard, and through participation, the audience is able to see and hear differently, and thus learn new ways to be and new ways to understand.

COMING TO SELF-TRANSFORMATION

hooks describes the act of coming to voice as a metaphor for self-transformation.[15] She observes that when women use their voice to speak they not only engage in an act of self-transformation but also in a rite of passage where she moves from being object to subject.[16] For women of colour, this is a particularly important process which allows for recovery of lost narratives and agency over their bodies. hooks notes that 'Only as subjects can we speak. As objects we remain voiceless – our beings defined and interpreted by others.'[17] For coming to movement, it is this process of transforming from object to subject that is most pertinent. While hooks focuses on this transformation occurring through the articulation of speech, within coming to movement it is an embodied process.

Speaking to me in 2015, Hemsley explained how she experiences the objectification of her body and her concerns around it,

> [its] like I have something I don't really know what it is, it's mine, it's my voice, but somehow people take it out of my hair, my appearance, my booty ... and they get to use it and I am super passive within that ... That's a really deep concern, I think about how to own my space.[18]

For the African or African diasporic woman her body is positioned within society as other and is objectified and oversexualised, subjectivity is not a given for her. The rite of passage from object to subject that hooks conceptualises is a necessary undertaking for African and African diasporic women. Ramsay Burt notes how the relationship between subjectivity and embodiment is one that is at the centre of the functionality of dance.[19] Hélène Cixous argues that 'by writing herself, woman will return to the body which has been more than confiscated from her'.[20] Moving becomes a way for women to disrupt power constructs that place her as object and *move* herself into subjectivity.

In 'Diasporic aesthetics and visual culture'[21] Kobena Mercer identifies the historical object/subject dichotomy and observes how whiteness often assumes 'universality' in its existence that aligns itself to a 'subject position of mastery', whereas Blackness has been 'fixed into the field of vision as an object for the gaze'.[22] For Black visual artists, the white gaze often operates as a denial of their artistic expression, especially if their art does not align with stereotypical or expected expressions of 'Blackness'. Dance artists also struggle with the white gaze. Hemsley expressed her frustration at this, 'It's so hard to navigate it all and come out at the end and feel like I've still been heard and not like I've just been "brown blur, brown blur moving her arms at me," they write black dance and [see] if I can fit it into [their] programme.'[23] While Seutin expressed her fatigue of her work having preconceived expectations, '[T]here is always this thing about identity associated with black dance constantly, I feel like, you always have to follow ... [They] look for the identity because you are a black, identity is here ... and the thing is every dance has an identity.'[24] As Seutin comments, all dances have a type of identity, but the objectification of African and African diasporic dancers within British Dance results in identity being the dominant topic of exploration, which closes down other ways of thinking about and interacting with their work.

In *O* we see a mix of improvisation and choreographed movement embodied by Hemsley and Johnson-Small. They combine their contemporary dance training with a variety of social dance forms as they wander and sing across the stage, they wear gold shiny hot pants and dance erotically. They form their body into shapes and their silhouette is projected onto the stage curtains. The variety of their movement vocabulary and the symbolism presented becomes a way for the duo to travel into the body, not only through their training but through embodied ancestral and cultural data.[25] An example of this is when the duo use a chair to project an image that resembles Saartjie Baartman;[26] the duo embody the issues of gaze, exoticism and objectification through this image.

Peggy Phelan explains that the process of moving from the 'grammar of words' to the 'grammar of the body' is a movement from metaphor to metonymy. While metaphor insists on the vertical reduction of turning two to one by 'erasing dissimilarity and negating difference',[27] metonymy works horizontally on an axis of contiguity and displacement. Metonymy is a somatic language of the body[28] which involves corporeality and embodiment.[29] Engaging with this language allows for the holistic body to digest new ideas into their being. For Rudolf Laban,[30] participation and corporeality were particularly important when accessing a political/cultural space through the body. Engaging in a process through the body

to access new ideas, space or revelations is one that has close connections with Heidegger's[31] circumspection. For Heidegger, it is through the
process of circumspection that the 'new' occurs. It is a practice of going
through to reveal, it is only through a process of doing that this can occur.
In the case of dance, it is the process of engaging through embodying
artistic practice that allows for 'something never-before-conceived to
be revealed'.[32] The 'new' in coming to movement is the self-transformed
woman who has shifted from object to subject.

During O, the duo invites audience members to paint their almost
naked bodies with black paint. For me, this was one of the most
poignant places of self-transformation within the piece. Hemsley and
Johnson-Small open themselves up to complete vulnerability in order to
confront the audience's objectification of their bodies. In my interview
with Johnson-Small, she described the tension between the discomfort in
revealing her vulnerabilities and the opportunity of taking agency when
choreographing out of her experiences, 'I usually find [performing]
traumatic and horrible ... [but] I think that it is important. There is
something about how amazing it is to be able to design a situation ...
you have control, I can make a world [in my work], and in everyday
life I cannot make a world.'[33] Vulnerability is not a decision without
its personal sacrifice, the duo perform out of their struggle, and bear
invisible wounds; however, in engaging with the various movement
vocabularies that exist within their bodies, we begin to see a subversive
process take place in which transformation occurs.

Asking the audience to engage in painting their brown skin black no
longer allows the audience to be passive in any opinions that they may
hold but to take ownership of their positionality. As we the audience
engage in this act, we go through a process of circumspection which
forces a new regard of the performers, one no longer sees them as object
and acknowledges their humanity. Hemsley explained the duo's hope to
increase awareness within the audience members,

> if we can access and somehow trigger or allow our many subjec-
> tivities and make them more present in the space of a theatre than
> they usually are, be more present in the space of the street than they
> usually are when I walk down it ... then somehow it is an invitation
> for the audience to realise their own subjectivity as spectators than
> as usual.[34]

These ideas are further reflected in *Ceci n'est pas Noire*. Seutin makes an offering to the audience. Taking off a head wrap made of African wax, Seutin reveals her dreadlocks. Taking the head wrap in her hands, she asks a member of the audience to smell it and pass it around. This is a generous act by Seutin which breaks down barriers between performer and audience. The show continues for some time. At a certain point, Seutin asks for the head wrap back, when she receives it she then says, 'African Wax made in Belgium.'[35] This has multiple connotations; it points to Alesandra herself, but it also points to the colonial/postcolonial relationship between Africa and Europe in which both cultures have been affected. The offering that Seutin presents to the audience normalises the head wrap, which before her sharing it with the audience alluded to the exotic, and afterwards, she 'de-exoticises' herself – she transforms from a signifier of object to a subject with agency and invites the audience into the metonymic space of multiplicity from which she is moving.

These artistic expressions engage in a process that facilitates self-transformation from object to subject through the circumspective process of corporeal and embodied movement. This does not just allow for a transformative state to occur for the performers, but through participation, an embodied knowledge transfers to those watching and participating. The nature of the audience participation in these cultural exchanges are a reminder that the dialogue and dichotomy are constantly shifting and being articulated in different ways as different audiences respond. In hooks' conceptualisation of coming to voice this can be framed as 'talking back',[36] which is simultaneously a gesture of resistance and an affirmation of struggle. This aids in establishing a unique liberatory movement of an African or African diasporic woman. The mind and voice are necessarily corporeal, by expanding hooks' theory of coming to voice, it is evident that it is *through* the body,[37] through a corporeal embodiment of movement that African and African diasporic women can experience freedom.

CONCLUSION

Using hooks' concept of coming to movement, this chapter has examined how artistic expressions of dance constitute an alternative medium of communication that can act as gestures of resistance. The choreographers and dancers I analysed, while having similar experience moving through the British landscape, are exemplary of the nuances to be found within the African and African diasporic communities in Britain. The embodiment of the experiences has manifested three unique shows with a movement language that is specific to each artist. Through their artistic expression in dance, these women transcend the insufficiencies of the spoken word and harness an environment that encourages reconciliation, renewal and reunion. The embodiment of their truth as African diasporic women allows for the tensions of their experience to coexist within the spaces they create. They move through their vulnerabilities in order to transform, resist and empower. These women create radical creative spaces in which audiences are no longer passive observers but are actively engaged and confronted with the reality of women of African diasporic heritage in Britain. These choreographers and dancers create spaces which challenges conventions, break down barriers and allow for embodiment as an alternative way of knowing to occur. It is a place in which we can feel more connected to each other and see our humanity. Through these artists we can see the radical acts of women of colour moving in their own truth, embodying their story and making visible their narratives that have been hidden from society. To come to movement is an act of resistance, empowerment and self-transformation.

NOTES

* Earlier versions of this chapter were presented at events in 2016, 2017 and 2018. T.-M. Uzor, 2016. 'Avoiding capture – brown women creating and defining their own spaces'. Presented at the ADAD Re:generations 4, Diasporic Dance: Legacies of Imagination, Midlands Arts Centre, Birmingham. T.-M., Uzor, 2017. 'Avoiding capture – brown women creating and defining their own spaces'. Presented at the 2nd Black Feminism, the Womanism and the Politics of Women of Colour in Europe, Binnenpret, Amsterdam. T.-M. Uzor, 2018. 'Avoiding capture, coming to movement: African diasporic women in British Dance'. Presented at the 30th Annual International Conference and Festival of Blacks in Dance, Sherton Gateway, Los Angeles. This work has been used in Ramsay Burt (2018). 'Avoiding capture'. *Dance Research Journal* 50(3), pp. 99–119.
1. Stuart Hall, 1990. 'Cultural identity and diaspora'. In Jonathon Rutherford (ed.), *Identity: Community, Culture, Difference*. Lawrence and Wishart, London, pp. 222–3.
2. bell hooks, 1989. *Talking Back: Thinking Feminist, Thinking Black*. South End Press, Boston, MA. bell hooks, 2015. *Yearning: Race, Gender, and Cultural Politics*. Routledge, New York.
3. Funmi Adewole, 2016. 'The construction of the Black dance/African peoples dance sector in Britain'. In Christy Adair and Ramsay Burt (eds), *British*

Dance: Black Routes. Routledge, London. Funmi Adewole, Dick Matchett and Colin Prescod, 2007. *Voicing Black Dance: The British Experience 1930s–1990s*. Association of Dance of the African Diaspora, London. Naseem Khan, Calouste Gulbenkian Foundation, Arts Council of Great Britain, Community Relations Commission, 1976. *The Arts Britain Ignores: The Arts of the Ethnic Minorities in Britain*. The Commission, London. Hermin McIntosh, Lorraine Yates, Claudette McDonald, Arts Council of England, Kajans Women's Enterprise and Association, 2000. *Time for Change: A Framework for the Development of African People's Dance Forms*. Arts Council of England, London. Pawlet Brookes (ed.), 2013. *Hidden Movement: Contemporary Voices of Black British Dance*. Serendipity, Leicester.

4. Tia-Monique Uzor, 2018. 'Negotiating African diasporic identity in dance: Brown bodies creating and existing in the British dance industry'. In Adesola Akinleye (ed.), *Narratives in Black British Dance: Embodied Practices*. Palgrave Macmillan, Cham, pp. 37–50.

5. hooks, *Yearning: Race, Gender, and Cultural Politics*, p. 146.

6. hooks, *Talking Back: Thinking Feminist, Thinking Black*, p. 12.

7. C.L.R. James, 1984. 'Africans and Afro-Caribbeans: A personal view'. *TEN* 8(16), p. 55.

8. Vicki Igbokwe, interview by Tia-Monique Uzor, 8 September 2015.

9. Thich Nhat Hahn, 2001. *The Raft is Not the Shore: Conversations Toward a Buddhist/Christian Awareness*. Orbis Books, New York, 129.

10. hooks, *Talking Back: Thinking Feminist, Thinking Black*, p. 14.

11. Ibid., p. 15.

12. Trinh Minh-ha, *When the Moon Waxes Red: Representation, Gender and Cultural Politics*. Routledge, London; New York, pp. 93–4.

13. Stuart Hall, 1995. 'Negotiating Caribbean identities'. *New Left Review* 209, pp. 3–14 (p. 8).

14. hooks, *Yearning: Race, Gender, and Cultural Politics*, p. 152.

15. hooks, *Talking Back: Thinking Feminist, Thinking Black*, p. 12.

16. Ibid.

17. Ibid.

18. Alexandrina Hemsley, interview by Tia-Monique Uzor, 8 October 2015.

19. Ramsay Burt, 2007. *The Male Dancer: Bodies, Spectacle, Sexualities*. 2nd edition. Routledge, London, p. 15.

20. Hélène Cixous, 2003. 'The laugh of Medusa'. In Matthew Calarco and Peter Atterton (eds), *The Continental Ethics Reader*. SUNY Press, Albany, NY, p. 279.

21. Kobena Mercer, 2005. 'Diaspora aesthetics and visual culture'. In Kennell A. Jackson and Harry J. Elam (eds), *Black Cultural Traffic: Crossroads in Global Performance and Popular Culture*. University of Michigan Press, Ann Arbor, pp. 141–61.

22. Kobena Mercer, 2016. *Travel & See: Black Diaspora Art Practices since the 1980s*. Duke University Press, Durham, p. 156.

23. Hemsley, interview.

24. Alesandra Seutin, interview by Tia-Monique Uzor, 19 September 2015.

272 · TO EXIST IS TO RESIST: BLACK FEMINISM IN EUROPE

25. These ideas are developed by H. Patten. Cultural knowledge, memory and ancestral data exist within the corporeal dancing body and can manifest as movement through engaging in dancing. H. Patten, 2016. 'Feel de riddim, feel de vibes: dance as a transcendent act of survival and upliftment'. In Christy Adair and Ramsay Burt (eds), *British Dance: Black Routes*. Routledge, London, pp. 99–124.

26. The South African woman who was exhibited within freak shows across Europe during the nineteenth century due to the shape of her body.

27. Peggy Phelan, 1993. *Unmarked: The Politics of Performance*. 1st edition. Routledge, Abingdon, p. 150.

28. Jane Blocker, 2004. *What the Body Cost: Desire, History, and Performance*. University of Minnesota Press, Minneapolis; London, p. 33.

29. Valerie M. Preston-Dunlop and Ana Sanchez-Colberg, 2010. *Dance and the Performative: A Choreological Perspective: Laban and Beyond*. Dance Books, Alton, p. 7.

30. As observed by Preston-Dunlop and Sanchez-Colberg (ibid.).

31. Martin Heidegger, 1996. *Being and Time* (J. Stambaugh, trans.). SUNY Press, Albany, NY, p. 65.

32. Barbara Bolt, 2011. *Heidegger Reframed: A Guide for the Arts Student*. I.B. Tauris, London, p. 94.

33. Jamila Johnson-Small, interview by Tia-Monique Uzor, 8 October 2015.

35. Belgium being the country in which Seutin grew up.

36. hooks, *Talking Back: Thinking Feminist, Thinking Black*, p. 18.

37. Carolyn McConnell, 2014. 'The body never lies'. In Sharon E. Friedler and Susan B. Glaze (eds), *Dancing Female: Lives and Issues of Women in Contemporary Dance*. Routledge, London, p. 221.

21

Through Our Lens:
Filming Our Resistance.

Does the Future Look Black in Europe?

Dorett Jones

Film as a moving image continues to be an ingenious way to tell a story, and as an art product and cultural producer, film remains a valuable mechanism for us as viewers and creators in its social, cultural and political significance. While creating and producing film, one is never certain of what will transpire once the process is complete. Regardless of the medium it is seen through, once a film is released out into the world, the filmmaker cannot control how it will be received, viewed and interpreted. However, as film auteurs we control the intention, content and narrative to create our own stories about us, by us, for us; by Black[1] women, about Black women. As experts in our own lives, we bring our own subjective artistic expression through whichever creative process, to convey, share, emote, learn, captivate, wonder, agitate and organise.

Through a number of British independent films, recently made by and about Black women and women of colour, this chapter briefly takes a look at some of the previous emergent British Black feminist thinking in the United Kingdom as a precursor to ways British Black women's resistance has been made visual specifically through the production and viewing of film. Included are *Nothing About Us Without Us*, by yours truly (Jones, 2016), which offers a snapshot of Black women resisting austerity measures and UK government cuts to specialist services for Black and minority ethnic women and girls who experience violence. The film focuses on women and children from Rotherham, England, along with other allies from different parts of the country, who march across central London to hand in a petition to the then Prime Minister, David Cameron at 10 Downing Street. The second short film, *'I'd just like to be free': Young Women Speak Out About Sexual Harassment* (Imkaan and

End Violence Against Women Coalition (EVAW), 2016), captures young Black women and women of colour reflecting on everyday experiences of sexual harassment, their attempts to avoid it and the impact and consequences of challenging it. I explore what is possible, namely, how Black women have and continue to resist creatively within our herstorical and current socio-political context, and the role film can play in capturing our herstories of solidarity and resistance through this medium. I assert that the method and journey Black women undertake as auteurs in the creation of this art form is a revolutionary act itself.

WE'VE BEEN HERE BEFORE

Black women organising and movement building in the United Kingdom have been present for a long time, such as the work of Trinidadian feminist, activist and Black communist Claudia Jones. The cultural iconography and visual by-product created by Jones, I argue, was a conscious advancement towards ownership and the development of a social and political currency, created by and for British Caribbeans and Asians. This collective organising would prove pivotal in the anti-racist movements of the 1970s and early 1980s where working class Caribbean, African and Asian communities unified to stand together as collective voices against oppression, racist policing and imperialism.

Jones and her colleagues used creative modes of production, such as print media and an annual carnival of costumes, music, dance and celebration, as a form of resistance and consciousness-raising. This provided a vehicle of commonality, familiarity and cohesion with Caribbean heritage peoples, produced through our lens for our gaze, which continued with the Notting Hill Carnival still going strong today. It is important to highlight that this self-celebration was an active space of solidarity and form of resistance, which has shifted over the last two decades with local gentrification and the co-option of that space of resistance. This has changed how the Carnival is spoken of, who is heard and seen as representing Carnival, and, more significantly. what and whom it is for. Recent debates on the Carnival have included people viewing old footage on YouTube as part of generating discussion to subvert against the gentrification and removal from its original authenticity.

As time passed, the 'product' of Carnival would ultimately be seen, referenced and used partially or otherwise as part of the fabric of British culture, including British film, which would use whiteness as a way to replace those forms and spaces of resistance, such as Roger Michell's *Notting Hill* (1999). In the narrative, the filmmakers relied on a universal *knowing* of the name that is synonymous with the Carnival, and then presented a visual narrative of the commodification of the locality, along with a complete absence of any representation of Carnival.[2]

As previously mentioned, the late 1970s was a time of collective organising and an autonomous Black women's organisation in Britain was formed – Organisation of Women of Asian and African Descent (OWAAD) – which provided a space for development and growth of political framings and Black feminism along with a link for Black women in Britain.[3] Although tensions around political Blackness and sexuality eventually led to its demise, OWAAD stood for and created an activist space for women to organise, campaign and movement build for African and Asian women's liberation. This unity represents an important aspect of Black women organising autonomously as a reflection of the power Black women hold and the potential to generate change through this form of political activism.[4] Over the decades this unity has reshaped and transformed to incorporate the broader intersections of our lives and oppressions we experience. Expanding anti-racist demands to incorporate similar agendas for lesbian, bisexual and trans women rights, ending violence against women and girls, forced detention of refugees and asylum seekers, Stop the War and Palestinian human rights movements, disability rights and prison abolition.

At the beginning of the 1980s, Black British artists were creating celluloid stories and representations of being young and Black (African Caribbean) in Britain. *Burning An Illusion* (Menelik Shabazz, 1981) captured the social and political consciousness of lived experiences and challenges of being young and heteronormative yet different. Shabazz weaves a story and imagery of Black and Empire, centring on Pat, a young Black British woman seeking freedom from the constraints of her life which collides with the reality of her boyfriend Del and his false arrest and cruel beating at the hands of the police.

In Britain as the 1980s continued, pioneering work by the Feminist Review Collective (1983–84) provided a platform for Black feminist scholars such as Amos and Parmar[5] to re-centre Black British feminism out of a legacy of white hetero-patriarchal imperialism. At the same time, Black women's herstories were being documented by Bryan, Dadzie and Scarfe[6] with Black women providing testimonies of the impact on their daily lives of racism, sexism and class domination, recording how they mobilised and found support. Black women's lives continued to be documented, later evolving through Amina Mama's re-imagined Black female subjectivity[7] and with the introduction of an anthology of lesbian and gay independent filmmakers and media,[8] this offered further expansions of subjectivity media and sexuality.

Intergenerational Black feminist frameworks offer us further analysis and understanding of our lives. Black feminists in Britain now utilise new media and push the limitations on ways we conduct our activism and engage with current Black feminist thought. Black-owned independent media organisations, like Media Diversified, have built their activism via an online community. Black feminists creating artistic exhibitions, writing columns in national newspapers or creating regular vlogs on mixed media platforms remind us of new technologies, the digital age and an increase in opportunities to further create and organise our own revolutions.

SPECTATORSHIP: WHO'S LOOKING AT WHOM?

Given the context of our lived realities and resistance of subjugation, in our explorations of what film can provide, for Black women, is it possible for the lens to capture an image of us that is not infused with a semiology of colonialist regurgitation? Film as an art form relies on the auteur's and the viewer's imagination and it is here in the conscious [re]imagining that the image can be [re]defined, [re]made and [re]told through our lens, evoking numerous possibilities and capturing some *thing* new.

Black women and women of colour speak about these forms of oppression and highlight some of the consequences on women's lives in the short documentaries *Nothing About Us Without Us* and *'I'd just like to be free'*. The women featured give voice to how our experiences of misogyny, violence and intersecting oppressions are not isolated or siloed instances but always connected and informed by a cross-section of racism, sexuality, gender, age, class and ableism. In one of the earlier scenes in *Nothing About Us Without Us*, we hear women shouting 'Sisters united will never be defeated', and shortly after we see an Asian woman in a wheelchair with a microphone vigorously chanting and shouting 'What do we want? Apna Haq, Apna Haq zindabad (long live) ... You can't silence us, We will rise'. Later on in the film, the CEO of Apna Haq, Zlakha Ahmed, who is wearing a hijab, walks through the gates towards 10 Downing Street and she looks directly at the camera, raises her British passport to the camera and says 'I may look like this but I've got one of these'. Similarly, in *'I'd just like to be free'*, a young woman of colour speaks about 'Men and boys feeling they have a level of entitlement and ownership over women and girl's bodies'.

The inscriptions assigned to our bodies remain in the imagination of white consumers. When we as Black women are seen, looked at and viewed, be it still or moving image, then we are also consumed and understood as that image through another's lens.[9] Therefore, if we are to create our own visual imagery and representations, then it is useful to consider how those images could possibly be interpreted. Film has been and must continue to be utilised in numerous ways to create alternative content and stories by us, and about us. From documentaries of our herstories on fighting against social injustice, sexual violence, police brutality and prison abolition, like in Pratibha Parmar's *A Place of Rage* (1991), to London-centric fictional narrative from Campbell X, *Stud Life* (2012) exploring the lives of a few Black lesbians, dykes and studs. These Black British filmmakers present Black women's lives within the complexities of our different social identities and experiences.

For Black women and women of colour in Britain, I propose a theory of what I refer to as *first look*; on spectatorship and looking relations, which always situates the viewer within her given context, and it is the contextual time, place and space in conjunction with the viewer which is also subjective, thus shifting the relationship of just looking to also encompass the contextuality of what is happening for the subjective viewer where the viewing is taking place. So, for instance, a young Black German woman in 1989 is watching a film in Berlin about Black resistance at the same time the Berlin Wall is coming down, and a Black British older lesbian is watching the same film in London. Both women will employ *first look*, spectate, and experience different looking relations based on their subjective positionality, place, space and time and their reference of 'looking'.

Lola Young addresses viewer identification from screen to self in her exploration of Black female sexuality in independent British film, the power of looking and control of Black bodies and their representations of Black female 'otherness' on screen.[10] Young's critique offers a cultural perspective of ways in which Black women are measured and viewed against dominant white hegemonic modes of production and viewing, specific to British film, with imperialist ideologies and complex legacies such as the Colonial Film Unit: 'Moving Images of the British Empire'.[11]

The Unit was instrumental in promoting 'propaganda' film to African audiences in support of the war effort, however, it was also a tool for the British government in utilising film as a means to control, shape and manipulate imperial citizens. The distribution and development of British film within African colonial territories post Second World War was another vehicle in which 'industry, modernisation and civilisation' were brought to African audiences. For Black women filmmakers in Britain today, the legacies of the Colonial Film Unit in 'bringing' film to the colonised remain as a historical site for Moving Images of the British Empire, where films can be viewed and referenced and valuable insight provided into early developments of how colonised peoples were visualised on celluloid.

It is incumbent on us within the context of Black British feminist frameworks to push the boundaries of looking relations further and expand our analysis to contextualise time, location and herstory of British and European Black women, whose legacies and pathways of movements and visual representation may present differently. For example, the years Audre Lorde spent in Berlin, Germany, with Katharina Oguntoye and May Ayim helped to foster an important cultural and political scene, the Black Afro German women's movement, where women could articulate and name something they had felt for a long time alongside social change.

I am not suggesting here to throw out the contents of the proverbial bath water, but rather to give attention to how we may look from a position of power when our subjective narratives are conveyed through our own lenses and we employ *first look*. This builds on spectatorship theory and offers another perspective on viewing relations which encompasses subjectivity, time, location and memory and power relations that affect the representation of Black women on screen. *First look* situates the act of spectatorship within our own unique intersecting frameworks of viewing that can never remain static as we are always negotiating our points of reference in which to 'look' from. Guyanese playwright, teacher and poet Cecile Nobrega, who sadly has now passed on, was the driving force behind Britain's first statue of a Black woman, located in Stockwell Memorial Gardens, south London. The Bronze Woman depicts a Black Caribbean woman holding her baby aloft and after 15 years work of fundraising and campaigning, Nobrega saw her dream become reality with the 10 feet tall monument to womanhood and motherhood.[12] The Bronze Woman remains for us all to view and also represents its own position and reference point of the geographical and allegorical journey of Caribbean women in Britain and in the struggle.

CREATIVE RESISTANCE

While contemplating what I wanted to contribute and say in this volume, I began to think about the numerous creative platforms used by Black women in England who bring our talent and own unique voices to our herstories of expansion and resistance. Artists like dancer Zinzi Minott, photographer, writer and activist Ingrid Pollard, artist and illustrator Olivia Twist, and social change activists, Sabrina Qureshi, founder of Million Women Rise,[13] Marai Larasi, Executive Director of Imkaan and Co-Chair of EVAW, and Amrit Wilson, writer and activist, all bring a rich eclectic mix of how *we do our activism*, which includes a photographic collection of Black British lesbians organising and protesting human rights in Britain from the 1970s onwards, and the founder of the only annual march in London to end male violence against women and girls, now in its eleventh year.

There is always room for expansion and growth, and as the socio-economic and political ground continues to shift under our feet, this is a moment for us to [re]claim our power and collective spaces. Diawara also speaks of the power held by Black spectators, and it seems appropriate at this point to return to the question of opportunities for representation and movement building across Europe, and using film as one type of creative platform to aid this. With this medium we can use our difference and power as auteurs to strengthen, connect and determine what our future looks like and how we share and archive it.

Documentary filmmaking as a genre holds a long history of identifying social injustices and providing diverse commentary. This film form in Britain, along with fictional and experiential narratives, have broadened the scope of ways Black women organise and resist through the use of film. We have often shaped our craft to tell untold stories and to counter and resist dominant damaging discourse, yet agitate while also creating.

In November 2015, Apna Haq,[14] a Black women's organisation in Rotherham, faced with closure due to increasing austerity cuts, and armed with a petition from former service users and allies, visited London, along with support from sister organisations, Imkaan and Million Women Rise, to deliver the list of signatories direct to the Prime Minister's office at Downing Street. Apna Haq was one of many organisations in the ending violence against Black women's sector across England, Wales and Scotland, facing similar threats due to the British government's austerity measures. When I attended the march with the Rotherham women to Downing Street, I borrowed my partner's camcorder, and my intention was to capture the protest and the march. Women and children had travelled from Rotherham, across the country to march for their lives.

On reflecting about the march, I realised I had captured a significant moment in time and not only for the organisation's history but also the history of Britain; listening to women speak passionately about the safety of Black women, and wanting to ensure the survival, agency and security of all the women and children Apna Haq serves, but equally the survival of the organisation itself. Although told through my unique lens, the act of filming also allowed me to witness and be part of a movement that day; a collective voice of resistance, captured and held in time and place. Being present also meant my own participation and connection to organised activism, illustrated here in some examples of women chanting strong messages on the day:

> You can't silence us,
> Together we are strong, together we will rise.
> We are here to create social change and we aren't going to stop just because you take the money away
>
> (*Nothing About Us Without Us*, 2016)

OUR CONTINUITY

When we speak about activism there is a plethora of creative imaginings and products that can be articulated as resistance; a piece of art, sculpture, photograph, film, blog. Resistance will be in whatever form we determine; what it looks like, how it is organised, what it feels like, the texture, the smells, the touch, how is it named, spoken about, drawn, danced, filmed, screamed, recorded, sang and played. It is only through identifying commonalities and differences, building solidarity in sharing craft, speaking tongues and making the connections from the legacies of Empire and European invasion that we can hope to survive. I use the word *survive* intentionally, as we are in a state of emergency, and creative processes like the films mentioned are examples of where we can continue to [re]claim [creative] space, build connections across Europe, and capture Black women's resistant creativity and revolt against the harm that is perpetrated against us.

In order to expand our reading and continue beyond what we already know about looking relations, and to create new meanings of visual text and imagery, in how we view and look at *self* and representations, I suggest alternative ways of viewing that allow us to incorporate the shifting positions of *first look*. This concept allows us to look from a non-fixed position and considers location, temporality and subjectivity. As one of the programmers and curators of the London Feminist Film Festival, it has been my privilege to engage with many talented and artistic independent filmmakers, and over the last year I have been in dialogue with other Black feminist friends, activists and colleagues about where we can create a platform for the breadth of our stories about us and for us. We are currently engaged in the analysis of what is needed to create a Black Feminist Film Festival in London, and this will also provide another route for our feminisms, activism and sharing space, where we can meet, galvanise and movement build within our intersectional lives. Although the current film festival provides some space for global independent films, what I suggest is missing is a space that is constructed solely for us as Black women and women of colour to showcase, critique, celebrate, debate and share collective, similar and different narratives.

As I close this chapter I am cognisant of the way this volume acts as a collective footprint and archive to the various social and political changes Black women are striving to create both here in the United Kingdom and across Europe. The continuation of cultural products and creative responses, like those I have discussed here, provide vital connectivities, voice and transformation, and as auteurs we are actively participating and contributing to create change. As movements build across the United Kingdom and Europe, and whether we call ourselves Black, women of colour, water spirit, womanist, feminist, infinite consciousness and/or activist, this moment provides us with opportunities for creative expansion, and it is incumbent on us to continue to create physical, psychic and ideological space for other Black women. We must collectively connect in order to have access to the varied narratives that make up our herstories and participate in current and emerging creative platforms in order to elicit much needed socio-economic and political change. My hope for us as auteurs of our lives and in producing creative resistance is to continue making the future Black with the creativity, work and feminist frameworks provided by so many groups, organisations and sisters like Sabrina Qureshi, Ingrid Pollard, May Ayim, Amrit Wilson, Marai Larasi and Katharina Oguntoye, both here in the United Kingdom and across Europe and those voices and Black herstories who are doing the 'work' but not mentioned in this chapter, as well as those we have yet to hear and visualise.

FILMOGRAPHY

A Place of Rage (Pratibha Parmar, 1991)
Burning An illusion (Menelik Shabazz, UK, 1981)
'I'd just like to be free': Young Women Speak Out About Sexual Harassment (Imkaan and End Violence Against Women Coalition (EVAW), UK, 2016)
Nothing About Us Without Us (Dorett Jones, UK, 2016)
Notting Hill (Roger Michell, UK, 1999)
Stud Life (Campbell X, UK, 2012)

NOTES

1. For the purposes of this chapter I shall use the term 'Black' politically in reference to what Paul Gilroy calls: 'A phenomenon of assertive decolonisation'. Paul Gilroy, 1987. 'There ain't no Black in the Union Jack'. In Bill Ashcroft, Gareth Griffiths and Helen Tiffin (eds), *The Postcolonial Studies Reader*. Routledge, London, pp. 227–9. This term will encompass herstories of women and peoples who originate from the Caribbean, Africa, Asia and indigenous peoples of the Pacific, Indian Oceans and Australasia and the Americas.
2. The *Independent* newspaper ran an article on Carnival on 28 August 2016, highlighting the roots of Carnival out of the social and political tensions in Britain, to what is now a British institution: 'Black culture is popular, but everyone should remember why Carnival started when partying this weekend.' www.independent.co.uk/voices/notting-hill-carnival-racism-dont-forget-why-it-started-a7210986.html (accessed 5 April 2018).
3. *Fowaad!* Newsletter of the Organisation of Women of Asian and African Descent. Issue 7 (November 1980).
4. Julia Sudbury, 1998. *Other Kinds of Dreams: Black Women's Organisations and the Politics of Transformation*. Routledge, London; New York.
5. Valerie Amos and Pratibha Parmar, 1984. 'Challenging imperial feminism, many voices, one chant: Black feminist perspectives'. *Feminist Review* 17(Autumn), pp. 3–19.
6. B. Bryan, S. Dadzie and S. Scafe, 1985. *The Heart of the Race: Black Women's Lives in Britain*. Virago Press, London.
7. Amina Mama, 1995. *Beyond the Masks: Race, Gender and Subjectivity*. Routledge, London.

8. Martha Gever, Pratibha Parmar and John Greyson (eds), 1993. *Queer Looks: Perspectives on Lesbian and Gay Film and Video*. Routledge, New York; London.

9. bell hooks, 1992. *Black Looks: Race and Representation*. South End Press, Boston, MA.

10. Lola Young, 1996. *Fear of the Dark; 'Race', Gender and Sexuality in the Cinema*. Routledge, London; New York.

11. The Colonial Film Unit (CFU) was instrumental in the production, distribution and exhibition of colonial films to primarily African audiences, and one of its many roles was to also promote film production within Britain's African colonies. The history of the unit represents broader changes in British colonial policies. www.colonialfilm.org.uk (accessed 5 April 2018).

12. www.guyaneseonline.wordpress.com (accessed 5 April 2018).

13. The largest all women march in Europe to end male violence against women and girls. www.millionwomenrise.com/ (accessed 11 December 2017).

14. Apna Haq is a specialist Black and 'minority-ethnic' service in the ending violence against women and girls sector based in Rotherham, England, that has existed for nearly 30 years. In 2015, it had its funding withdrawn from the local city council and staff, management and volunteers as well as service users, friends and allies all organised to create a day of action in London's Whitehall.

22

When We Heal: Creative Practice as a Means of Activism and Self-Preservation

Stacie CC Graham

There is an abundance of research literature on the subject of art and activism focusing on the question of art's ability to function as a medium for political protest and social justice. Due to the limitations of what can be identified as art, protest and activism, these discussions largely overlook the social – if not political – impact that creative spaces, more generally, can have on groups of people and entire communities. Creative space, as used here, is a broad notion that seeks to include physical, mental, emotional and soulful/spiritual environments, within which creativity is facilitated, fostered and promoted. Creative spaces are not limited to spaces in which arts and culture are cultivated, developed, exhibited and formed. That means that arts and culture can take place in creative spaces, however, creative spaces must not necessarily include arts and cultural expression. For the purposes of this chapter, arts and culture encompass artistic disciplines, including the humanities, as well as an array of cultural expressions specific to Black communities and communities of colour as they vary across Europe. Due to the specificity of the Black experience, a certain critical consciousness accompanies creative spaces, arts and culture stemming from the Black experience. Critical consciousness includes taking action against the oppressive elements in one's life, illuminated by increased understanding.[1]

As community wellbeing and cultural vitality are interdependent,[2] this chapter, with the help of a few empirical examples, demonstrates the extent to which community-focused initiatives prioritising the creativity, visibility and healing of its members forge both community wellbeing as well as cultural vitality. It must be acknowledged that in both academic research as well as between the cities that are of interest in this chapter, terms such as activism, creative space, cultural activism, critical consciousness and others are not subject to one objective standard. Readers are advised not to see the use of these terms in a strict context, rather they are more flexibly put forth as commonly used within the local communities explored.

CREATIVE PRACTICE

The greatest social impacts of participation in the arts – and the ones which programmes cannot achieve – arise from their ability to help people think critically about and question their experiences and those of others, not in a discussion group but with all the excitement, danger, magic, colour, symbolism, feeling, metaphor and creativity that understanding and social inclusiveness are promoted.[3]

Creative practice as representation

Implied in the word marginalised is the statement of proximity to the centre, to the norm. Marginalised groups, and more specifically Black women and women of colour, rarely find themselves represented in mainstream establishments, from mainstream media to the wellness industry. Perhaps a more subtle form of discrimination and marginalisation, it is, however, no less detrimental to their wellbeing and self-understanding than more overt examples of oppression. Many mainstream outlets deny their role in this process by highlighting the trope figures that are used to maintain an appearance of diversity. However, tropes are merely representations of stereotypes and deny Black women and women of colour their multi-dimensionality and depth. Further, in such faux-representation the question must be continually posed and attended to of who is telling whose stories.

As bell hooks explains:

We keep coming back to the question of representation because identity is always about representation. People forget that when they wanted white women to get into the workforce because of the world war, what did they start doing? They started having a lot of commercials, a lot of movies, a lot of things that were redoing the female image, saying, 'Hey, you can work for the war, but you can still be feminine.' So what we see is that the mass media, film, TV, all of these things, are powerful vehicles for maintaining the kinds of systems of domination we live under, imperialism, racism, sexism, etc. Often there's a denial of this and art is presented as politically neutral, as though it is not shaped by a reality of domination.[4]

If we can assume that growing up in a globally connected society means that, after a certain age, no one remains untainted by the consequences of Western hegemony, patriarchy, anti-Black racism, heteronormative standards of living out gender, sexuality and intimacy, as well as other forms of oppression, how can spaces guarantee that they are not simply replicating these (unconscious) forms of oppression that are understood as the norm? Lifting the silence that has served for so long as a survival strategy and telling their stories is a powerful practice towards dismantling those oppressive structures and internal healing. In the following, a few example projects in two European cities will be described that are working to create their own spaces, while simultaneously penetrating and/or impacting mainstream spaces and thereby undermining their hold on storytelling.

BERLIN

Precarious Art

The Precarious Art series was initiated in 2014 in order to provide a platform for Black women artists and women artists of colour to promote their work while critiquing the mainstream art establishment of Berlin. alpha nova-kulturwerkstatt & galerie futura, which was founded in 1986 as a Berlin-based art space for exhibitions and cultural events with an explicit gender-critical perspective, invited artists, who self-identify as women, to discuss pertinent topics that specifically affect women artists within the framework of a two-day workshop on the subject of 'art, crisis & feminism'. The four major subjects were: feminist (art) spaces today, the problematisation of the Western art canon, how to work in self-organised groups, and community from an intersectional perspective. As workshop participation was on an invite-only basis, workshop facilitators, gallery directors and the participating artists worked from an unspoken assumption that a common socio-political understanding was given. However, fundamental notions of discrimination and oppression were challenged throughout the discussions. These differences threatened the completion of group work which included designing a zine and writing a manifesto. One of the major takeaways from that workshop was that a separate space needed to be created in order to address themes that are specific to Black women artists and women artists of colour.

The two gallery directors at that time, Dr Katharina Koch and Dr. Marie-Anne Kohl, as well as myself worked with local activists, artists and academics to construct and curate the programme for 'Precarious Art: Protest and Resistance', which consisted of a visual arts exhibition, event series and two-day symposium that took place from September through October 2015. While the gallery itself is considered an off space in the Berlin art scene, the two gallery directors recognised the privilege that they experience as white German women. For this reason, they did not take an active role in the different events. At the same time, it was important to them that such privilege be acknowledged, especially in consideration of the fact that the audiences at the symposium would be mixed. Thus, one speaker, who specialises in critical whiteness, was invited to speak from her perspective as a white woman and, more generally, on the role of allies with great emphasis on their personal self-work and unlearning processes. With those three exceptions, all active contributors to the programme identified as Black women or women of colour.

'Precarious Art: Protest and Resistance' confronted the subject of structural and everyday racism within the Berlin art establishment. At the centre of this inquiry was the concept of intersectionality, meaning of interaction of varying identifying characteristics (for example, race and gender) that must be examined at their intersections rather than individually.[5] The project sought to highlight and introduce long-term changes in discriminating structures, as was acknowledged by contributors.

Some quotes by contributing artists as a takeaway were:[6]

It is important to consider the question 'who is speaking about whom?' and how to frame binary positions that are ultimately used as borders of segregation in the landscape of both the media and in public space. (Christa Joo Hyun D'Angelo)

The strategy that I find most productive is storytelling. Stories do not need visas or a plane ticket – they can cross the Black Atlantic and move through otherwise impermeable borders. An international perspective to our local struggles is key for me at the moment. (Karina Griffith)

Accordingly, the three curators continued the Precarious Art project with a second visual arts exhibition and workshop series entitled 'Precarious Art: Artificial Boundaries', which took place in Berlin from October through November 2017 and in London in December 2017. The curators sought to fulfil an obligation to not only further the discussion but also to foster the creation of art as well as subject-, medium- and cross-regional exchange and collaboration among Black women artists and women artists of colour. The project aimed to generate and disseminate knowledge in such a way that members of the underserved and underrepresented communities were not put in a position of educating those from socio-politically privileged points of departure. Instead, it was meant to raise the visibility of these artists and those they represent within a context of the 'norm' rather than from the gaze of a deviant political object. The artists were offered the space to present their work and themselves as a part of the 'norm' and simultaneously as specific political subjects. This positioning is especially important in Berlin and, more broadly, Germany. It has proven extremely difficult to reverse the equivalence of whiteness with Germanness in the collective mind. Black women have always been at the forefront of this push beginning with *Farbe Bekennen*, the first book published by and coining the term Afro-Germans. In a majority white population, the burden of proof (or education) is often left to the marginalised. With the Precarious Art series that presumption was rejected.

LONDON

Black Blossoms

Black Blossoms, founded by Bee Tajudeen, is a collective as well as travelling art exhibition which highlights the voices of Black women. In 2015 Tajudeen put out a call for artists. The inaugural showcase took place in London at UAL Showroom, University of the Arts Holborn from 11 July through 2 October 2016. After the exhibition closed, the artists felt they were not done; they had formed a community and chosen family. Again, Tajudeen put out an open call and received over 80 applications from which she selected 25 artists, one DJ and one poet to take part in the touring exhibition *If We Are Going to Heal, Let It Be Glorious.*

Tajudeen aspires to normalising Black art. 'By default you should be able to go to Ikea and get pictures of cornrows on bedsheets like Habiba Nabisubi's work. It's about commercialising it without exploiting the artist.'[7]

The following are example quotes from people who have participated in the exhibition and collective work:[8]

I have thoroughly enjoyed being part of such a strong collective of beautiful empowered black women of all shades. The most important lesson I learnt this year is that being mixed race doesn't negate my blackness and being part of the Black Blossoms collective has further cemented that view. Today was the last day of the exhibition but there will be many more things to come from us!

Blown away by the #BlackBlossoms exhibition! In a word EMPOW-ERING. (Neleswa Mclean-Thorne)

While Tajudeen explicitly states that she seeks to showcase art created by Black women and men, she has also inevitably created community. For example, a group of Black women were invited to a photoshoot for a particular art project, and in the process had the opportunity to take part in talks, yoga, mindfulness as well as rehabilitative and rejuvenating stretching sessions at no cost to them. Other Black women who attended the art exhibitions returned for the extra activities offered on the touring exhibition. Many of the women exclaimed on their social media channels that their excitement is due to the fact that they have rarely seen art as 'for them'. Mainstream art establishments in the United Kingdom have not consistently targeted this audience in the past.

Arts Council England, a funding body that invests in artistic and cultural experiences in England, claims to prioritise diversity with its Creative Case for Diversity, which requires that any institutions or organisations receiving funding must exhibit a commitment to diversity, equality and inclusion. Yet even when those institutions choose to target underrepresented audiences, they severely underestimate audience interest and engagement. Recent examples include Tate Modern's unpre-paredness for the large numbers that showed up for their Tate Late event that aligned with the exhibition *Soul of a Nation: Art in the Age* of *Black Power* in August 2017 or to listen to Reni Eddo-Lodge's talk on her book *Why I'm No Longer Talking to White People About Race* in November 2017. When such audiences recognise that their experiences are the subject of an event – taken from a similar point of departure rather than from the white gaze – they come out in large numbers to support, explore and exchange. It is also important to prioritse that the entertainer(s) and the consumer(s) of such entertainment have shared experiences, in order to dismantle the previously exploitative nature of entertainment provided by Black and People of Colour (BPoC) to white audiences.

The Cocoa Butter Club

The Cocoa Butter Club is a (neo-)burlesque cabaret evening celebrating and showcasing queer BPoC performers. It was founded by Sadie Sinner in London in September 2016. Its mission is to better demonstrate representation in a number of genres from spoken word and singing to voguing and burlesque dance. It has been overwhelmingly successful, which can be seen in their accumulation of bookings for festivals and performances across the United Kingdom as well as on Continental Europe. Yet there is still scepticism as to whether it is truly necessary to create a separate space for such performers.

The website states:

> As Creatives, when faced with issues of cultural appropriation, lack of representation and even black-facing in cabaret, we had no choice but to create! – create something beautiful in response. So, we set up the alternative option for those who don't want to see trivialising, appropriating or clowning of our cultures, but perhaps experience how fabulous our histories and cultures are, as told by us.[9]

In an interview with 21st Century Burlesque, Sinner explained some of the major motivating factors in her founding the cabaret evening:

> Ultimately, I wanted a space where I could be unapologetically black in cabaret and pay homage to my past and I want that for everybody – to be themselves shamelessly. I could see all these POC thinking their art wasn't valid, because our current scene didn't recognise it or perhaps they simply don't consider it art. All these people going

un-booked because their art, their story, doesn't come in a package some non-POC producers bother to decipher.[10]

In one performance, an artist was testing new material that targeted homophobia in the family and how that can affect a young person coming of age and discovering their sexuality. The artist played several different roles in the piece including the homophobic 'mother/aunty' figure. A member of the audience yelled at the figure – out of turn – which was unexpected for the artist. Other members of the audience intervened, so that the piece could continue. Afterwards, Sinner reminded audience members that artists have complete creative freedom. Further, she stated that it is important for artists to be able to bring those experiences into the space created by the Cocoa Butter Club, as there are few spaces where queer BPoC performance artists have the opportunity to do so in front of a predominantly queer BPoC audience.

Sinner often points to the Club showcasing the art of BPoC performers as well as providing a networking hour, so that the non-BPoC cabaret producers have the opportunity to meet, greet and consequentially book BPoC performers rather than allowing others to 'clown' their identities, for example, by using blackface. More importantly, however, the Club has given a stage for the Other to no longer be othered. Queer BPoC performers use the platform to test new material that they would not nec-essarily feel comfortable performing in other environments. And diverse audiences that are predominantly queer and BPoC have the opportunity to openly and supportingly consume their own culture and find their experiences demonstrated and expressed onstage in a non-commercial and non-exploitative environment.

CREATIVE PRACTICE AS SURVIVAL

Health and wellbeing are innate desires that we share as human beings. The use of arts and creativity to support health and wellbeing is increas-ingly advocated, as art is often experienced as beneficial due to its therapeutic quality. Some people turn to alternative practices, such as Reiki, yoga and massage, to facilitate their healing and wellbeing. And a growing body of research demonstrates that any of these practices will positively impact an individual's physical and mental health. However, prescribed arts and creativity therapies are still under great scrutiny due to the challenges of the evaluation process.[11] Many people are thus denied access to these benefits – most conspicuously on account of costs. Costs for training in these specialties are so high that they create a socio-economic barrier. Individuals who have completed training seek to recoup those costs and as such their services cannot reach every part of the population. Members of particular communities may not access these services because they are not familiar with them and do not see other members of their communities offering or receiving alternative treatments and therapies beyond what a doctor can and/or will prescribe. In the following, creative spaces that serve marginalised communities in these areas are detailed.

LONDON

OYA: Body-Mind-Spirit Retreats, an example of preventive/proactive wellbeing

OYA: Body-Mind-Spirit Retreats, founded by myself in February 2016, creates holistic wellness experiences for Black women and women of colour communities in the United Kingdom and abroad. OYA Retreats has been founded as a platform for Black women and women of colour providers of a variety of holistic healing mechanisms, such as Ayurveda, massage, Reiki, sex education, yoga and others, to serve the communities that they stem from. While such projects do exist in the United States, such as Black Girl in Om or Chelsea Jackson Robert's Yoga, Literature & Art Camp, at the time that OYA Retreats was founded no such project existed in the United Kingdom.

Movement and exercise are important for physical wellbeing. Mindful activities, such as meditation, are essential for mental wellbeing.[12] Many people, however, are denied access to these practices and thus their benefits. That denial often takes place quite overtly in the costs for practicing in a gym or yoga studio. More subtly, exclusion is maintained through the micro aggressions conveyed by teachers in a class. While London is one of the most racially and ethnically diverse cities in Europe, that diversity is not reflected in mainstream health and wellness spaces. Yoga, for example, in its ancient form originated from India. With its introduction into the West, it has been excessively commercialised and commodified over the last century. The image of yoga in the collective Western mind has become one of a flexible white woman in an unachievable posture which has no connection to yoga's pre-colonial roots.

OYA Retreats seeks to make movement and mindfulness practices more accessible to Black women and women of colour. This group is addressed as it is often the most underserved and underrepresented in wellness spaces. Traditionally, women have been expected to be the caretakers of society. And in the United Kingdom, many professional carers are women of Black and minority ethnic backgrounds who, after professionally caring for people during the day, go home to care for their families. Due to the nature of their work and perhaps, in some cases, intergenerational patterns of behaviour, these women do not take the time or acknowledge the importance in taking care of themselves. For this reason, OYA Retreats delivers holistic wellness experiences by offering weekend residential retreats, urban day retreats, as well as community yoga classes. The different offers are important to address the social and financial circumstances of the target audience.

As the household, personal, religious and socio-economic circumstances, among others, are different for each of the women who seek to participate and/or contribute, OYA Retreats endeavours to ameliorate those concerns by offering different types of events. In 2016, for example, a queer-centred workshop was offered. A four-part urban retreat series was offered in the autumn and winter of 2017/18 and followed a theme of embodied awareness and sexual pleasure. Weekly community yoga classes are offered as venues become available. Across all of the events women are encouraged to be guided by the needs of their bodies and their intuition:

> It's really hard to describe what happens when you get a group of women together at a retreat but it feels like Healing. When this is with women who perhaps share your culture, ethnicity or experiences then this retreat becomes a place of implicit knowing and acceptance – like the Healing is growing from a place of overwhelming love. There is nothing quite like this. (Mariam, Muslim women's group organiser)

The unexpected consequence of such a holistic wellness project is the creation of a network of Black women and women of colour healing practitioners. There are a wealth of doulas, massage therapists, movement coaches, osteopaths, Reiki masters, yoga teachers and more working throughout London, however, most participants are not aware of such offerings. Email requests are regularly received by people who seek to work with a specialist who identifies as a woman of colour. Similarly, contributors reach out regularly to connect with the platform and find ways to actively bring their knowledge and expertise into the community. Furthermore, OYA is currently offering a women of colour yoga teacher training with the British Wheel of Yoga, the national governing body of yoga, at a heavily subsidised rate. Raising visibility and building community and network is fundamental to enabling the mission of the project.

Grenfell Healing Zone, an example of responsive wellbeing

A west London tower block, Grenfell Tower was engulfed in fire in the early morning of 14 June 2017. The 24-storey building in north Kensington was difficult to escape from for a still unknown number of residents. It is assumed that approximately 350 people would have been in the tower at that time, but there is no way to be confident of that number. Due to the extent of the fire and its damage to the building, it took an extensive amount of time to identify all of the people who may have succumbed to the tragic fire, but officials expect the number to remain at around 80. The tower was built in 1974, however, an £8.6 million refurbishment was completed in 2016 on behalf of the Royal Borough of Kensington and Chelsea Council. The work included a new exterior cladding that was the source of much debate, as it is assumed it was added to make the 'eyesore' more aesthetically pleasing to the wealthier residents of the area while completely neglecting the fact that it did not meet basic fire safety requirements.

Any fire that results in the loss of life is tragic, yet this particular tragedy was experienced by many residents of the borough as well as London, more generally, as especially devastating due to the fact that a group of residents had already warned of it in November 2016.

Unfortunately, the Grenfell Action Group have reached the conclusion that only an incident that results in serious loss of life of KCTMO [Kensington and Chelsea Tenant Management Organisation] residents will allow the external scrutiny to occur that will shine a light on the practices that characterise the malign governance of this non-functioning organisation.[13]

While the community found itself inundated with donations of clothing, food and other tangible items, it was a Black woman who recognised the urgency of a space needed for calm in order to support processing and enable healing. On 22 June 2017, Lenéa Herew created the Grenfell Healing Zone which offered several different forms of therapy to those affected – both directly and indirectly – by the fire. On the first day, treatments were offered in homeopathy, massage, osteopathy and yoga at no charge to the community. As more volunteers came forward, the offer was spread to a diverse mix of healing practices and outlets, such as Yoruba ancestor prayers and drumming, Buddhist chanting and even youth boxing.

From July 2017, the Healing Zone was moved to new centres and offered every Wednesday and Saturday throughout the summer. The stated purpose of continued services was free healing and creative therapies and activities for survivors of Grenfell, the affected and every member of the community who needed the services. The project, which served the entire community, was founded by and predominantly led by Black women and women of colour healers and facilitators.

Example quotes from some of those who utilised the healing sessions:

Dear Lenéa, thank you very much for your magic hand and your time with my mum on Saturday, she said your work on her was the best she ever experienced. She said she felt so deeply relaxed after very long time and it is still with her. (The daughter of an elderly woman who received Reiki and massage)[14]

The power of touch. Humans need humans. We need to love and support each other especially when in trauma. Thanks to our loving volunteer therapists for making this available to the Grenfell community.[15]

The people affected by the Grenfell Tower fire are diverse, but a large part of that community identify as Black or as an ethnic minority. With the diversity of the practitioners who came forward to offer their services, there was an opportunity to ignite a genuine healing process from within the community, as the tragedy itself is steeped in institutional racism and classism. Due to a lack of consistent funding and coordinated efforts between the Council and community members, the Healing Zone was not able to continue in the way described above.

Since the fire, many initiatives have been created to help those directly and indirectly affected. Given the extent of issues that were present before the fire and their consequent exacerbation after the fire, there is a lack of targeted support, especially for women. However, some groups are working diligently to make cohesive the very fragmented community and services landscape. Most notably, the Women for Grenfell Network, founded and chaired by Idil Hassan, which works to build, maintain and nourish a network of women, who are in varying capacities providing care, help and support to people in the community and the borough.

CONCLUSION

There are a number of events, spaces and collectives creating space across Europe. Other examples include the Black women-led projects such as: the PoC community choir in Berlin, the Soul Sisters Berlin collective and Black Arts Retreat, the Mwasi Collectif Afroféministe of Paris that regularly holds activities, actions, events and workshops, Black Women in Europe with chapters and meet-ups across Europe, Amsterdam Black Women, The Rabbani Project (London) and so forth. What they have in common is a mission to build community, support their members and provide a space for creativity, exchange and healing.

Participating in the arts and creative spaces benefits both individuals and communities. On an individual level, self-confidence and self-expression increases, while creative and transferable skills are learned. Such individual benefits translate to greater social impact in that marginalised groups are empowered through acquiring new skills, building and maintaining confidence, as well as becoming more (equitably) involved in local and community affairs.[16]

In common with the findings that the Book Café in Harare[17] fostered civic engagement and activism through four main channels – providing a platform for freedom of expression and debate, empowering marginalised groups, especially women and youth, serving as a meeting place and thereby enabling collaborations and exchange, as well as nurturing art and artists committed to work with social impact – the projects described above, while not running to a comparable extent of time and consistency, utilise similar channels of community engagement and amplify public discourse and collective awareness of the challenges they are committed to confronting.

NOTES

1. Elena Mustakova-Possardt, 2003. *Critical Consciousness: A Study of Morality in Global, Historical Context.* ABC-Clio, London, pp. 3–4.

2. Maria Rosario Jackson, Florence Kabwasa-Green and Joaquín Herranz, 2006. *Cultural Vitality in Communities: Interpretation and Indicators*. The Urban Institute, Washington, DC, pp. 12–15.

3. François Matarasso, 2003. *Use or Ornament? The Social Impact of Participation in the Arts*. Comedia, Gloucester, p. 90.

4. bell hooks, 1996. *Reel to Real: Race, Sex, and Class at the Movies*. Routledge, New York, p. 221.

5. Kimberlé Crenshaw, 1991. 'Mapping the margins: Intersectionality, identity politics, and violence against women of color'. *Stanford Law Review* 43, pp. 1242–5.

6. Stacie CC Graham, Katharina Koch and Marie-Anne Kohl (eds), 2016. *Prekäre Kunst: Protest & Widerstand Eine Ausstellung und Veranstaltungsreihe in der alpha nova & galerie futura*. Self-published, Berlin, p. 65.

7. Victoria Sanusi, 2016. 'A woman created an exhibition that embodies Black girl magic', 11 October. www.buzzfeed.com/victoriasanusi/a-woman-created-an-exhibition-that-embodies-black-girl-magic?utm_term=.yim5440kd4#.eq6GvvmOBv (accessed 18 September 2017).

8. https://blackblossomsexhibition.tumblr.com/ (accessed 18 September 2017).

9. https://thecocoabutterclub.com/welcome/ (accessed 17 September 2017).

10. Ivy Wilde, 2017. 'Sadie Sinner: Cocoa butter queen'. *21st Century Burlesque*, 3 March. http://21stcenturyburlesque.com/sadie-sinner-cocoa-butter-club-poc/ (accessed 17 September 2017).

11. Norma Daykin, Karen Gray, Mel McCree and Jane Willis, 2017. 'Creative and credible evaluation for arts, health, and well-being: Opportunities and challenges of co-production'. *Arts & Health* 9, pp. 124–8.

12. Christina Congleton, Britta K. Hölzel and Sara W. Lazar, 2015. 'Mindfulness can literally change your brain'. *Harvard Business Review*, January.

13. Grenfell Action Group. https://grenfellactiongroup.wordpress.com/2016/11/20/kctmo-playing-with-fire/ (accessed 18 September 2017).

14. Public post retrieved from www.facebook.com/grenfellhealingzone/photos/a.1076404645826535.1073741827.1075074765959523/1091743140959352/?type=3&theater (accessed 18 September 2017).

15. Public post on Grenfell Healing Zone Facebook profile (accessed 18 September 2018).

16. Matarasso, *Use or Ornament*. Humanist Institute for Development Cooperation (HIVOS), Zimbabwe, pp. 92–5.

17. Anne Gadwa Nicodemus and Florence Mukanga-Majachani, 2015. *How Creative Spaces Foster Civic Engagement: A Case Study of the Book Café (Harare, Zimbabwe)*. Harare, pp. 28–38.

Notes on Contributors

Ego Ahaiwe Sowinski is a London/Minneapolis-based mixed-media artist/designer, archivist and organiser.

Cyn Awori Othieno is an independent artist and activist with Mwasi Collectif, France.

Gabriella Beckles-Raymond is a Senior Lecturer in Womanist Theology, Philosophy, and Culture at Canterbury Christ Church University, UK.

Kesiena Boom is an independent writer and masters student in Gender Studies at Lund University, Sweden.

Cruel Ironies Collective is based in the Netherlands.

Annette Davis is an activist with Mwasi Collectif, France.

Yesim Deveci is a Senior Lecturer at the University of East London, UK.

Oda-Kanage Midtvåge Diallo is a PhD candidate at the Norwegian University of Science and Technology, Norway.

Akwugo Emejulu is Professor of Sociology at the University of Warwick, UK.

Stacie CC Graham is a curator, culture producer, writer and public speaker, UK.

Nicole Grégoire is an FNRS Postdoctoral Researcher at Laboratoire d'Anthropologie des Mondes Contemporains, Université Libre de Bruxelles, Belgium.

Melody Howse is a filmmaker and a PhD candidate in Anthropology at Universität Leipzig, Germany.

Claire Heuchan is an independent writer and researcher in the UK.

Nazmia Jamal is an A level English teacher in London, UK.

Dorett Jones is an activist and filmmaker and works at Imkaan, UK.

Johanna Melissa Lukate is a PhD candidate in Psychology at the University of Cambridge, UK.

Alecia McKenzie is an award-winning Jamaican writer, journalist and artist, based in France.

Nadia Nadesan is an independent activist, writer and researcher currently affiliated with Working On Our Power, Spain.

Modi Ntambwe is an award-winning activist and Chair of the ReFI–oe, Belgium.

Chijioke Obasi works at Northumbria University, UK.

Pamela Ohene-Nyako is a PhD candidate at the University of Geneva and founder of Afrolitt', Switzerland.

Sadiah Qureshi is a Senior Lecturer in Modern History at the University of Birmingham, UK.

Francesca Sobande is a Digital Media Studies Lecturer at Cardiff University, UK.

Tia-Monique Uzor is a PhD candidate and part-time Lecturer at De Montfort University, UK.

Lubumbe Van de Velde is a PhD candidate at Canterbury Christ Church University, UK.

Viki Zaphiriou-Zarifi is an independent researcher and activist in the UK and Greece.

Index

Holocaust, 58
Homans, Liesbeth, 142
homelessness, 94
Honneth, Axel, 120
hooks, bell, 5, 14, 15, 22, 172, 201, 202, 236, 252, 259–63, 266, 269, 285
Hoover, Edgar, 152
Howse, Melody, 8
Hudson-Weems, 229, 232, 240
Hughes, Langston, 47
Hurston, Zora Neale, 190, 198

ICTs, 39–41
identity, 3, 83, 111, 112, 114, 116–28, 169, 184, 185, 189, 210, 216, 219, 224–6
  African identity, 22, 31, 238, 265, 267
  Black identity, 144, 182, 222, 233, 235, 260
  British identity, 93
  Caribbean identity, 92
  cultural identity, 24
  hooks, bell, 275–6
  national identity, 13, 26, 28, 29, 34, 146
'I'd just like to be free': Young Women Speak Out About Sexual Harassment (film), 273, 276, 277, 282
Igbokwe, Vicki, 259, 261, 262–4
Imkaan, 273, 279, 282
imperialism, 93, 274, 275, 286
Independent (newspaper), 154
Instagram, 39, 40
intersection, 4, 6, 7, 14, 35–6, 38, 64, 65, 69, 70, 71–3, 79, 117, 118, 120, 182–5, 188–7, 198, 191, 232–3, 253, 275, 281, 286, 287
  Crenshaw, Kimberlé W., 208, 232
  Denmark, 219, 225
Isin, Engin F., 13–14
Islamophobia, 51, 54, 62n8, 220, 227. See also Charlie Hebdo (magazine)

International Refugee Day, 20
International Women's Day (IWD), 15, 24, 26 fig 2.7, 28 fig 2.8, 35–8, 55 fig 4.4
internet, 14, 30, 52, 60, 61, 79, 81, 87
Irish oppression, 234

Jackson, Sarah J., 79
Jagger, Bianca, 77
Jain, Dimpal, 231
Jamaica, 93, 97
  Kingston, 151, 152, 153
Jamal, Nazmia, 8
James, C.L.R., 261
Jarmon, Renina, 81–2, 87
Jezebel (magazine), 254
Johannes Gutenberg University Mainz, 202
Johnson, Lyndon B., 152
Johnson-Small, Jamilia, 259, 261–2, 267, 268
Jones, Claudia, 4, 9, 274
Jones, Dorett, 8
Jordan, June, 129, 172, 178–9
journalists, 19 fig 2.3, 23, 47, 49, 50, 51, 117, 152, 153

King, Denise, 160–61
King, Martin Luther, 4, 83
Kitt, Eartha, 8, 151–63
K-neter, 104
Ko, Aph, 81
Koch, Katharina, 287
Ko-fi, 81
Kohl, Marie-Anne, 287
Kramer, Pascal, 104
Ku Klux Klan, 58
Kwanzaa, 35, 38

Laban, Rudolf, 267
La Cancha es Nuestra (The Court is Ours), 38–9
La Cene Littéraire, 104, 108
Ladies Rock!, 131–2, 136, 137
Ladyfest, 131, 133, 139n5
Lambeth Women's Project, 130–40